The Roswell Report

CASE CLOSED

Headquarters United States Air Force

This edition published by Barnes & Noble, Inc.,
by arrangement with the U.S. Government Printing Office.

This edition is an exact facsimile of *The Roswell Report: Case Closed* written by Captain James McAndrew and published by the U.S. Government Printing Office in June 1997.

1997 Barnes & Noble Books

ISBN 0-7607-0814-2

Printed and bound in the United States of America

97 98 99 00 01 M 9 8 7 6 5 4 3 2 1

MV

The Cover
A solarized image taken from a U.S. Air Force motion picture of experiments conducted for Project High Dive. This image, unsolarized, appears on page 34 (Figure 37).

Foreword

The "Roswell Incident" has assumed a central place in American folklore since the events of the 1940s in a remote area of New Mexico. Because the Air Force was a major player in those events, we have played a key role in executing the General Accounting Office's tasking to uncover all records regarding that incident.

Our objective throughout this inquiry has been simple and consistent: to find all the facts and bring them to light. If documents were classified, declassify them; where they were dispersed, bring them into a single source for public review.

In July 1994, we completed the first step in that effort and later published *The Roswell Report: Fact vs. Fiction in the New Mexico Desert.* This volume represents the necessary follow-on to that first publication and contains additional material and analysis. I think that with this publication we have reached our goal of a complete and open explanation of the events that occurred in the Southwest many years ago.

Beyond that achievement, this inquiry has shed fascinating light into the Air Force of that era and revitalized our appreciation for the dedication and accomplishments of the men and women of that time. As we celebrate the Air Force's 50th Anniversary, it is appropriate to once again reflect on the sacrifices made by so many to make ours the finest air and space force in history.

SHEILA E. WIDNALL
Secretary of the Air Force

Guide For Readers

This publication contains the complete report as submitted to the Secretary of the Air Force. The exceptions are the statements found in Appendix B. Due to Privacy Act restrictions and by request, the addresses of the individuals making these statements have been deleted.

This volume is divided into two sections, eight subsections, eleven sidebar discussions, and three appendices. Section One examines alleged events at two locations in rural New Mexico. Section Two examines the alleged activities at the Roswell Army Airfield Hospital.

Appendix A is a table listing the launch and landing locations of test equipment for U.S. Air Force scientific research projects HIGH DIVE and EXCELSIOR. Appendix B is a collection of signed sworn statements based on in-person interviews conducted for this report by U.S. Air Force researchers. The exception is the statement of Lt. Col. William C. Kaufman, which was not sworn due to equipment failures at the time of interview.

Appendix C contains transcripts of interviews of alleged witnesses presented by UFO theorists. The interviews of Gerald Anderson, Alice Knight, and Vern Maltais were excerpted in their entirety from unedited interviews used to prepare the video, *Recollections of Roswell, Part II* (1993), and appear courtesy of the Fund for UFO Research. The interview of Mr. W. Glenn Dennis was provided by the interviewer, Karl T. Pflock. The transcript of the interview of Mr. James Ragsdale was provided by Kevin Randle, the coauthor of the *Truth About the UFO Crash at Roswell* (Avon Books, 1994), in which direct quotes from this transcript appear.

A selected bibliography of technical reports and how to obtain them are found on page 221. For additional information on this subject, see Headquarters United States Air Force, *The Roswell Report: Fact vs. Fiction in the New Mexico Desert* (Washington D.C.: U.S. Government Printing Office, 1995).

The Author

CAPTAIN JAMES McANDREW serves as an Intelligence Applications Officer assigned to the Secretary of the Air Force Declassification and Review Team, The Pentagon, Washington, D.C.. Captain McAndrew was the coauthor, with Col. Richard L. Weaver, of *The Roswell Report: Fact vs. Fiction in the New Mexico Desert* (1995), the first Air Force work on the alleged "Roswell Incident." He participated in the declassification of the *Gulf War Air Power Survey* (1993) and has served special tours of duty with the Drug Enforcement Administration and High Intensity Drug Trafficking Area (HIDTA) Task Force. He holds a BS degree with honors, from Metropolitan State College, Denver, Colo. and is a native of Washington, D.C..

Contents

APPENDIX A

Anthropomorphic Dummy Launch and Landing Locations

APPENDIX B

Witness Statements

APPENDIX C

Interviews

Tables

Figures

SECTION ONE

SECTION TWO

Introduction

In July 1994, the Office of the Secretary of the Air Force concluded an exhaustive search for records in response to a General Accounting Office (GAO) inquiry of an event popularly known as the "Roswell Incident." The focus of the GAO probe, initiated at the request of New Mexico Congressman Steven Schiff, was to determine if the U.S. Air Force, or any other U.S. government agency, possessed information on the alleged crash and recovery of an extraterrestrial vehicle and its alien occupants near Roswell, N.M. in July 1947.

Reports of flying saucers and alien bodies allegedly sighted in the Roswell area in 1947, have been the subject of intense domestic and international media attention. This attention has resulted in countless newspaper and magazine articles, books, a television series, a full-length motion picture, and even a film purported to be a U.S. government "alien autopsy."

The July 1994 Air Force report concluded that the predecessor to the U.S. Air Force, the U.S. Army Air Forces, did indeed recover material near Roswell in July 1947. This 1,000-page report methodically explains that what was recovered by the Army Air Forces was not the remnants of an extraterrestrial spacecraft and its alien crew, but debris from an Army Air Forces balloon-borne research project code named MOGUL.[1] Records located describing research carried out under the MOGUL project, most of which were never classified (and publicly available) were collected, provided to GAO, and published in one volume for ease of access for the general public.[*]

Although MOGUL components clearly accounted for the claims of "flying saucer" debris recovered in 1947, lingering questions remained concerning anecdotal accounts that included descriptions of "alien" bodies. The issue of "bodies" was not discussed extensively in the 1994 report because there were not any bodies connected with events that occurred in 1947. The extensive Secretary of the Air Force-directed search of Army Air Forces and U.S. Air Force records from 1947 did not yield information that even suggested the 1947 "Roswell" events were anything other than the retrieval of the MOGUL equipment.[2]

---

[*] MOGUL records which ultimately lead to the identification of the origin of the 1947 claims of "flying saucer" debris, described balloon research that was never classified. Other MOGUL records, describing military applications of balloon-borne acoustical sensors, were declassified, along with millions of pages of other unrelated executive branch documents by Executive Order 11652, issued on March 6, 1972 by President Richard M. Nixon.

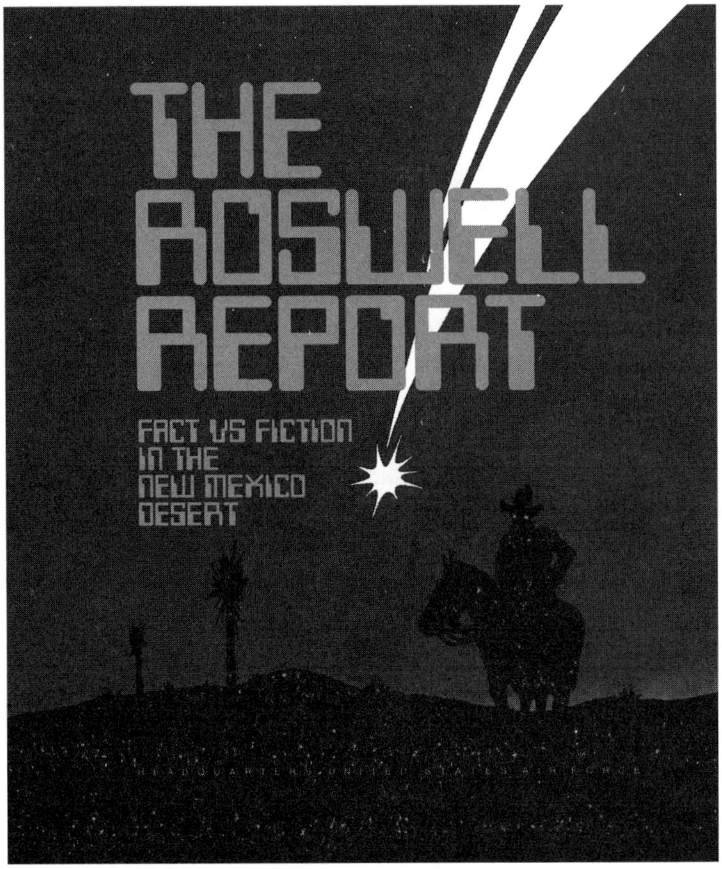

Fig.1. *The Roswell Report: Fact vs. Fiction in the New Mexico Desert* contains, in its entirety, the report submitted to the Secretary of the Air Force in July 1994. It is available for sale from the U.S. Government Printing Office, Superintendent of Documents, Washington, D.C., 20402-9328. Stock No. 008-070-00697-9, ISBN 0-16-048023-X.

Subsequent to the 1994 report, Air Force researchers discovered information that provided a rational explanation for the alleged observations of alien bodies associated with the "Roswell Incident." Pursuant to the discovery, research efforts compared documented Air Force activities to the incredible claims of "flying saucers," "aliens" and seemingly unusual Air Force involvement. This in-depth examination revealed that these accounts, in most instances, were of actual Air Force activities but were seriously flawed in several major areas, most notably: the Air Force operations that inspired reports of "bodies" (in addition to being earthly in origin) did not occur in 1947. It appears that UFO proponents have failed to establish the accurate dates for these "alien" observations (in some instances by more than a decade) and then erroneously linked them to the actual Project Mogul debris recovery.

This report discusses the results of this further research and identifies the likely sources of the claims of "alien" bodies. Contrary to allegations that the Air Force has engaged in a cover-up and possesses dark secrets involving the Roswell claims, some of the accounts appear to be descriptions of unclassified and widely publicized Air Force scientific achievements. Other descriptions of bodies appear to be descriptions of actual incidents in which Air Force members were killed or injured in the line of duty.

The conclusions of the additional research are:

- Air Force activities which occurred over a period of many years have been consolidated and are now represented to have occurred in two or three days in July 1947.
- "Aliens" observed in the New Mexico desert were probably anthropomorphic test dummies that were carried aloft by U.S. Air Force high altitude balloons for scientific research.
- The "unusual" military activities in the New Mexico desert were high altitude research balloon launch and recovery operations. The reports of military units that always seemed to arrive shortly after the crash of a flying saucer to retrieve the saucer and "crew," were actually accurate descriptions of Air Force personnel engaged in anthropomorphic dummy recovery operations.
- Claims of bodies at the Roswell Army Air Field hospital were most likely a combination of two separate incidents:
  1) a 1956 KC-97 aircraft accident in which 11 Air Force members lost their lives; and,
  2) a 1959 manned balloon mishap in which two Air Force pilots were injured.

This report is based on thoroughly documented research supported by official records, technical reports, film footage, photographs, and interviews with individuals who were involved in these events.

Fig. 2. Roswell, N.M. (pop. 37,000), boasts competing "museums" focusing on the Roswell Incident, including this one, The International UFO Museum and Research Center.

SECTION ONE

Flying Saucer Crashes and Alien Bodies

The most puzzling and intriguing element of the complex series of events now known as the Roswell Incident, are the alleged sightings of alien bodies. The bodies turned what, for many years, was just another flying saucer story, into what many UFO proponents claim is the best case for extraterrestrial visitation of Earth. The importance of bodies and the assumptions made as to their origin is illustrated in a passage from a popular Roswell book:

Crashed saucers are one thing, and could well turn out to be futuristic American or even foreign aircraft or missiles. But alien bodies are another matter entirely, and hardly subject to misinterpretation.[3]

The 1994 Air Force report determined that project MOGUL was responsible for the 1947 events. MOGUL was an experimental attempt to acoustically detect suspected Soviet nuclear weapon explosions and ballistic missile launches.[4] MOGUL utilized acoustical sensors, radar reflecting targets and other devices attached to a train of weather balloons over 600 feet long. Claims that the U.S. Army Air Forces recovered a "flying disc" in 1947, were based primarily on the lack of identification of the radar targets, an element of weather equipment used on the long MOGUL balloon train. The oddly constructed radar targets were found by a New Mexico rancher during the height of the first U.S. flying saucer wave in 1947.[5] The rancher brought the remnants of the balloons and radar targets to the local sheriff after he allegedly learned of the broadcasted reports of flying discs. However, following some initial confusion at Roswell Army Air Field, the "flying disc" was soon identified by Army Air Forces officials as a standard radar target.[6]

From 1947 until the late 1970s, the Roswell Incident was essentially a non-story. The reports that existed contain only descriptions of mundane materials that originated from the Project MOGUL balloon train— "tinfoil, paper, tape, rubber, and sticks."[7] The first claim of "bodies" appeared in the late 1970s, with additional claims made during the 1980s and 1990s. These claims were usually based on anecdotal accounts of second-and third-hand witnesses collected by UFO proponents as much as 40 years after the alleged incident. The same anecdotal accounts that referred to bodies also described massive field operations conducted by the U.S. military to recover crash debris from a supposed extraterrestrial spaceship.

A technique used by some UFO authors to collect anecdotal corroboration for their theories was to solicit cooperating witnesses through newspaper announcements. For example, one such solicitation appeared in the *Socorro* (N.M.) *Defensor Chieftan* on November 4, 1992, on behalf of

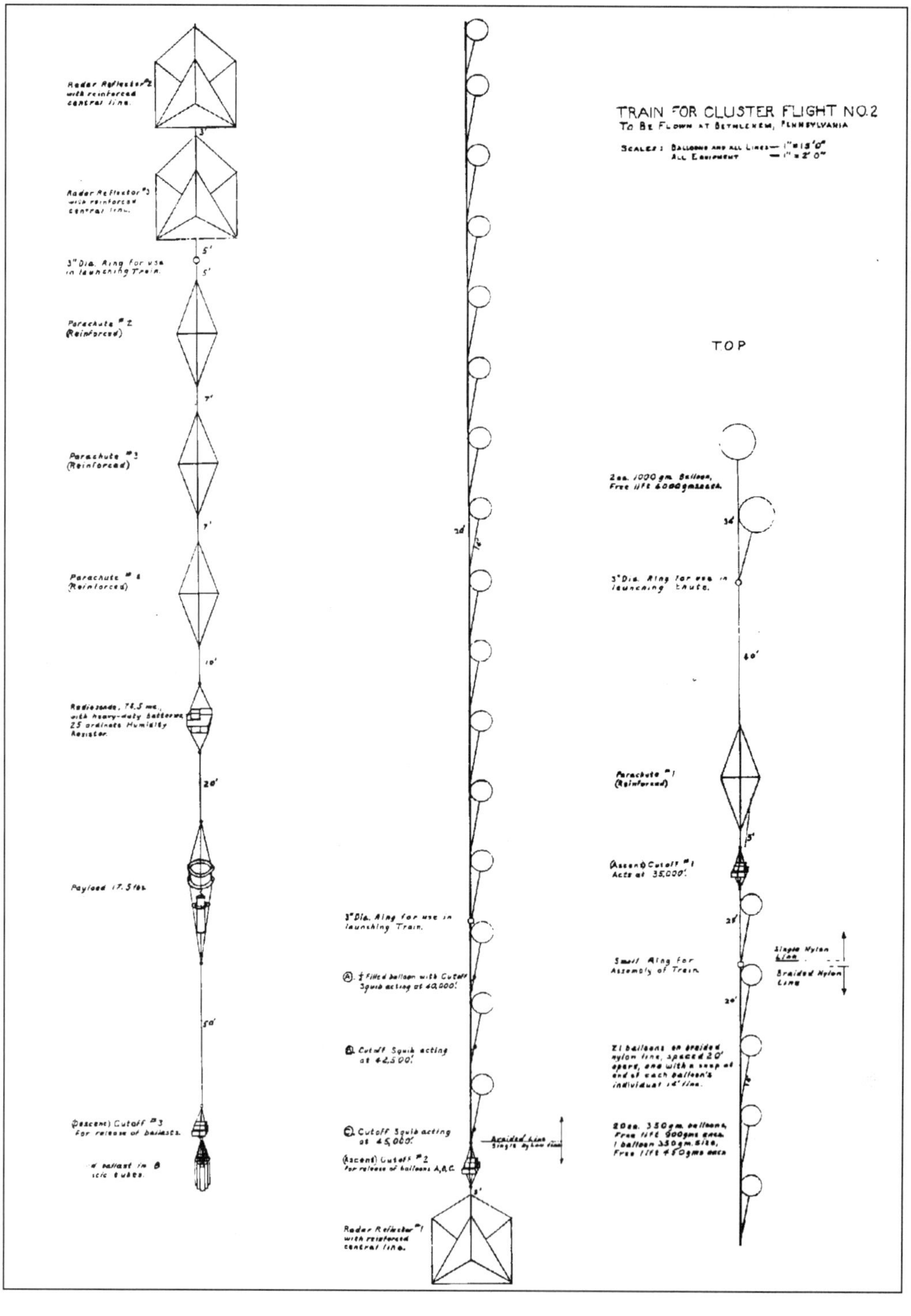

Fig. 3. An illustration of a Project MOGUL balloon train similar to one found on a ranch 75 miles northwest of Roswell, N.M. in June 1947, which contains all of the "strange" materials described as part of a "flying disc." Initial confusion at Roswell AAF and delayed identification of this equipment was the first in a series of unrelated events now known as the "Roswell Incident."

Fig. 4. *(Right)* Maj. Jesse Marcel, an intelligence officer from Roswell Army Air Field, with the debris found 75 miles northwest of Roswell in June 1947. When compared to a standard radar target used by project Mogul, it is clear that they are the same object. (*Courtesy, Special Collections Division, the University of Texas at Arlington Libraries, Arlington, Tex.*)

Fig. 5 & 6. *(Below, left and right)* Constructed of aluminized paper glued and taped to a balsa wood frame, several ML-307B/AP radar targets were used on the Mogul balloon train to make it visible to radar. *(U.S. Air Force photos)*

Harassed Rancher who Located 'Saucer' Sorry He Told About It

W. W. Brazel, 48, Lincoln county rancher living 30 miles south east of Corona, today told his story of finding what the army at first described as a flying disk, but the publicity which attended his find caused him to add that if he ever found anything else short of a bomb he sure wasn't going to say anything about it.

Brazel was brought here late yesterday by W. E. Whitmore, of radio station KGFL, had his picture taken and gave an interview to the Record and Jason Kellahin, sent here from the Albuquerque bureau of the Associated Press to cover the story. The picture he posed for was sent out over AP telephoto wire sending machine specially set up in the Record office by R. D. Adair, AP wire chief sent here from Albuquerque for the sole purpose of getting out his picture and that of sheriff George Wilcox, to whom Brazel originally gave the information of his find.

Brazel related that on June 14 he and an 8-year old son, Vernon were about 7 or 8 miles from the ranch house of the J. B. Foster ranch, which he operates, when they came upon a large area of bright wreckage made up on rubber strips, tinfoil, a rather tough paper and sticks.

At the time Brazel was in a hurry to get his round made and he did not pay much attention to it. But he did remark about what he had seen and on July 4 he, his wife, Vernon and a daughter Betty, age 14, went back to the spot and gathered up quite a bit of the debris.

The next day he first heard about the flying disks, and he wondered if what he had found might be the remnants of one of these.

Monday he came to town to sell some wool and while here he went to see sheriff George Wilcox and "whispered kinda confidential like" that he might have found a flying disk.

Wilcox got in touch with the Roswell Army Air Field and Maj. Jesse A. Marcel and a man in plain clothes accompanied him home, where they picked up the rest of the pieces of the "disk" and went to his home to try to reconstruct it.

According to Brazel they simply could not reconstruct it at all. They tried to make a kite out of it, but could not do that and could not find any way to put it back together so that it would fit.

Then Major Marcel brought it to Roswell and that was the last he heard of it until the story broke that he had found a flying disk.

Brazel said that he did not see it fall from the sky and did not see it before it was torn up, so he did not know the size or shape it might have been, but he thought it might have been about as large as a table top. The balloon which held it up, if that was how it worked, must have been about 12 feet long, he felt, measuring the distance by the size of the room in which he sat. The rubber was smoky gray in color and scattered over an area about 200 yards in diameter.

When the debris was gathered up the tinfoil, paper, tape, and sticks made a bundle about three feet long and 7 or 8 inches thick, while the rubber made a bundle about 18 or 20 inches long and about 8 inches thick. In all, he estimated, the entire lot would have weighed maybe five pounds.

There was no sign of any metal in the area which might have been used for an engine and no sign of any propellers of any kind, although at least one paper fin had been glued onto some of the tinfoil.

There were no words to be found anywhere on the instrument, although there were letters on some of the parts. Considerable scotch tape and some tape with flowers printed upon it had been used in the construction.

No strings or wire were to be found but there were some eyelets in the paper to indicate that some sort of attachment may have been used.

Brazel said that he had previously found two weather observation balloons on the ranch, but that what he found this time did not in any way resemble either of these.

"I am sure what I found was not any weather observation balloon," he said. "But if I find anything else besides a bomb they are going to have a hard time getting me to say anything about it."

Fig. 7. This account from the July 9, 1947 *Roswell Daily Record*, described the materials "tinfoil, paper, rubber, tape, and sticks" found on the ranch 75 miles northwest of Roswell, in June 1947.

Don Berliner and Stanton T. Friedman the authors of the book *Crash at Corona*. This request solicited persons to provide information about the supposed crashes of alien spacecraft in the Socorro area.[8*]

In response to the newspaper announcement, two scientists central to the actual explanation of the "Roswell" events, Professor Charles B. Moore, a former U.S. Army Air Forces contract engineer, and Bernard D. Gildenberg, retired Holloman AFB Balloon Branch Physical Science Administrator and Meteorologist, came forward with pertinent information.[9] According to Moore and Gildenberg, when they met with the authors their explanations that some of the Air Force projects they participated in were most likely responsible for the incident, they were summarily dismissed. The authors even went so far as to suggest that these distinguished scientists were participants in a multifaceted government cover-up to conceal the truth about the Roswell Incident.

---

*Socorro, N.M. is situated at the northwest boundary of White Sands Missile Range, the largest military test range in the United States. Since the 1940s, White Sands and the surrounding areas of New Mexico have been the site of a high volume of military test and evaluation activity, including the launch and recovery of anthropomorphic dummies carried aloft by high altitude balloons.

Authors seek UFO witnesses

Co-authors of a major book on the 1947 crash of at least one alien spacecraft in the New Mexico desert will be at the Golden Manor Motel in Socorro on Monday, Nov. 16 to seek out additional witnesses to these events.

Nuclear physicist Stanton T. Friedman and aviation/science writer Don Berliner, whose "Crash at Corona" is now in its second printing, want to meet with people having knowledge of the 1947 crashes.

Their book, being published in August by Paragon House of New York, is being prepared for a made-for-TV movie. It is the story of the discovery, retrieval, shipping and cover-up of what the authors call the most important scientific discovery of the past thousand years.

It is based on dozens of interviews with first- and second-hand civilian and ex-military witnesses to various parts of what is referred to as a very complex series of events.

In order to strengthen their case for government knowledge of what they call "the truth behind almost 50 years of UFO sightings," the authors are seeking out additional, reliable witnesses. It remains their policy to honor requests to keep the names of witnesses private.

For more information, contact Don Berliner, 1202 S. Washington St., Alexandria, VA., 22314 (703-548-0405); or Stanton T. Friedman, 79 Pembroke Crescent, Fredericton, New Brunswick E3B 2V1, Canada (506 457-0232).

Witnesses are invited to call either author collect or to make arrangements to meet them at any of their stops in New Mexico, which include the cities of Santa Fe, Albuquerque, Las Cruces, Alamogordo and Roswell.

Fig. 8. Announcement from the November 4, 1992 *Socorro* (N.M.) *Defensor Chieftan* soliciting witnesses of flying saucer crashes in New Mexico. When former Air Force scientists responded to advise the authors that Air Force projects were most probably responsible for the UFO accounts, they were summarily dismissed by the authors who placed the announcement, and then were accused of participating in a cover-up.

Fig. 9. *(Left)* B.D. "Duke" Gildenberg served as the civilian meteorologist, engineer, and physical science administrator for the Holloman AFB Balloon Branch from 1951-1981. Gildenberg actively participated in thousands of high altitude balloon operations, including the flights that dropped anthropomorphic dummies at off-range locations throughout New Mexico. Gildenberg, the "father" of Air Force scientific ballooning, was instrumental in identifying the many actual Air Force activities now known as the "Roswell Incident."

Fig. 10. *(Right)* Charles B. Moore, Professor Emeritus of Atmospheric Physics at the New Mexico Institute of Mining and Technology, was the project engineer for New York University under contract to the U.S. Army Air Forces to develop high altitude balloon technology for Project Mogul. Moore launched the balloon train on June 4, 1947, that when combined with other events, are now known as the "Roswell Incident."

Since many of the Roswell accounts and allegations were collected by irregular methods and are not specifically documented, the series of events as alleged by UFO theorists has become very complex and requires clarification. Therefore, the following section will briefly examine some of the more confusing elements of the Roswell stories, specifically, the multiple crash sites and complex scenarios, in order to facilitate an objective analysis of actual events.

1.1
The "Crash Sites," Scenarios, and Research Methods

The "Crash Sites"

From 1947 until the late 1970s, the Roswell Incident was confined to one alleged crash site. This site, located on the Foster Ranch approximately 75 miles northwest of the city of Roswell, was the actual landing site of a Project MOGUL balloon train in June 1947.[10] The MOGUL landing site is referred to in popular Roswell literature as the "debris field."

In the 1970s, the 1980s and throughout the 1990s, additional witnesses came forward with claims and descriptions of two other alleged crash sites. One of these sites was supposedly north of Roswell, the other site was alleged to have been approximately 175 miles northwest of Roswell in an area of New Mexico known as the San Agustin Plains.[11] What distinguished the two new crash sites from the original debris field were accounts of alien bodies.

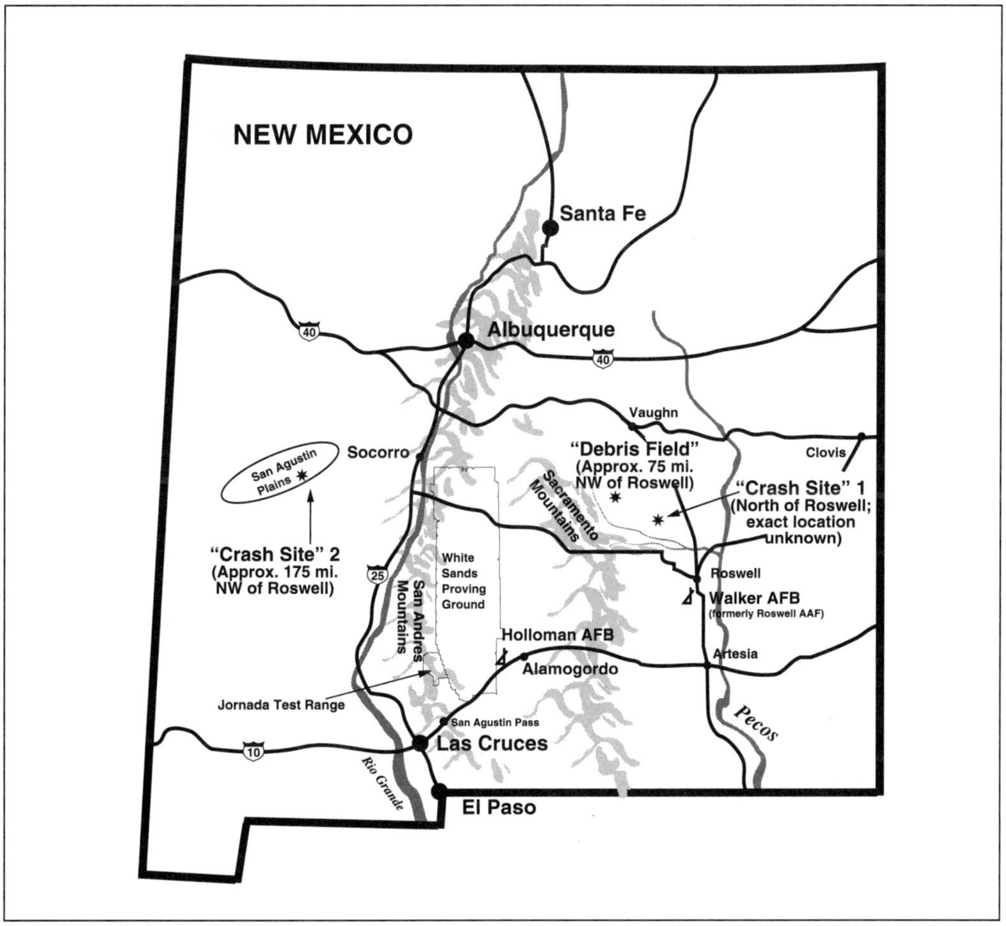

Fig. 11. Map of New Mexico depicting the "crash sites" and "debris field."

The Scenarios

UFO enthusiasts have attempted to explain the obvious contradiction of multiple impact sites involving only one alien craft through the introduction of complicated scenarios . These scenarios have become increasingly convoluted since the proponents of each crash site must make allowances to have "their" flying saucer at the correct time and place—the actual MOGUL balloon train landing site in early July, 1947— in order to "fit" with the rest of the story. The actual Project MOGUL landing site, 75 miles northwest of Roswell, lends credibility, and more importantly establishes a *time frame,* for the other accounts that include reports of bodies. Flying saucer enthusiasts use the documented presence of U.S. Army Air Forces personnel at the MOGUL site in July 1947, who were there to retrieve the MOGUL balloon train, to provide the nucleus of unrelated and much later accounts that include reports of "bodies." It must be emphasized that the claims of "bodies" only became part of the Roswell Incident after 1978, when they were erroneously linked to the July 1947 retrieval of Project MOGUL components.

"It must be emphasized that the claims of bodies only became part of the Roswell Incident after 1978, when they were erroneously linked to the July 1947 retrieval of Project MOGUL components."

In general, "Roswell Incident" scenarios claim that a disabled alien craft momentarily touched down at the site 75 miles northwest of Roswell, leaving behind parts of the spaceship (material that has been subsequently identified as components of a MOGUL balloon train) to create the original "debris field." The scenarios further contend that the damaged craft again became airborne and flew to its final crash site, at either the location north of Roswell or 175 miles northwest of Roswell on the San Agustin Plains.

Regardless of the dispute over the location, an element common to most scenarios was that, once recovered, the bodies were supposedly transported to the hospital at Roswell Army Air Field for autopsy. Also common to these theories is that the bodies were later shipped from Roswell AAF to another facility, usually Wright-Patterson AFB, Ohio (or a host of other facilities—this is another area of further disagreement among UFO theorists) for further evaluation and ultimate deep-freeze storage.

Research Methods

In an attempt to untangle this collection of complicated assertions and determine if there was any validity to the reports of bodies, Air Force researchers faced the task of sorting through and examining anecdotal testimony of hundreds of witnesses. However, a large number of the accounts were eliminated by applying previously established facts to the testimonies. The July 1994 report to the Secretary of the Air Force clearly presented and documented these facts:

a. The U.S. Army Air Forces did not recover an extraterrestrial vehicle and alien crew. This conclusion was based on extensive research that included a thorough review of both classified and unclassified materials at record depositories, archives, libraries and research facilities throughout the nation. Of the millions of pages of material reviewed, there was no mention of any activities that even tangentially suggested such an event. Additionally, former and retired Air Force members and civilian contract scientists were located and released from any possible nondisclosure agreements they may have entered into regarding past classified activities. This release allowed them to freely discuss with Air Force researchers, or any other persons, information related to this issue. These releases were issued at the express written direction of the Secretary of the Air Force. Interviews with these persons yielded no information supporting extraterrestrial claims or any other unusual activities.

b. The reports of bodies were not associated with Project MOGUL. The MOGUL balloon train did not, was not designed to, nor could it carry passengers. Neither did it carry hazardous materials that would have caused injury, death, or mutilation to persons who may have come in contact with any of its components.

c. Actual events, if any, that inspired reports of bodies did not occur in 1947. Based on extensive examinations of U.S. Army Air Forces activities in 1947, no evidence was found to support allegations that the Army Air Forces was involved in any uncommon operations other than the retrieval of the MOGUL balloon train in the Roswell area in July 1947. Examination of research and development projects, aircraft crashes, errant missiles and possible nuclear accidents yielded no information to support a 1947 claim.

In light of these documented facts, the hundreds of anecdotal accounts were reduced to a few. Eliminated were accounts that were likely descriptions of materials known to be part of the Project MOGUL balloon train and accounts describing transportation of these materials.

From the remaining testimony, Air Force researchers developed the following set of working hypotheses to assist in identifying the actual events, if any, matching those described by the witnesses.

a. Due to the number and great detail provided in some of the accounts, it was likely that some event(s) actually did occur.

b. Due to the many similarities of the two crash site descriptions and the considerable distance between them, it was likely that more than one event with similar characteristics was the basis for these accounts.

c. Since the account of bodies at the Roswell Army Air Field hospital did not contain elements similar to reports of the two crash sites, it was likely that this account was unrelated to the crash site accounts. (The hospital account will be addressed separately in Section Two of this report.)

The remaining testimony was examined with regard both to the facts and to working hypotheses to determine if there were common threads or links connecting any of the accounts. If similarities were found, the next step was to determine if they were related to an actual event. Finally, if there were actual event(s), were they part of U.S. Air Force or U.S. Government activities?

Common Threads

Careful examination of the testimony revealed that primary witnesses of the two "crashed saucer" locations contained descriptions common to both. These areas of commonality contained both general and detailed characteristics. However, before continuing, the accounts were carefully examined to determine if the testimony related by individual witnesses were of their own experiences and not a recitation of information given by other persons. While many aspects of the remaining accounts were judged to be similar, other aspects were found to be significantly different. The accounts on which the analysis is based were determined, in all likelihood, to have been independently obtained or observed by the witnesses.

General Similarities. The testimony presented for both crash sites generally followed the same sequence of events. The witnesses were in a rural and isolated area of New Mexico. In the course of their travels in this area, they came upon a crashed aerial vehicle. The witnesses then proceeded to the area of the crash to investigate and at some distance they observed strange looking "beings" that appeared to be crewmembers of the vehicle. Soon thereafter, a convoy of military vehicles and soldiers arrived at the site. Military personnel allegedly instructed the civilians to leave the area and forget what they had seen. As the witnesses left the area, the military personnel commenced with a recovery operation of the crashed aerial vehicle and "crew."

Detailed Similarities. Along with general similarities in the testimonies, there also existed a substantial amount of similar detailed descriptions of the "aliens," and the military vehicles and procedures allegedly used to recover them.

The first obvious similarity was the descriptions of the aliens. Mr. Gerald Anderson, an alleged witness of events at the site 175 miles northwest of Roswell, recalled, "I thought they were plastic dolls." [12] Mr. James Ragsdale, an alleged witness of the site north of Roswell, stated, "They were using dummies in those damned things." [13] Another alleged witness to a "crash" north of Roswell, Frank J. Kaufman, recalled that there was "talk" that perhaps an "experimental plane with dummies in it" was the source of the claims.[14]

Additional similarities were also noted. Mr. Vern Maltais, a secondhand witness of the site 175 miles northwest of Roswell, described the hands of the "aliens" as, "They had four fingers."[15] Anderson characterized the hands as, "They didn't have a little finger."[16] He also described the heads of the aliens as "completely bald"[17] while Maltais described them as "hairless."[18] The uniforms of the aliens were independently described by Anderson as "one-piece suits...a shiny silverish-gray color"[19] and by Maltais as "one-piece and gray in color."[20] The date of this event was also not precisely known. Maltais recalled that it may have occurred "around 1950"[21] and another secondhand witness, Alice Knight stated, "I don't recall the date."[22]

Witnesses of different sites also used the terms "wrecker"[23] and "six-by-six"[24] when they described the military vehicles present at the different recovery sites. One witness described seeing a "medium sized Jeep/truck"[25] and another witness described seeing a "weapons carrier"[26] (a weapons carrier is a mid-sized Jeep-type truck).

The Research Profile

When the general and specific similarities were combined, a profile emerged describing the event or activity that might have been observed. The profile, which contains elements common to at least two, and in some cases, all of the accounts, established a set of criteria used to determine what the witnesses may have observed. The profile is as follows:

a. An activity that, if viewed from a distance, would appear unusual.

b. An activity of which the exact date is not known.

c. An activity that took place in two rural areas of New Mexico.

d. An activity that involved a type of aerial vehicle with dolls or dummies that had four fingers, were bald, and wore one-piece gray suits.

e. An activity that required recovery by numerous military personnel and an assortment of vehicles that included a wrecker, a six-by-six, and a weapons carrier.

Based on this profile, research was begun to identify events or activities with these characteristics. Due to the location of the sites, attention was focused on Roswell AAF (renamed Walker AFB in 1948), White Sands Missile Range and Holloman AFB, N.M. The aerial vehicles assigned or under development at these facilities were aircraft, missiles, remotely-piloted drones, and high altitude balloons. The operational characteristics and areas where these vehicles flew were researched to determine if they played a role in the events described by the witnesses.

Missiles and Drones. Missiles and drones were determined not to have been responsible for the accounts.* The areas where the alleged crashes took place were, in all likelihood, too far from the White Sands Missile Range. Missiles were equipped with a self-destruct mechanism that was activated if it strayed off-course or out of the White Sands Missile Range. There was never a program that required a dummy or doll to be placed inside a missile or a drone. However, missiles were launched from White Sands carrying monkeys and other small animals aloft for scientific research.[27] These projects were well documented, and none of these missiles landed near either of the two crash sites.

Aircraft. Aircraft seemed just as unlikely as missiles to have been responsible for the extraterrestrial claims as outlined in the profile. Although additional research revealed the significant role dummies played in the test and evaluation of aircraft emergency escape systems, these dummies were used on board aircraft and on the high-speed test track at Holloman AFB. However, aircraft test flights demanded strict adherence to established flight profiles over the instrumented portions of the White Sands Missile Range, many miles from the alleged crash sites. Dummies used on the high-speed track remained in the immediate vicinity of the track facilities at Holloman AFB. This geographical impossibility ruled out dummies that were ejected from aircraft and those used on the high-speed track as a cause of alleged alien sightings. (Aircraft accidents will be discussed extensively in Section Two of this report.)

Figs. 12 & 13. Missiles *(left)* and drones *(right)* under development at Holloman AFB, N.M. were determined not to have been involved in the "Roswell Incident." *(U.S. Air Force photos)*

*From September 1961 until March 1965 12 Atlas F intercontinental ballistic missiles (ICBMs) were deployed by the 579th Strategic Missile Squadron in areas surrounding Walker AFB, N.M. These missiles were determined not to have been involved in the Roswell Incident.

High Altitude Research Balloons. The only vehicles not yet evaluated as a possible source of the accounts were high altitude research balloons. Previous reviews of early research balloon flight records revealed that trajectories of high altitude balloons were, at times, unpredictable and did not usually remain over Holloman AFB or White Sands Missile Range.[28] Many of the scientific payloads required recovery so the data collected during flight could be returned to the laboratory for analysis.

These characteristics seemed to fit at least some of the research profile. Atmospheric sampling apparatus or weather instruments, the typical payload of many high altitude balloons, could hardly have been mistaken for space aliens. A careful examination of the instruments carried aloft by the high altitude balloons revealed that one unique project used a device that very likely could be mistaken for an alien—an anthropomorphic dummy.

An anthropomorphic dummy is a human substitute equipped with a variety of instrumentation to measure effects of environments and situations deemed too hazardous for a human. These abstractly human dummies were first used in New Mexico in May 1950, and have been used on a continuous basis since that time.[29]

In the 1950s, anthropomorphic dummies were not widely exposed outside of scientific research circles and easily could have been mistaken for something they were not. Today, anthropomorphic dummies, better known as crash test dummies, are easily identifiable and are even the "stars" of their own automotive safety advertising campaign. During the 1950s when the U.S. Air Force dropped the odd-looking test devices from high altitude balloons in its program to study high altitude human free-fall characteristics, public awareness and stardom were decades away. It seems likely that someone who unexpectedly observed these dummies at a distance would believe they had seen something unusual. In retrospect, when interviewed over 40 years later, they could accurately report that they had seen something *very unusual.*

With the introduction of anthropomorphic dummies as a possible explanation for the reports of bodies, another element of the research profile appeared to be satisfied. Specific information that described the locations, methods, and procedures used to employ the dummies was required before any definitive conclusions could be drawn. To gather this detailed information, research efforts were concentrated on high altitude balloon operations and the specific projects that utilized balloon-borne anthropomorphic dummies.

Fig. 14. *(Left)* Example of an anthropomorphic dummy carried aloft by U.S. Air Force high altitude balloons. These dummies landed at numerous locations throughout New Mexico during the 1950s. *(U.S. Air Force photo)*

Fig. 15. *(Right)* Newspaper advertisement depicting anthropomorphic dummies "Vince and Larry" "stars" of the successful advertising campaign by the National Highway Traffic Safety Administration to encourage use of safety belts. *(Courtesy of NHTSA)*

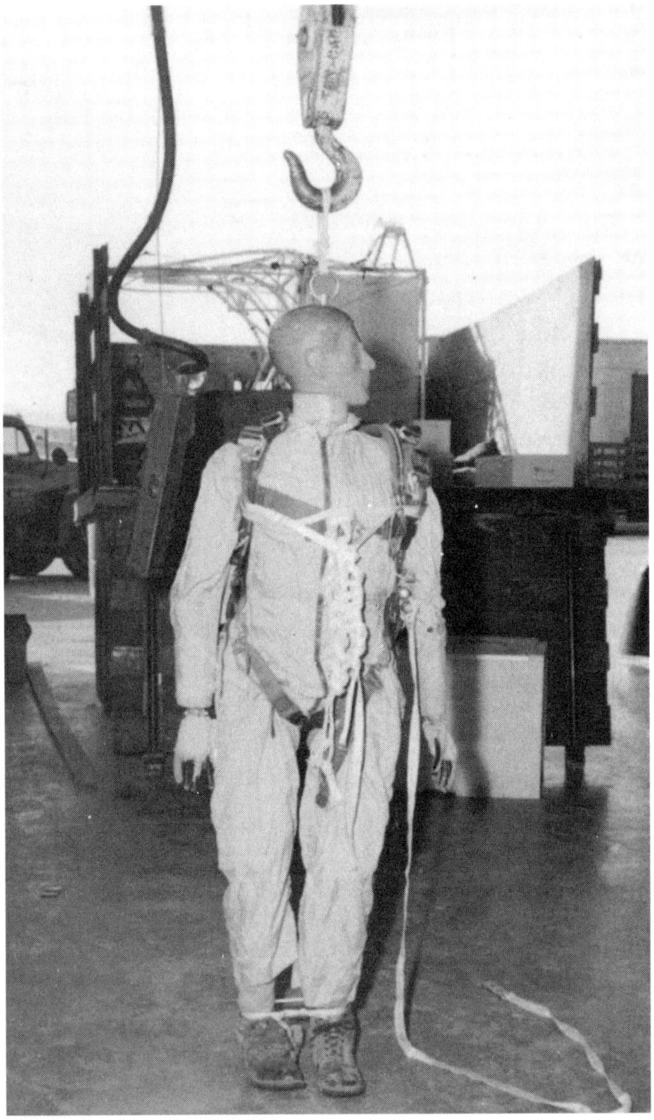

Test Dummies Used by the U.S. Air Force

Since the beginning of manned flight, designers have sought a substitute for the human body to test hazardous new equipment. Early devices used by the predecessors of the U.S. Air Force were simply constructed parachute drop test dummies with little similarity to the human form. Following World War II, aircraft emergency escape systems became increasingly sophisticated and engineers required a dummy with more humanlike characteristics.

Parachute Drop Dummies

During World War I research and development of the first U.S. military parachute was underway at McCook Field, Ohio. To test the parachute, engineers experimented with several types of dummies, settling on a model constructed of three-inch hemp rope and sandbags with the approximate proportions of a medium-sized man.[30] The new invention was soon known by the nickname "Dummy Joe." Dummy Joe is said to have made more than five thousand "jumps" between 1918 and 1924.[31]

By 1924, parachutes were required on military aircraft with their serviceability tested by dummies dropped from aircraft.[32] For this routine testing, several types of dummies were used. The most common type is shown in figures 17 and 18. Parachutes were individually drop-tested from aircraft until the early stages of World War II, when, due both to increased reliability and large numbers of parachutes in service, this routine practice was discontinued. Nonetheless, test dummies were still used frequently by the Parachute Branch of Air Materiel Command (AMC) at Wright Field, Ohio, to test new parachute designs.

Fig. 16. "'Dummy Joe,' the hero of five thousand jumps" is shown here with engineers J.J. Higgins *(left)* and Guy Ball at McCook Field, Ohio in 1920. *(U.S. Air Force photo)*

Fig. 17. *(Left)* Early rope and sandbag dummy used to test parachutes. *(U.S. Air Force photo)*

Fig. 18. *(Right)* Parachute drop dummies in use at Wright Field, Ohio. The historic Flight Test hangars, Hangars 1 and 9, can be seen in the background. *(U.S. Air Force photo)*

Anthropomorphic Dummies

The ejection seat had been developed and used successfully by the German Luftwaffe during the latter stages of World War II. The utility of this invention was realized when the U.S. Army Air Forces obtained an ejection seat in 1944.[33] To properly test the ejection seat, the Army Air Forces required a dummy that had the same center of gravity and weight distribution as a human, characteristics that parachute drop dummies did not possess. In 1944, the USAAF Air Materiel Command contracted with the Ted Smith Company of Upper Darby, Pa. to design and manufacture the first dummy intended to accurately represent a human.[34] The dummy had the same basic shape as a human, but with only abstract human features, and "skin" made of canvas.

In 1949, the U.S. Air Force Aero Medical Laboratory submitted a proposal for an improved model of the anthropomorphic dummy.[35] This request was originated by the renowned Air Force scientist and physician John P. Stapp, now a retired Colonel, who conducted a series of landmark

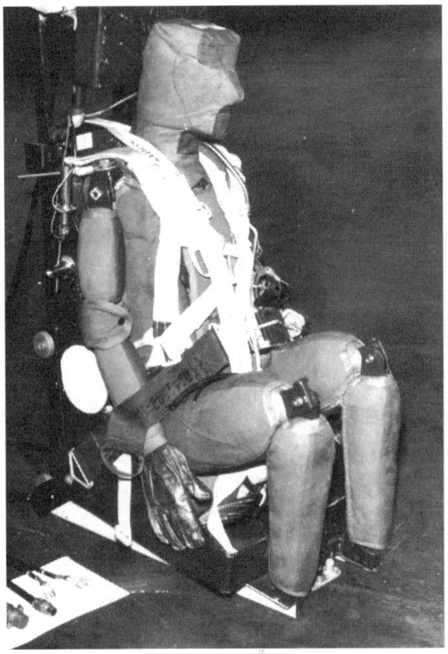

Figs. 19 & 20. *(Left & Right)* These early anthropomorphic dummies, manufactured by the Ted Smith Co., of Upper Darby, Pa., were used by the Army Air Forces beginning in 1944. They were replaced by a more realistic dummy in 1949.

(Right) "Oscar Eightball," the name given to this early model anthropomorphic dummy by Col. John P. Stapp, is shown following a run of the high-speed track at Muroc AAF (now Edwards AFB), Calif., in 1947. *(U.S. Air Force photos)*

experiments at Muroc (now Edwards) AFB, Calif., to measure the effects of acceleration and deceleration during high-speed aircraft ejections.[36] Stapp required a dummy that had the same center of gravity and articulation as a human, but, unlike the Ted Smith dummy, was more human in appearance. A more accurate external appearance was required to provide for the proper fit of helmets, oxygen masks, and other equipment used during the tests. Stapp requested the Anthropology Branch of the Aero Medical Laboratory at Wright Field to review anthropological, orthopedic, and engineering literature to prepare specifications for the new dummy.[37] Plaster casts of the torso, legs, and arms of an Air Force pilot were also taken to assure accuracy.[38] The result was a proposed dummy that stood 72 inches tall, weighed 200 pounds, had provisions for mounting instrumentation, and could withstand up to 100 times the force of gravity or 100Gs.

In 1949, a contract was awarded to Sierra Engineering Company of Sierra Madre, Calif., and deliveries began in 1950.[39] This dummy quickly became known as "Sierra Sam."

In 1952, a contract for anthropomorphic dummies was awarded to Alderson Research Laboratories, Inc., of New York City.[40] Dummies constructed by both companies possessed the same basic characteristics: a skeleton of aluminum or steel, latex or plastic skin, a cast aluminum skull, and an instrument cavity in the torso and head for the mounting of strain gauges, accelerometers, transducers, and rate gyros.[41] Models used by the Air Force were primarily parachute drop and ejection seat versions with center of gravity tolerances within one quarter inch.

Over the next several years the two companies improved and redesigned internal structures and instrumentation, but the basic external appearance of the dummies remained relatively constant from the mid 1950s to the late 1960s. Dummies of these types were most likely the "aliens" associated with the "Roswell Incident."

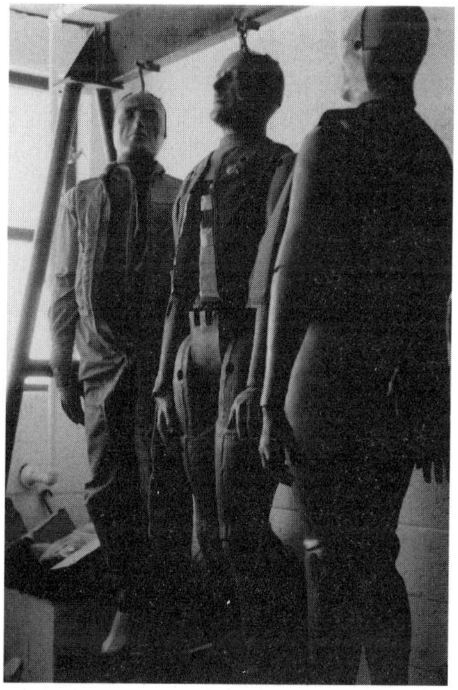

Figs. 21& 22. Examples of a "Sierra Sam" *(left)* and Alderson Laboratories anthropomorphic dummies *(right)* of the type dropped from balloons at off-range locations throughout New Mexico during the 1950s. *(U.S. Air Force photos)*

1.2
High Altitude Balloon Dummy Drops

From 1953 to 1959, anthropomorphic dummies were used by the U.S. Air Force Aero Medical Laboratory as part of the high altitude aircraft escape projects HIGH DIVE and EXCELSIOR.[42] The object of these studies was to devise a method to return a pilot or astronaut to earth by parachute, if forced to escape at extreme altitudes.[43]

Fig. 23. Project HIGH DIVE anthropomorphic dummy launch, White Sands Proving Ground, N.M., June 11, 1957. *(U.S. Air Force photo)*

Anthropomorphic dummies were transported to altitudes up to 98,000 feet by high altitude balloons. The dummies were then released for a period of free-fall while body movements and escape equipment performance were recorded by a variety of instruments. Forty-three high altitude balloon flights carrying 67 anthropomorphic dummies were launched and recovered throughout New Mexico between June 1954 and February 1959.[44] Due to prevailing wind conditions, operational factors and ruggedness of the terrain, the majority of dummies impacted outside the confines of military reservations in eastern New Mexico, near Roswell, and in areas surrounding the Tularosa Valley in south central New Mexico.[45] Additionally, 30 dummies were dropped by aircraft over White Sands Proving Ground, N.M. in 1953. In 1959, 150 dummies were dropped by aircraft over Wright-Patterson AFB, Ohio (possibly accounting for alleged alien "sightings" at that location). [46]

Anthropomorphic Dummy Launch and Landing Locations

△ Anthropomorphic Dummy Launch Locations
□ Anthropomorphic Dummy Landing Locations

Locations approximate; numbers within symbols correspond to listing of locations found in Appendix A

Source: Test records of U.S. Air Force aeromedical project no. 7218, task 71719 (HIGH DIVE) and project no. 7222, task 71748 (EXCELSIOR).

A number of these launch and recovery locations were in the areas where the "crashed saucer" and "space aliens" were allegedly observed.

Following the series of dummy tests, a human subject, test pilot Capt. Joseph W. Kittinger, Jr., now a retired Colonel, made three parachute jumps from high altitude balloons. Since free-fall tests from these unprecedented altitudes were extremely hazardous, they could not be accomplished by a human until a rigorous testing program using anthropomorphic dummies was completed.

Fig. 25. "Lord, take care of me now," were Capt. Joseph W. Kittinger, Jr.'s words as he exited the EXCELSIOR III balloon gondola at 102,800 feet on August 16, 1960, over White Sands Proving Ground, N.M. Kittinger's courageous scientific achievement remains, to this day, the highest parachute jump ever accomplished. *(U.S. Air Force photo)*

A Cover-Up?

Countering claims of a cover-up, Air Force projects that used anthropomorphic dummies and human subjects were unclassified and widely publicized in numerous newspaper and magazine stories, books, and television reports. These included a book written by test pilot Kittinger, *The Long, Lonely Leap*, another book, *Man High*, by MAN HIGH Project Scientist, Lt. Col. David G. Simons (MC), a feature article in *National Geographic*, and cover stories in *Life, Collier's, Popular Mechanics,* and *Time*.[47] A characterization of Kittinger's record parachute jump even appeared in the adolescent magazine, *MAD*.[48] The intense public interest in HIGH DIVE, EXCELSIOR and other aero medical projects conducted at Holloman AFB also resulted in a 1956 Twentieth Century Fox full-length motion picture, *On the Threshold of Space* (see page 38).

Fig. 26. This photo of Capt. Joseph W. Kittinger, Jr. taken by a remotely operated camera on the EXCELSIOR III gondola, was featured in the December 1960 *National Geographic*.

The Long, Lonely Leap

World's highest jump tests a new type of parachute for high-altitude flyers and scientists returning from the threshold of space

By CAPT. JOSEPH W. KITTINGER, JR., USAF

Illustrations by National Geographic photographer VOLKMAR WENTZEL

OVERHEAD my onion-shaped balloon spread its 200-foot diameter against a black daytime sky. More than 18½ miles below lay the cloud-hidden New Mexico desert to which I shortly would parachute.

Sitting in my gondola, which gently twisted with the balloon's slow turnings, I had begun to sweat lightly, though the temperature read 36° below zero Fahrenheit. Sunlight burned in on me under the edge of an aluminized antiglare curtain and through the gondola's open door.

In my earphones crackled the voice of Capt. Marvin Feldstein, one of our project's two doctors, from ground control at Holloman Air Force Base:

"Three minutes till jump, Joe."

I was ready to go, for more reasons than one. For about an hour—as the balloon rose from 50,000 to 102,800 feet above sea level—I had been exposed to an environment requiring the protection of a pressure suit and helmet, and the fear of their failure had always been present. If either should break, unconsciousness would come in 10 or 12 seconds, and death within two minutes.

In our altitude-chamber flights at the laboratory, I always

"Lord, take care of me now," I pray, then take the big step-off that begins my return from the edge of space, a 13-minute, 45-second plunge to an earth wrapped in clouds. The lanyard attached to my parachute pack is my last link with the gondola. It starts a timer on a small stabilization chute that will open 16 seconds later and prevent horizontal spinning. Without stabilization, man could not survive a jump from these high altitudes.

A National Geographic camera mounted above the gondola took this remarkable photograph at 102,800 feet.

854

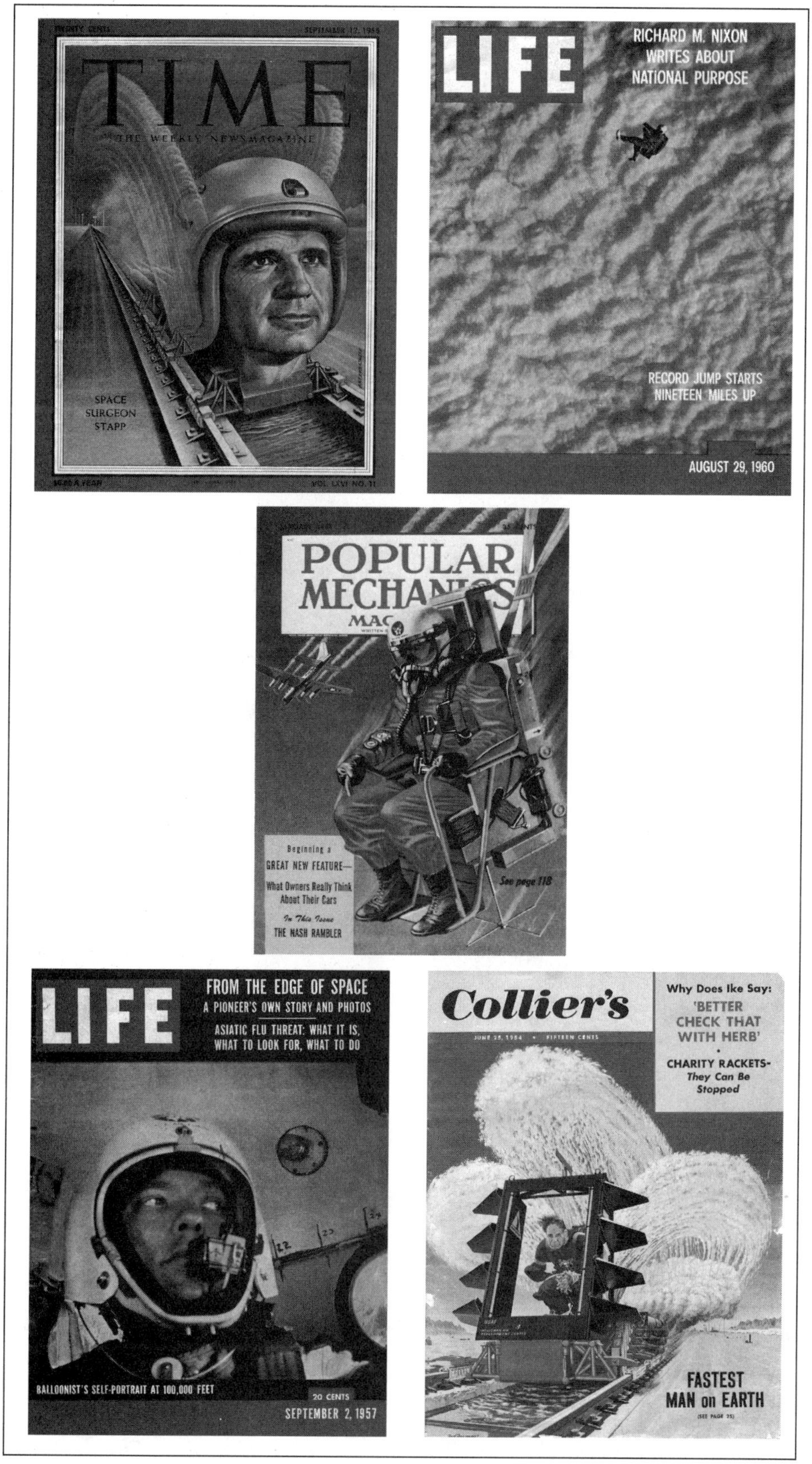

Fig. 27. Contemporary magazines that featured experiments at Holloman AFB, N.M. *Clockwise from top left, Time,* September 12, 1955; *Life,* August 29, 1960; *Popular Mechanics Magazine, (center)* January 1951; *Collier's*, June 25,1954; and *Life*, September 2, 1957.

Dummy Drop Procedures

For the majority of the tests, dummies were flown to altitudes between 30,000 and 98,000 feet attached to a specially designed rack suspended below a high altitude balloon.[49] On several flights the dummies were mounted in the door of an experimental high altitude balloon gondola.[50] Upon reaching the desired altitude, the dummies were released and free-fell for several minutes before deployment of the main parachute.

The dummies used for the balloon drops were outfitted with standard equipment of an Air Force aircrew member. This equipment consisted of a one-piece flightsuit, olive drab, gray (witnesses had described seeing aliens in gray one-piece suits) or fuchsia in color, boots, and a parachute pack.[51] The dummies were also fitted with an

Fig. 28. *(Left)* Witnesses at both flying saucer "crash" sites stated that a "wrecker" was used in the recovery of the "alien" craft. This was a likely reference to the M-342 five-ton wrecker, used to launch and recover anthropomorphic dummies.

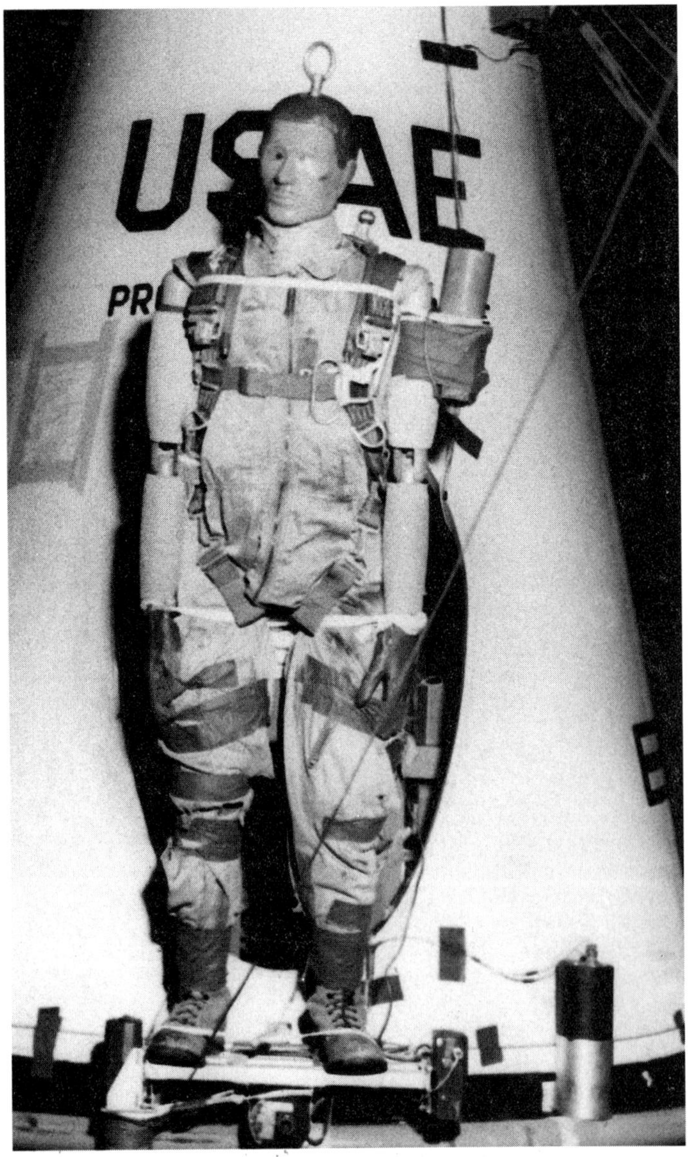

Fig. 29. *(Right)* Three tests utilized anthropomorphic dummies mounted in the door of an experimental Project HIGH DIVE gondola. This launch took place on October 8, 1957, in front of curious onlookers at the public picnic area of White Sands National Monument, N.M. *(U.S. Air Force photo)*

Fig. 30. A "Sierra Sam" with HIGH DIVE Project Officers 1st Lts. Eugene M. Schwartz *(left)* and Raymond A. Madson *(right)*. This dummy is outfitted in a "sage green" colored flightsuit (a shade of gray) with red tape sealing its neck, wrists, and ankles. *(U.S. Air Force)*

instrumentation kit that contained accelerometers, pressure transducers, an ocscillograph, and a camera to record movements of the dummy during free-fall.[52]

Recoveries of the test dummies were accomplished by personnel from the Holloman AFB Balloon Branch.[53] Typically, eight to twelve civilian and military recovery personnel arrived at the site of an anthropomorphic dummy landing as soon as possible following impact. The recovery crews operated a variety of aircraft and vehicles. These included a wrecker, a six-by-six, a weapons carrier, and L-20 observation and C-47 transport aircraft—the exact vehicles and aircraft described by the witnesses as having been present at the crashed saucer locations.[54] On one occasion, just southwest of Roswell, a High Dive project officer, 1st Lt. Raymond A. Madson, even conducted a search for dummies on horseback[55] (see statement in Appendix B).

To expedite the recoveries, crews were prepositioned with their vehicles along a paved highway in the area where impact was expected.[56]

Fig. 31. An M-35 2½-ton cargo truck, commonly referred to as a "six-by-six," were used by the Holloman Balloon Branch to launch and recover anthropomorphic dummies and suspension racks at numerous locations throughout New Mexico. *(U.S. Air Force photo)*

Fig. 32. M-37 ¾-ton utility trucks, known as "weapons carriers," were used for high altitude balloon recoveries by the Holloman Balloon Branch during the 1950s. Here, recovery technicians use an M-37 to retrieve an Aero Medical gondola from a location on Holloman AFB, N.M. *(U.S. Air Force photo)*

On a typical flight the dummies were separated from the balloon by radio command and descended by parachute.[57] Prompt recovery of the dummies and their suspension racks, which usually did not land in the same location resulting in extensive ground and air searches, was essential for researchers to evaluate information collected by the instrumentation and cameras. To assist the recovery personnel, a variety of methods were used to enhance the visibility of the dummies: smoke grenades, pigment powder, and brightly colored parachute canopies.[58] Also, recovery notices promising a $25 reward were taped to an exposed portion of a dummy.[59] Local newspapers and radio stations were contacted when equipment was lost.[60]

The Bravest Man

America was introduced to Col. John Paul Stapp on December 10, 1954, when he became known as both the "the bravest" and "the fastest" man on earth. Stapp earned these titles following a rocket sled test that accelerated him to 632 miles per hour. He reached this speed in just five seconds—faster than a .45 caliber bullet—and was decelerated to a stop in 1.4 seconds, subjecting his body to more than 42 times the force of gravity! While this was America's introduction to Col. Stapp, the 1954 rocket sled test that examined aircraft restraint devices and human responses to accelerative/decelerative forces and windblast, was just one of many achievements of this legendary Air Force physician.

Born in Bahia, Brazil to American missionary parents, Stapp sold pots and pans door to door during the Depression while he earned both undergraduate and graduate degrees in zoology and chemistry at Baylor University. He went on to earn a doctorate in biophysics from the University of Texas, and a doctorate in medicine from the University of Minnesota.

In 1944 Stapp entered the U.S. Army Air Forces and became a flight surgeon. From 1946 to 1963, due to his unique qualifications in biophysics and medicine, he conducted a series of acceleration/deceleration experiments on the high-speed track at Muroc (now Edwards AFB), Calif.,[61] and later at Holloman AFB, N.M. Developments from these and other studies resulted

Fig. 33. The first "space doctor," Lt. Col. John P. Stapp (now a retired Colonel) being strapped into the rocket sled Sonic Wind Nº 1, on December 10, 1954, at Holloman AFB, N.M. Courageously, Stapp was his own volunteer subject on 29 rocket sled tests and earned two awards of the Legion of Merit and the Cheney Award for valor and self-sacrifice. *(U.S. Air Force photo)*

in innovations which have saved many lives. These included improved safety belt restraint systems and design specifications for aircraft and automobiles, aircraft ejection and emergency escape systems, refinement of automobile airbag systems, and development of the modern anthropomorphic test dummy.

As commander of the U.S. Air Force Aeromedical Field Laboratory at Holloman AFB, N.M. and later the Aero Medical Laboratory at Wright-Patterson AFB, Ohio, Stapp won support for the Air Force manned high altitude balloons projects—Man High and Excelsior. As a testament to his thorough safety preparations, these and other extremely hazardous projects administered by Stapp, did not result in a single debilitating injury to a test subject. These projects helped pave the way for future flights of both high altitude aircraft such as the X-15, and of spacecraft for the Mercury, Gemini, and Apollo programs. In fact, Stapp's expertise was called upon to assist in the selection of the initial cadre of astronauts, the "Mercury Seven."

He retired from the Air Force in 1970, but not before amassing a collection of awards and honors. These included two awards of the Legion of Merit for rocket sled experiments, the Cheney Award for 1954, and membership in the National Aviation Hall of Fame.

In association with the Society of Automotive Engineers, Stapp continues to participate in annual conferences in which industry experts assemble to discuss vehicle safety issues. The conferences, now in their 40th year bear his name: the Stapp Car Crash Conferences.

In 1991, in recognition of a lifetime of unselfish dedication to scientific research, Stapp was awarded the National Medal of Technology, bestowed upon him at the White House by President George Bush.

He is married to the former Lillian Lanese, a former soloist with the Ballet Theater of New York, and resides in Alamogordo, N.M. At 87 years old he continues to maintain a dizzying pace of travel and lectures.

It is not an exaggeration that virtually every person who has safely operated, or ridden in, an automobile, aircraft, or spacecraft, has benefited from the genius of Col. John Paul Stapp, and owes this brave scientist, physician, and visionary, a great deal of thanks.

Fig. 34. September 12, 1955 edition of *Time* featuring Col. John P. Stapp and his rocket sled experiments at Holloman AFB, N.M.

Despite these efforts, the dummies were not always recovered immediately; one was not found for nearly three years and several were not recovered at all.[62] When they were found, the dummies and instrumentation were often damaged from impact.[63] Damage to the dummies included loss of heads, arms, legs and fingers.[64] This detail, dummies with missing fingers, appears to satisfy another element of the research profile—aliens with only four fingers.

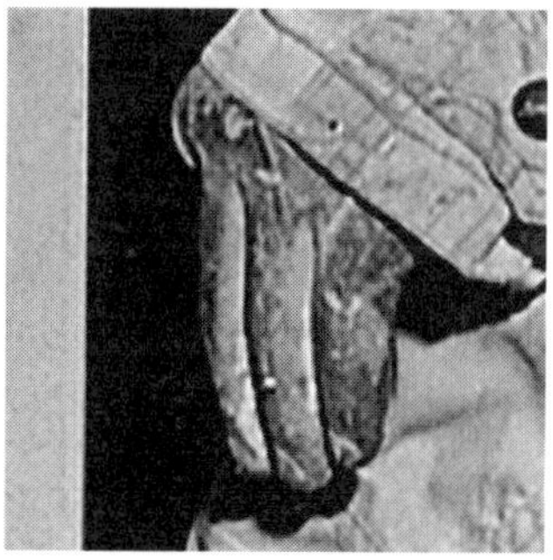

Fig. 35. Rough treatment and parachute failures during balloon drops often caused damage to the hands of the dummies. This detail, "beings" with "four fingers," was related by two witnesses as a distinguishing feature of the Roswell aliens.
(U.S. Air Force photo)

Figs. 36-38. Actual photographs of an Alderson Laboratories type anthropomorphic dummy falling away from its suspension rack at high altitude over New Mexico. Fig. 37 *(center)* appears on the cover of this publication. *(U.S. Air Force photos)*

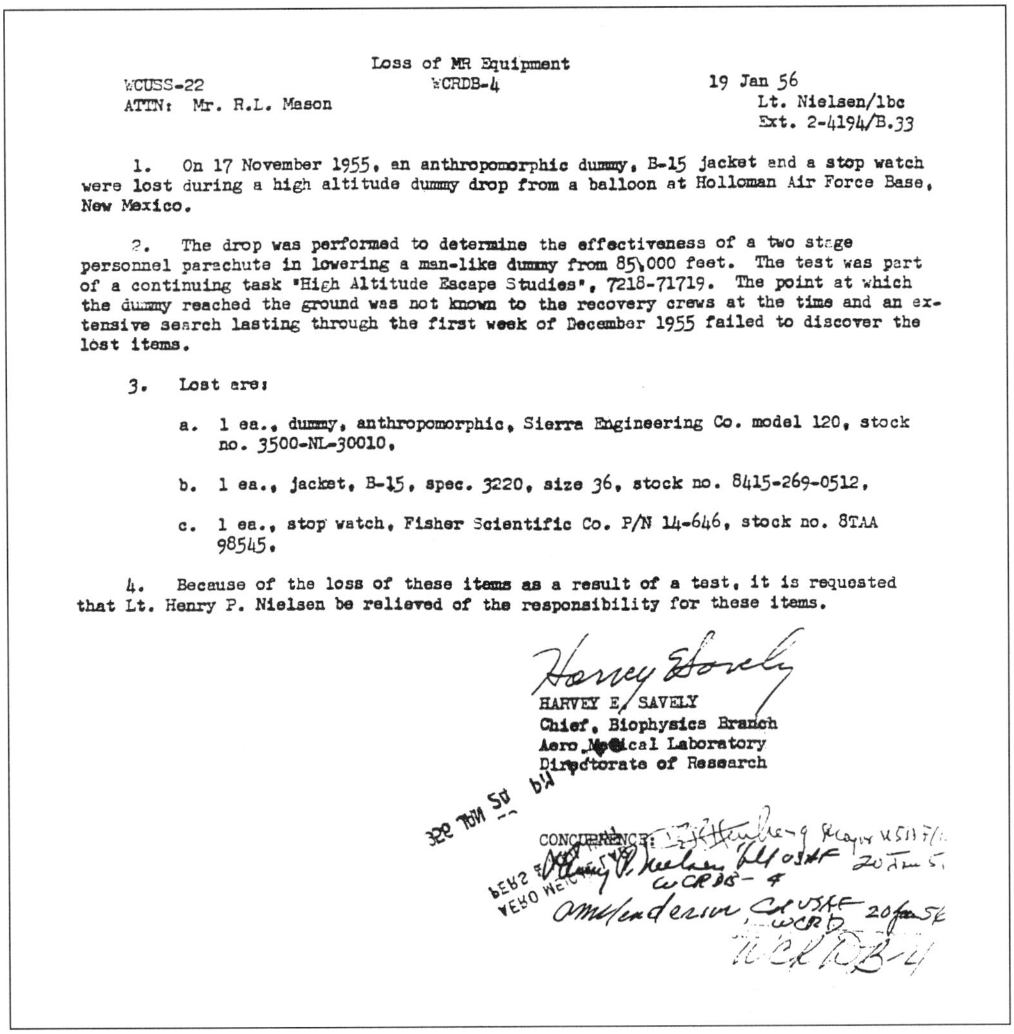

Loss of MR Equipment

WCUSS-22 WCRDB-4 19 Jan 56
ATTN: Mr. R.L. Mason Lt. Nielsen/lbc
Ext. 2-4194/B.33

1. On 17 November 1955, an anthropomorphic dummy, B-15 jacket and a stop watch were lost during a high altitude dummy drop from a balloon at Holloman Air Force Base, New Mexico.

2. The drop was performed to determine the effectiveness of a two stage personnel parachute in lowering a man-like dummy from 85,000 feet. The test was part of a continuing task "High Altitude Escape Studies", 7218-71719. The point at which the dummy reached the ground was not known to the recovery crews at the time and an extensive search lasting through the first week of December 1955 failed to discover the lost items.

3. Lost are:

a. 1 ea., dummy, anthropomorphic, Sierra Engineering Co. model 120, stock no. 3500-NL-30010,

b. 1 ea., jacket, B-15, spec. 3220, size 36, stock no. 8415-269-0512,

c. 1 ea., stop watch, Fisher Scientific Co. P/N 14-646, stock no. 8TAA 98545.

4. Because of the loss of these items as a result of a test, it is requested that Lt. Henry P. Nielsen be relieved of the responsibility for these items.

HARVEY E. SAVELY
Chief, Biophysics Branch
Aero Medical Laboratory
Directorate of Research

CONCURRENCE:

Fig. 39. Memo taken from Project HIGH DIVE files explaining the loss of a dummy near Roswell, N.M. in November 1955.

What may have contributed to a misunderstanding if the dummies were viewed by persons unfamiliar with their intended use, were the methods used by Holloman AFB personnel to transport them. The dummies were sometimes transported to and from off-range locations in wooden shipping containers, similar to caskets, to prevent damage to fragile instruments mounted in and on the dummy.[65] Also, canvas military stretchers and hospital gurneys were used (a procedure recommended by a dummy manufacturer) to move the dummies in the laboratory or retrieve dummies in the field after a test.[66] The first 10 dummy drops also utilized black or silver insulation bags, similar to "body bags" in which the dummies were placed for flight to guard against equipment failure at low ambient temperatures of the upper atmosphere.[67]

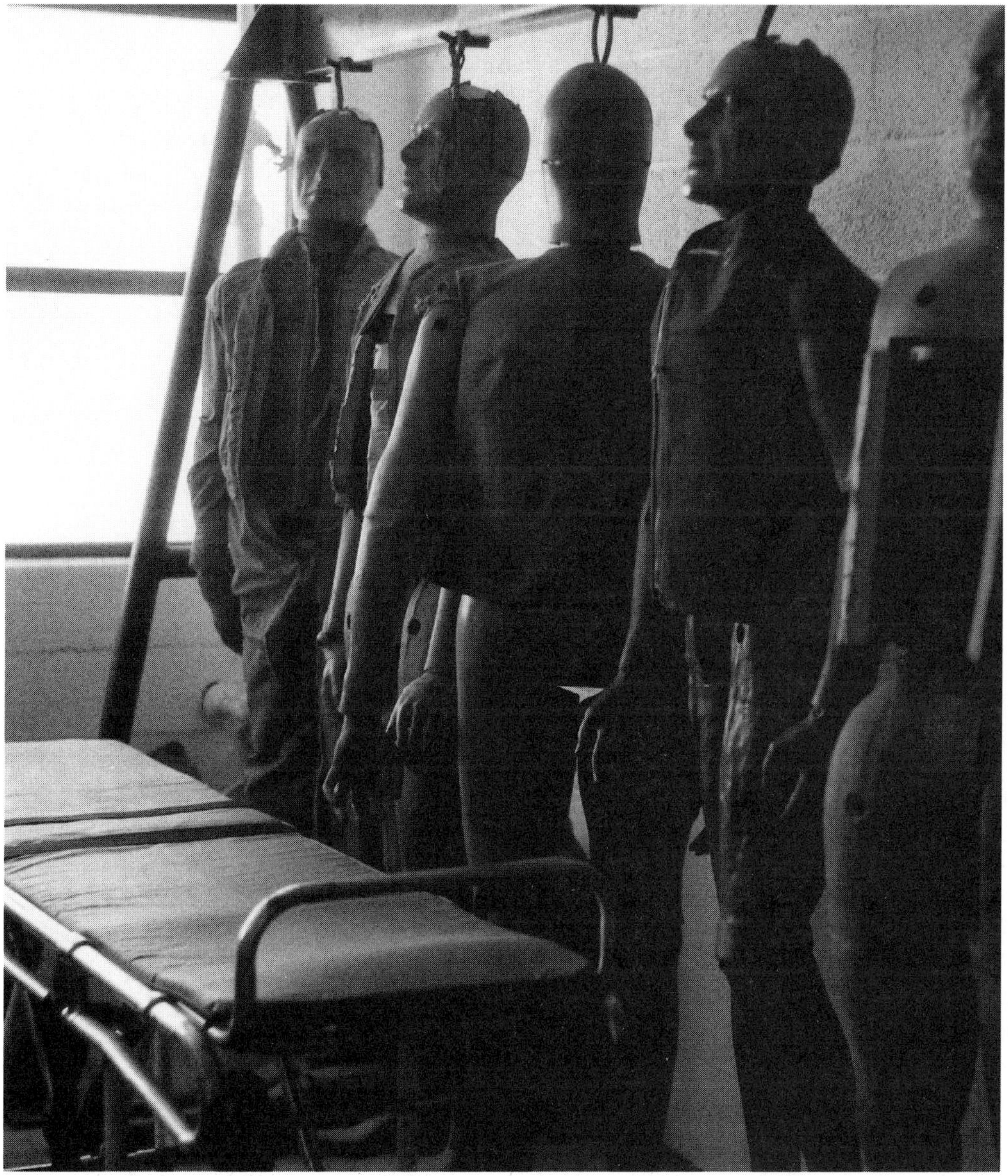

Fig. 40. Air Force personnel used stretchers and gurneys to pick up 200-pound dummies in the field and to move them in the laboratory.
(U.S. Air Force photo)

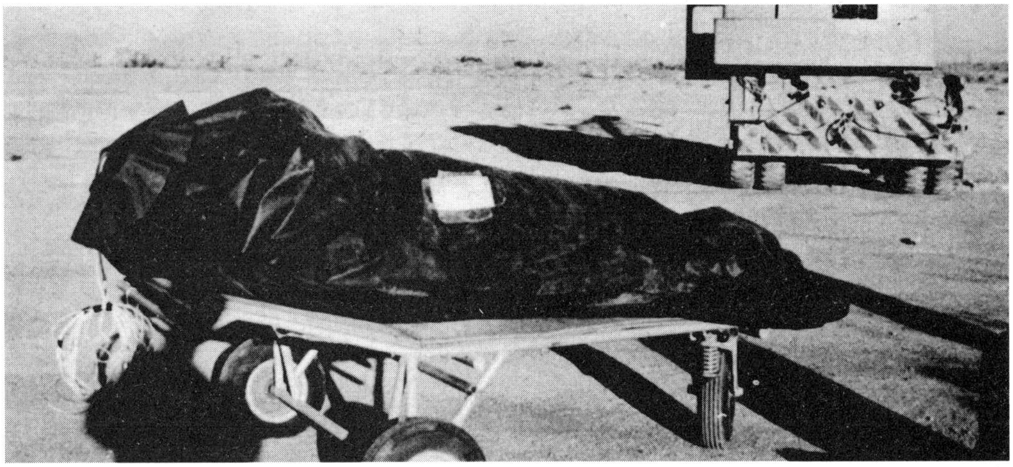

Fig. 41. For the first 10 balloon flights, dummies were placed in insulation bags to protect temperature-sensitive equipment. These bags may have been described by at least one witness as "body bags" used to recover alien victims from the crash of a flying saucer. *(U.S. Air Force photo)*

On one occasion northwest of Roswell, a local woman unfamiliar with the test activities arrived at a dummy landing site prior to the arrival of the recovery personnel.[68] The woman saw what appeared to be a human embedded head first in a snowbank and became hysterical. The woman screamed, "He's dead!, he's dead!"[69]

It now appeared that anthropomorphic dummies dropped by high altitude balloons satisfied the requirements of the research profile. However, the review of high altitude balloon operations revealed what appeared to be explanations for some other sightings of odd objects in the deserts and skies of New Mexico.

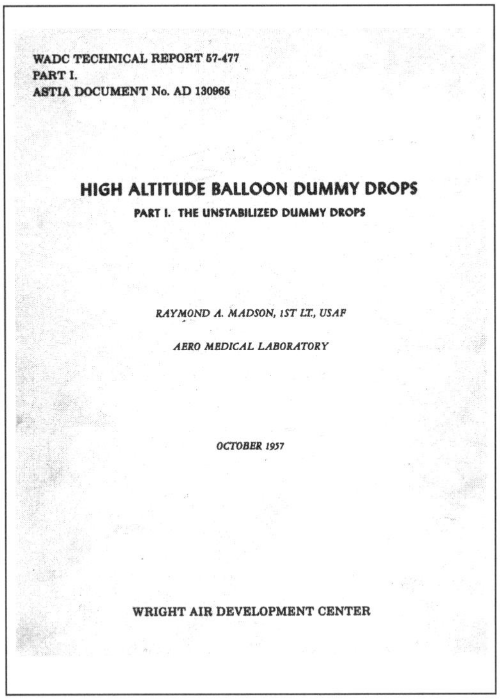

WADC TECHNICAL REPORT 57-477
PART I.
ASTIA DOCUMENT No. AD 130965

HIGH ALTITUDE BALLOON DUMMY DROPS

PART I. THE UNSTABILIZED DUMMY DROPS

RAYMOND A. MADSON, 1ST LT., USAF

AERO MEDICAL LABORATORY

OCTOBER 1957

WRIGHT AIR DEVELOPMENT CENTER

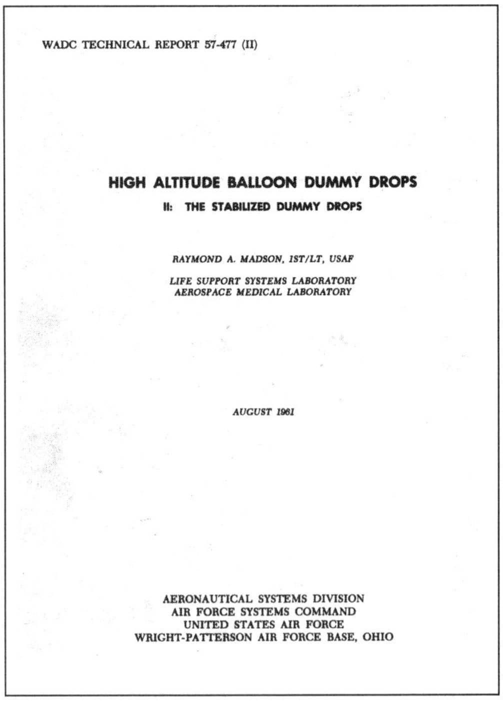

WADC TECHNICAL REPORT 57-477 (II)

HIGH ALTITUDE BALLOON DUMMY DROPS

II: THE STABILIZED DUMMY DROPS

RAYMOND A. MADSON, 1ST/LT, USAF

LIFE SUPPORT SYSTEMS LABORATORY
AEROSPACE MEDICAL LABORATORY

AUGUST 1961

AERONAUTICAL SYSTEMS DIVISION
AIR FORCE SYSTEMS COMMAND
UNITED STATES AIR FORCE
WRIGHT-PATTERSON AIR FORCE BASE, OHIO

Figs. 42 & 43. These reports detailed the methods and procedures used for the dummy tests. They may be obtained from the National Technical Information Service (NTIS), Springfield, Va.

1.3
High Altitude Balloon Operations

Research has shown that many high altitude balloons launched from Holloman AFB, N.M., were recovered in locations, and under circumstances, that strongly resemble those described by UFO proponents as the recovery of a "flying saucer" and "alien" crew. When these descriptions were carefully examined, it was clear that they bore more than just a resemblance to Air Force activities. It appears that some were actually distorted references to Air Force personnel and equipment engaged in scientific study through the use of high altitude balloons.

Since 1947, U.S. Air Force research organizations at Holloman AFB, N.M., have launched and recovered approximately 2,500 high altitude balloons. The Air Force organization that conducted most of these activities, the Holloman Balloon Branch, launched a wide range of sophisticated, and from most perspectives, odd looking equipment into the stratosphere above New Mexico. In fact, the ***very first*** high altitude data gathering balloon flight launched from Alamogordo Army Airfield (now Holloman AFB), N.M., on June 4, 1947, was found by the rancher and was the first of many unrelated events now collectively known as the "Roswell Incident."

Fig. 44. Inflation of a U.S. Air Force 626 ft. long, 34.6 million cu. ft. research balloon on August 13, 1972. This balloon was launched from Roswell Industrial Air Center (formerly Roswell AAF), Roswell, N.M., to test components of the NASA VIKING space probe. *(photo by Ole Jorgeson)*

On the Threshold of Space

In 1956, Twentieth Century Fox released *On the Threshold of Space,* a full-length motion picture based on Air Force aero medical projects conducted at Holloman AFB, N.M. Starring Guy Madison, John Hodiak, and Dean Jagger, this drama chronicled the high altitude balloon experiments of projects HIGH DIVE/EXCELSIOR and the high-speed track studies conducted by Col. John P. Stapp. Filmed on location at Holloman AFB, Air Force personnel, high altitude balloons, aircraft, vehicles, and other equipment, including the actual anthropomorphic dummies responsible for sightings of aliens, were used in the making of this film.

In an ironic twist, in 1990 the television program *Unsolved Mysteries,* featured a segment on the Roswell Incident. The program, hosted by actor Robert Stack, depicted a dramatized version of the claims of "aliens," space ships and mysterious government recovery crews. Interestingly, a review of newspapers from 1956 announcing the Hollywood premiere of *On the Threshold of Space,* listed Stack among the persons scheduled to attend this star-studded event.[70]

Fig. 45. Lobby card of the 1956 Twentieth Century Fox release, *On the Threshold of Space* starring Guy Madison *(seated)* and Martin Milner *(right).*

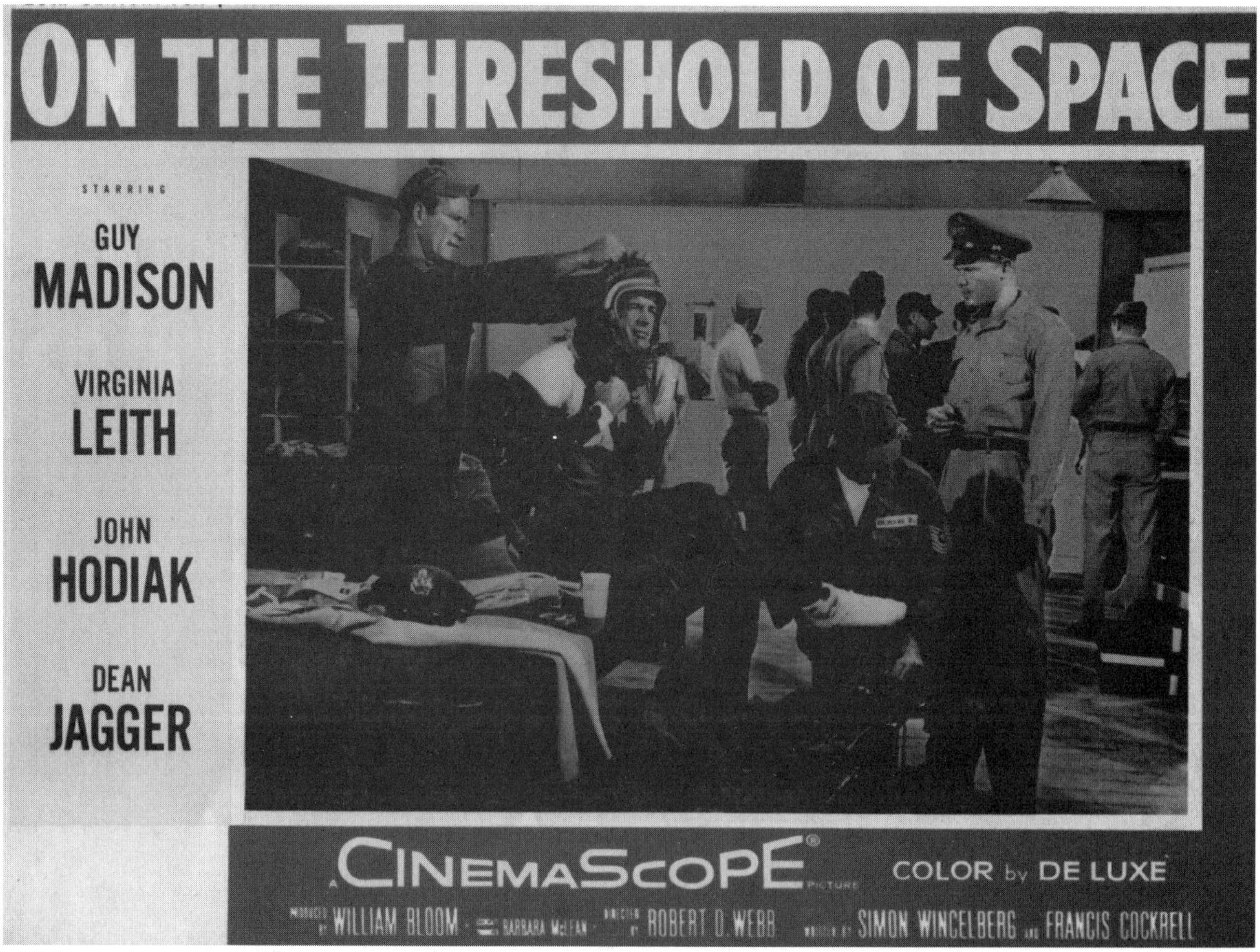

Fig. 46. Publicity photograph from *On the Threshold of Space* with *(from left)* Cameron Mitchell, Guy Madison and Dean Jagger. Scenes from the movie clearly depict the actual anthropomorphic dummies described nearly 40 years later as extraterrestrial "aliens."

Fig. 47. Col. J. P. Stapp's historic 1954 rocket sled test was re-created for *On the Threshold of Space (see figure 33, page 31).*

High Altitude Polyethylene Research Balloons

In 1946, as a result of research conducted for project MOGUL, Charles B. Moore, a New York University graduate student working under contract for the U.S. Army Air Forces, made a significant technological discovery: the use of polyethylene for high altitude balloon construction.[71] Polyethylene is a lightweight plastic that can withstand stresses of a high altitude environment that differed drastically from, and greatly exceeded, the capabilities of standard rubber weather balloons used previously. Moore's discovery was a breakthrough in technology. For the first time, scientists were able to make detailed, sustained studies of the upper atmosphere. Polyethylene balloons, first produced in 1947 for Project MOGUL, are still widely used today for a host of scientific applications.

High altitude polyethylene balloons and standard rubber weather balloons differ greatly in size, construction, and utility. The difference between these two types of balloons historically has been the subject of misunderstandings in that the term "weather balloon" is often used to describe both types of balloons.

High altitude polyethylene balloons are used to transport scientific payloads of several pounds to several tons to altitudes of nearly 200,000 feet. Polyethylene balloons do not increase in size and burst with increases in volume as they rise, as do standard rubber weather balloons. They are launched with excess capacity to accommodate the increase in volume. This characteristic of polyethylene balloons makes them substantially more stable than rubber weather balloons and capable of sustained constant level flight, a requirement for most scientific applications.

The initial polyethylene balloons had diameters of only seven feet and carried payloads of five pounds or less.[72] As balloon technology advanced, payload capacities and sizes of balloons increased. Modern polyethylene balloons, some as long as several football fields when on

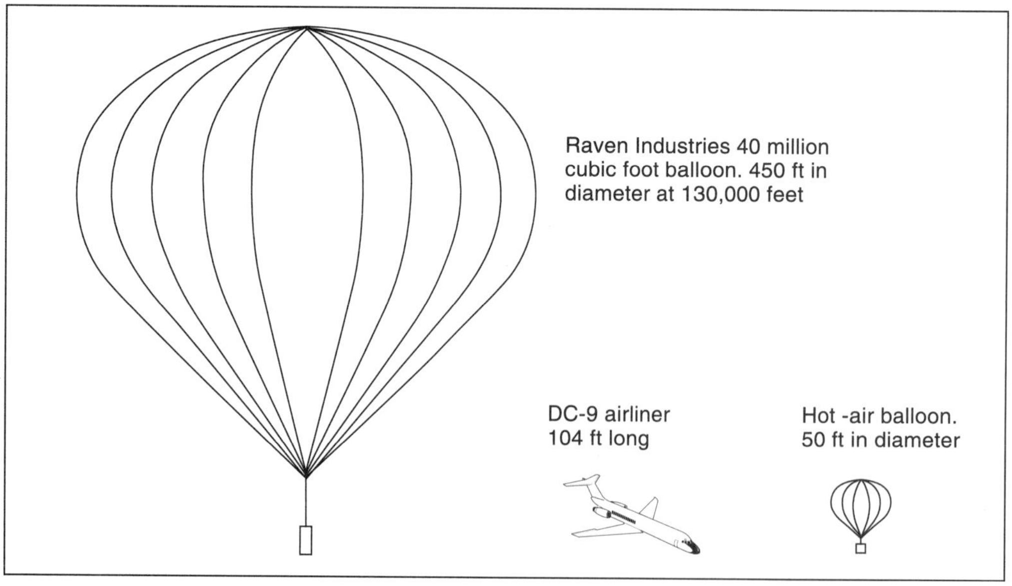

Fig. 48. Relative sizes of a modern high altitude poyethelyne research balloon, an airliner, and a hot-air balloon. Inaccurate characterizations of the giant high altitude research balloons as "weather balloons" (which are typically 15 feet in diameter) has historically been the source of confusion. *(courtesy of Mike Smith, Raven Industries)*

the ground, expand at altitude to volumes large enough to contain many jet airliners. Polyethylene balloons flown by the U.S. Air Force have reached altitudes of 170,000 feet and lifted payloads of 15,000 pounds.[73]

During the late 1940's and 1950's, a characteristic associated with the large, newly invented, polyethylene balloons, was that they were often misidentified as flying saucers.[74] During this period, polyethylene balloons launched from Holloman AFB, generated flying saucer reports on nearly every flight.[75] There were so many reports that police, broadcast radio, and newspaper accounts of these sightings were used by Holloman technicians to supplement early balloon tracking techniques.[76] Balloons launched at Holloman AFB generated an especially high number of reports due to the excellent visibility in the New Mexico region. Also, the balloons, flown at altitudes of approximately 100,000 feet, were illuminated before the earth during the periods just after sunset and just before sunrise. In this instance, receiving sunlight before the earth, the plastic balloons appeared as large bright objects against a dark sky. Also, with the refractive and translucent qualities of polyethylene, the balloons appeared to change color, size, and shape.

The large balloons generated UFO reports based on their radar tracks.[77] This was due to large metallic payloads that weighed up to several tons and echoed radar returns not usually associated with balloons. In later years, balloons were equipped with altitude and position reporting transponders and strobe lights that greatly diminished the numbers of both visual and radar UFO sightings.

One classic misidentification of a Holloman balloon that was mistaken for a UFO, was launched on October 27, 1953.[78] According to the following account published in a widely distributed 1958 history of Air Force balloon operations, *Contributions of Balloon Operations to Research and Development at the Air Force Missile Development Center Holloman Air Force Base, N. Mex. 1947-1958,* a suspected Holloman balloon was tracked both visually and by radar over London, England on November 3, 1953.

"English accounts of the incident contained such statements as 'tremendous speed,' 'practically motionless,' 'circular or spherical and white in color,' 'emitting or reflecting a fierce light.' Altitude was reported as 61,000 feet—and as no research balloon had recently been sent up from Britain, there was ample room for local saucer enthusiasts to claim the 'unidentified flying object' as proof of their theories. A much likelier explanation, however, is that this was really the balloon launched from Holloman on 27 October."[79]

High Altitude Balloon Payloads

Over the years, payloads transported by high altitude polyethylene balloons ranged from simple radio transmitters to anthropomorphic dummies to sophisticated satellite components and NASA interplanetary space probes. Many of these payloads, some of which weighed many tons, were not what someone would typically envision as being associated with a balloon. Examples of payloads flown in New Mexico by Air Force high altitude balloons can be found on pages 52 and 53 at the end of this section.

Research projects of the late 1940's and 1950's conducted at Holloman AFB which began with the Project MOGUL flights in June 1947, covered a wide spectrum of scientific research. One important experiment in space biology measured the effects of exposure to cosmic ray particles on living tissues.[80] Other projects gathered meteorological data and collected air samples to determine the composition of the atmosphere.[81] The first high altitude photographic reconnaissance project, a forerunner to today's reconnaissance satellites, Project 119L, also used high altitude balloons launched at Holloman AFB.[82]

As early as May 1948, polyethylene balloons coated or laminated with aluminum were flown from Holloman AFB and the surrounding area.[83] Beginning in August 1955, large numbers of these balloons were flown as targets in the development of radar guided air to air missiles.[84] Various accounts of the "Roswell Incident" often described thin, metal-like materials that when wadded into a ball, returned to their original shape. These accounts are consistent with the properties of polyethylene balloons laminated with aluminum. These balloons were typically launched from points west of the White Sands Proving Ground, floated over the range as targets, and descended in the areas northeast of White Sands Proving Ground where the "strange" materials were allegedly found.

In 1958 the first manned stratospheric balloon flights were made from Holloman AFB (see page 102). In 1960, balloon tests of components of the first U. S. reconnaissance satellite were also flown at Holloman AFB. In the 1960's, 70's, and 80's high altitude balloons were used in support of Air Force, and other U.S. Government and university sponsored research projects. Instrument testing of atmospheric entry vehicles for the National Aeronautics and Space Administration (NASA) space probes is one prominent example.

Fig. 49. Holloman Balloon Branch personnel prepare a polyethelyne balloon laminated with aluminum to serve as a target for radar guided missiles over White Sands Proving Ground, N.M. *(U.S. Air Force photo)*

High Altitude Balloons and America's First Satellite

An illustration of the important contributions of the Holloman AFB Balloon Branch, and the necessity for a rapid recovery of a high altitude balloon payload, were evaluations of components of the first U.S. satellite-based reconnaissance system, code named CORONA.

The Soviet Union had already beaten the U.S. into space with the launch and orbit of SPUTNIK I on October 4, 1957. The next achievement in the quest for space superiority were the physical recovery of a payload that had been in orbit.[85] The DISCOVERER satellite, the sensor used in the CORONA program, was to be propelled into orbit and then eject a capsule containing an American flag to enable the U.S. to claim this honor.[86]

The DISCOVERER program had been plagued by failure with 10 unsuccessful missions in 1959 and 1960. With the eyes of the nation watching, and the Soviets testing a similar system, more failures could not be tolerated. To test the faulty components of the DISCOVERER, U.S. Air Force high altitude balloons at Holloman AFB were determined to be the most expedient method of conducting the evaluations.

In April 1960, DISCOVERER XI, on the launch pad at Vandenberg AFB, Calif., was put into a hold pending results of the balloon tests.[87] The first test at Holloman AFB on April 5th was unsatisfactory due to a parachute failure.[88] On April 8th, with pressure mounting, the Balloon Branch launched another balloon with the DISCOVERER capsule. This test, in which the capsule was dropped over White Sands Missile Range and recovered immediately, was a total success.[89] The results were relayed by telephone from the Balloon Control Center at Holloman AFB to the launch pad at Vandenberg AFB where the countdown resumed.[90] Despite the successful balloon drop, DISCOVERER XI and DISCOVERER XII were failures.[91] Therefore, balloon testing continued throughout the summer of 1960.

Fig. 50. *(Left).* A Holloman Balloon Branch launch crew prepares a nosecone of the DISCOVERER satellite for a high altitude balloon flight at Holloman AFB, N.M. in April 1960. *(U.S. Air Force photo)*

Fig. 51. *(Right).* A U.S. Navy helicopter aboard the *USS Haiti Victory* is shown here with the capsule from the DISCOVERER XIII satellite. It was recovered from the Pacific Ocean 330 miles northwest of Hawaii on August 11, 1960. *(U.S. Air Force photo)*

Finally, on August 11,1960, DISCOVERER XIII successfully ejected a capsule and, amid much fanfare, the first recovery of a manmade object that had orbited the earth was accomplished.[92] This first successful mission of an American satellite, made possible in part by Holloman AFB high altitude balloons, enabled the U.S. to beat the Soviets and claim the honor of the first space recovery by only nine days.[93]

The SURVEYOR (Moon), VOYAGER-MARS (Mars), VIKING (Mars), PIONEER (Venus), and GALILEO (Jupiter) spacecraft were tested by Air Force high altitude balloons before they were launched into space.

VIKING and VOYAGER-MARS Space Probes. Examples of unusual payloads, not likely to be associated with balloons, were qualification trials of NASA's VOYAGER-MARS and VIKING space probes. Both of these spacecraft looked remarkably similar to the classic dome-shaped "flying saucer."

In 1966-67 and 1972, eight of the UFO lookalikes were launched by the Balloon Branch from the former Roswell Army Air Field (now Roswell Industrial Air Center), N.M.[94] The spacecraft were transported by Air Force balloons to altitudes above 100,000 feet and released for a period of self-propelled, supersonic, free-flight prior to landing on the White Sands Missile Range.[95] While the origins of the "Roswell" scenarios cannot be specifically traced to these vehicles, their flying saucer-like appearance, and the fact that they were launched exclusively from the original "Roswell Incident" location, leaves an impression that perhaps these odd balloon payloads may have played some role in the unclear and distorted stories of at least some of the "Roswell" witnesses.

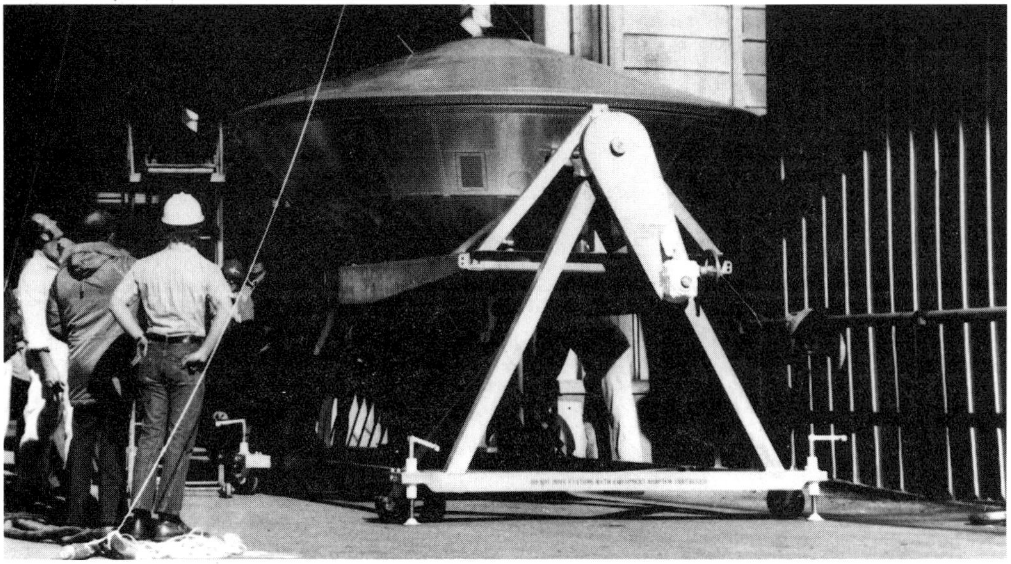

Fig. 52. A NASA VIKING space probe is rolled out of its assembly building at Martin Marietta Corporation in Denver, Colo. *(NASA)*

Fig. 53. *(Above Left)* The aeroshell of a NASA VOYAGER-MARS space probe just prior to launch at Walker AFB, N.M. (formerly Roswell AAF). *(U.S. Air Force photo)*

Fig. 54. *(Above Right)* This NASA VIKING flying saucer-like space probe was test flown by U. S. Air Force high altitude balloons in 1972 at the former Roswell Army Air Field. *(NASA)*

Fig. 55. *(Right)* Following a supersonic test flight in 1972, a VIKING space probe awaits recovery at White Sands Missile Range, N.M. *(NASA)*

Tethered Balloons. The Holloman Balloon Branch, in addition to high altitude research activities, also conducted low altitude tethered balloon flights. It appears that descriptions of these balloons may have become part of the "Roswell Incident."

Most standard shaped tethered balloons are readily identified when near the ground or when the tether is visible. Other experimental tethered balloons are not so easily identified. During the 1960s, Balloon Branch personnel flew experimentally shaped tethered balloons from deep canyons of central New Mexico. To a distant observer, from a vantage point above the canyon rim, where the tether and ground anchors are not visible, an experimental tethered balloon might lead some persons to speculate as to the oddly shaped balloon's origin and purpose. One design of a low altitude tethered balloon may have inspired at least one account of an "alien" craft. In *The Truth About the UFO Crash at Roswell,* the authors published a drawing of a crashed alien spaceship allegedly based on a drawing given to them by an anonymous witness.[96] When this drawing is compared to a photograph of an experimental tethered balloon flown at Holloman AFB in March 1965, the similarities are undeniable.[97] The tethered balloon and the NASA space probes are just two examples of the uncommon technologies that were flown in New Mexico by the Holloman Balloon Branch.

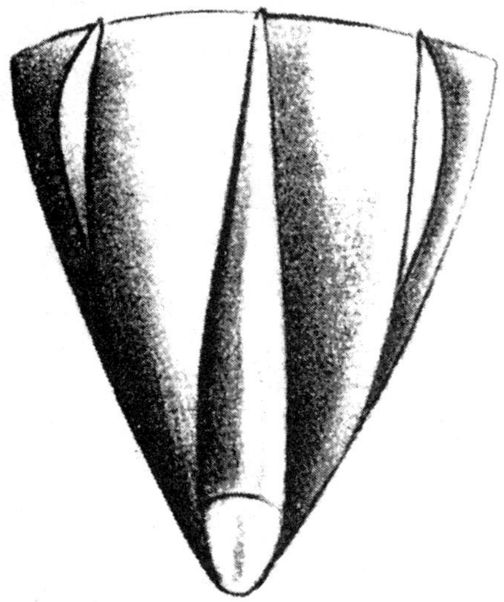

Fig. 56. *(Left)* A drawing from a popular UFO book, *The Truth About the UFO Crash at Roswell*, depicts an alien spacecraft allegedly drawn by an anonymous witness. *(The Truth About the UFO Crash at Roswell)*

Fig. 57. *(Right)* A tethered "Vee" balloon shown here at Holloman AFB, N.M. in March 1965. This experimental balloon, is strikingly similar to the "alien" craft. *(U.S. Air Force photo)*

Today, the Air Force maintains a reduced but still highly capable high altitude balloon program at Holloman AFB. The Space and Missile Command, Test and Evaluation Unit (SMC/TE, OL-AC) represents the sole Department of Defense high altitude research balloon capability. The ability of a U.S. Air Force high altitude balloon to lift a scientific payload to more than 100,000 feet, above 99 per cent of the earth's atmosphere, for days at a time, presents a profoundly useful scientific tool at a fraction of the cost of a space research platform. Recent tests that utilized Holloman balloons included atmospheric sampling and gravity measurement experiments, high altitude astronomic studies, weapons systems evaluations, and gamma ray detection experiments. While most tests continue to be launched from the permanent balloon launch facility at Holloman AFB, U.S. Air Force balloon crews have recently launched balloons from numerous field locations in the U.S. (including two sites in Roswell), as well as Alaska, Panama, and Antarctica.

Fig. 58. Present members of the Holloman Balloon Branch in front of the Balloon Operations Center, Building 850, at Holloman AFB, N.M., *(from left)* TSgt. Roger J. Welch, Mr. Joseph Fumerola, Mr. Alvin W. Hodges, Mr. Joseph Longshore, MSgt. Ray A. Pitts, Sr. Amn. John Witkop, and Mr. Harvey L. Harris. *(U.S. Air Force photo)*

Balloon and Payload Recoveries

UFO theorists support their claims of an extraordinary occurrence in the New Mexico desert by describing mysterious U.S. military personnel, operating a variety of vehicles and aircraft that always seem to arrive shortly after the crash of a "flying saucer." When carefully scrutinized, the descriptions of the mystery crews, their equipment, methods, and the areas where the recoveries allegedly occurred—in targeted high altitude balloon recovery areas—indicates that Holloman Balloon Branch activities were most likely responsible for the claims.

To successfully recover high altitude balloons, balloon recovery technicians regularly ventured far from Holloman AFB. In most instances the balloons and their scientific payloads were recovered from predetermined recovery areas. These regularly targeted areas, located in Arizona, West Texas, and New Mexico, included the area surrounding Roswell.[98] From 1947 to the present, the Roswell area has been the site of hundreds of balloon and payload recoveries (including those that carried anthropomorphic dummies).[99]

The regularly targeted areas were the result of the evolution of high altitude balloon control techniques developed at Holloman AFB. These techniques were based on meteorological, geographical, and operational conditions that exist in New Mexico. These factors, combined with ample amounts of skill and experience of balloon controllers at Holloman AFB, determined the impact points of Holloman high altitude balloons.

Many of the procedures used to position Air Force balloons are described in *General Philosophy and Techniques of Balloon Control,* and *Meteorological Aspects of Constant-Level Balloon Operations in the Southwestern United States,* both by Bernard D. Gildenberg (see statement in Appendix B).[100] Gildenberg served as the Holloman Balloon Branch Meteorologist, Engineer, and Physical Science Administrator from 1951 until 1981. During this period, Gildenberg, a recognized world expert in upper atmospheric wind patterns, pioneered methods to launch, control, track, and recover high altitude balloons. Many of these methods are still used today by the U.S. Air Force and by research organizations throughout the world.

Interaction with Civilians

In several accounts, unsubstantiated allegations have been made that military personnel who retrieved equipment from rural areas of New Mexico intimidated and threatened civilians. Contrary to these charges, Balloon Branch personnel enjoyed good relations with the local community and often solicited their assistance in the area of a balloon or payload

Fig. 59. Bernard D. "Duke" Gildenberg *(center)* Balloon Branch Meteorologist, is shown here in May 1957 in front of the MAN HIGH I gondola. With Gildenberg are MAN HIGH I pilot Capt. Joseph W. Kittinger, Jr. *(left),* and MAN HIGH project scientist/pilot, Lt. Col. David G. Simons (MC). When Gildenberg attempted to inform UFO theorists that high altitude balloon projects were likely responsible for some of the UFO claims, his explanations were rejected, *see also* pages 8 & 9. *(U.S. Air Force photo)*

landing. In the flat, featureless desert areas of southeastern New Mexico near Roswell, the parachutes, payloads, the balloons themselves, and circling chase aircraft often drew crowds of curious onlookers from the local community. In fact, so many civilians were often present at balloon or payload landing sites, the scene was described by longtime civilian Balloon Branch recovery supervisor, Robert Blankenship, as being like the "circus coming to town."[101]

Allegations that civilians were threatened or told to "forget what they saw" are profoundly inaccurate. Threats, intimidation, or other types of misconduct by Balloon Branch personnel would have served no purpose since without the cooperation of local persons, many recoveries would not have been possible.[102]

Most balloon recoveries were coordinated in advance with local law enforcement agencies.[103] If a balloon or payload landed on private property and the owner could not be located, Balloon Branch operating instructions dictated that the local sheriff or police must be contacted.[104] In situations where local persons arrived at balloon landing sites before the recovery crews, they were simply asked to "step back" to allow recovery personnel to secure the balloon equipment.[105] If these persons inquired as to the purpose of a balloon flight, they were informed by technicians that it was a U.S. Air Force scientific study and were given a telephone number at Holloman AFB if they required additional information. At Holloman AFB, individuals qualified to answer detailed questions responded to these

Fig. 60. *(Right)* This ranch family assisted in the recovery of a Project STARGAZER high altitude balloon payload and is shown here with a panel from the unmanned gondola. *(U.S. Air Force photo)*

inquiries. There was never a reason to mislead or threaten individuals who observed balloon operations. Relations with local citizens were good, and Balloon Branch personnel and equipment were a common sight to residents in areas with high incidences of balloon operations.

In a few instances, situations arose when persons not familiar with the procedures and equipment used by the Balloon Branch misunderstood their activities. Such misunderstandings occurred several times during the 1970s and 1980s when recovery crews not only attracted the attention of local citizens while coordinating balloon recoveries, but also drew the attention of federal law enforcement agencies.[106]

Checks with the local sheriff revealed that the trucks and circling aircraft in the desert near Roswell were part of a balloon recovery mission, and not a drug smuggling operation. Apparently, balloon recoveries appeared to be something suspicious even to federal agents.

Fig. 61. A typical Holloman Balloon Branch recovery crew is shown here with a man known as "The hermit" who assisted them in a balloon recovery northwest of Silver City, N.M. in the 1960s. *(photo collection of Robert Blankenship)*

Fig. 62. A mule (named Ida) was borrowed from a local rancher when a balloon payload landed in difficult terrain 20 miles north of Wickenburg, Ariz. in October 1966. *(U.S. Air Force photo)*

Fig. 63. On occasion, Air Force balloon recovery crews rented or borrowed equipment from local residents. This bulldozer was rented for one recovery in the Sacramento mountains west of Roswell. *(photo collection of Robert Blankenship)*

Fig. 64. Balloon Branch vehicle at roadside café. This M-43 3/4-ton field ambulance, converted by the Holloman Balloon Branch into a communications vehicle, was a common sight in the areas surrounding Roswell during the 1950s and early 1960s. *(photo collection of Ole Jorgeson)*

Figs. 65 & 66. Examples of unusual payloads flown by Air Force high altitude balloons at Holloman AFB, N.M. *(U.S. Air Force photos)*

Fig. 67. *(Left)* This U.S. Army communications payload was flown at Holloman AFB, N.M. on September 30, 1976. (U.S. Army photo)

Fig. 68. *(Right)* Payload launched by an Air Force high altitude balloon from Holloman AFB, N. M. on March 20, 1965. This payload was a scientific experiment for The John Hopkins University Astrophysics Laboratory. *(U.S. Air Force photo)*

Fig. 69. High altitude balloon payload launched from Holloman AFB on September 14, 1976. *(U.S. Air Force photo)*

1.4
Comparison of Witnesses Accounts to U.S. Air Force Activities

Were they aliens or dummies? This question can be answered by comparing witness testimony and the Air Force projects of the 1950s, HIGH DIVE and EXCELSIOR. Both of these projects employed anthropomorphic dummies flown by high altitude balloons and appeared to satisfy the requirements of the previously established research profile:

a. An activity that if viewed from a distance would appear unusual.
b. An activity for which the exact date was not likely to have been known because many dummies were dropped over a six-year period (1953-1959).
c. An activity that took place in many areas of rural New Mexico.
d. An activity that involved a type of aerial vehicle with dummies that had four fingers, were bald and wore one-piece gray suits.
e. An activity that required recovery by numerous military personnel and an assortment of vehicles that included a wrecker, a six-by-six, and a weapons carrier.

The testimony used in the following comparison, an undocumented mixture of firsthand and secondhand re-countings, are the actual statements, not the interpretations of UFO proponents, that are presented to "prove" the Earth was visited by extraterrestrial beings and the U.S. Air Force has covered up this fact since 1947. This comparison is augmented by references to photographs whenever possible to illustrate the undeniable similarities between the descriptions provided by the witnesses and the equipment and methods employed by the Air Force projects.

Fig. 70. Project HIGH DIVE anthropomorphic dummy launch. *(U.S. Air Force photo)*

"Crash" Site 1

(Allegedly North of Roswell)

This summarized account is the basis for the alleged "flying saucer" crash site north of Roswell.* The exact location is not known since the witness, Mr. James Ragsdale, in two separate sworn statements, has described two different sites, many miles apart.[107] This account was excerpted from an interview with Mr. Ragsdale by author Donald Schmitt. A transcript of the complete interview is included in Appendix C.

The Account

James Ragsdale

"They was using dummies in those damned things"[108]

Testimony attributed to Ragsdale, who is deceased, states that he and a friend were camping one evening and saw something fall from the sky. The next morning, when they went to investigate, they saw a crash site:

"One part [of the craft] was kind of buried in the ground and one part of it was sticking our [out] of the ground." "I'm sure that [there] was bodies... either bodies or dummies." "The federal government could have been doing something they didn't want anyone to know what this was. They was using dummies in those damned things...they could use remote control...but it was either dummies or bodies or something laying there. They looked like bodies. They were not very long... [not] over four or five foot long at the most." "We didn't see their faces or nothing like that... we had just gotten to the site and the Army...and all [was] coming and we got into a damned jeep and took off."

This testimony then describes an assortment of military vehicles used to recover the "bodies": "It was two or three six-by-six Army trucks a wrecker and everything. Leading the pack was a '47 Ford car with guys in it... It was six or eight big trucks besides the pickup, weapons carriers and stuff like that." Ragsdale also said that before he left the area he observed the military personnel "gathering stuff up" and "they cleaned everything all up."

Assessment

In his testimony, Ragsdale made numerous references to equipment, vehicles, and procedures consistent with documented anthropomorphic dummy recoveries for projects High Dive and Excelsior. The repeated use of the term "dummy" and the witness' own admission that "they was using dummies in those damned things" and "I'm sure that was bodies...either bodies or dummies"

---

* In *The Truth About the UFO Crash at Roswell* (Avon Books, 1994, p. 131), the authors provided a corroborating account for this testimony from a 96-year-old man who was in ill health, whose interview was not tape recorded, and has since died. According to the book, the man's "wife and daughter said that he was easily confused" and "memories of his life were jumbled and reordered."

leaves little doubt that what he described was an anthropomorphic dummy recovery.

Based on testimony attributed to this witness, the confusion could have resulted from the fact that he observed these activities from a distance. If the witness was even a short distance from the odd looking anthropomorphic dummies, it would be logical for him to believe, when interviewed 35 to 40 years after the event, that he "thought they were dummies or bodies or something." Also, for some of the high altitude drops, the dummies did not separate from the suspension rack and "rode the rack" to the ground without deployment of a parachute.[109] If the parachutes of the dummies or parachutes of the rack assembly did not deploy (a common occurrence during the early dummy drops), then they free-fell from up to 98,000 feet.[110] As a result of these malfunctions, the arms and legs of the dummies were often separated from the body on impact.[111] This may account for the witness' description of bodies [not] "over four or five foot" tall.

Another portion of his testimony suggesting that the witness observed an Air Force high altitude balloon and dummy recovery was the statement: "The federal government could have been doing something because they didn't want anyone to know what this was...they was using dummies in those damned things...they could use remote control." Balloon controllers used remote control to relay commands to the balloon control package to valve gas and drop ballast.[112] The dummies themselves were also dropped from the suspension rack by remote control.[113]

The witness also described a Balloon Branch procedure that required the area of a balloon or payload landing to be restored to its original condition. It was evident in the statements "They cleaned everything all up" and "They began gathering the stuff up." Thoroughly cleaning a balloon or dummy landing site and removing any debris

Fig. 71. Numerous vehicles and various types of equipment, were often present at high altitude balloon and anthropomorphic dummy launch and recovery locations. (photo collection of Ole Jorgeson)

deposited there was a standard procedure to maintain good community relations and avoid legal claims that could arise over property damages or livestock losses.[114] Cattle were known to ingest scraps of polyethylene balloon material that sometimes littered entire fields following a balloon failure or flight termination.[115]

The military vehicles described were also consistent with recovery and communications vehicles used during the 1950s to retrieve anthropomorphic dummies and suspension racks.[116] The witness stated he saw a "wrecker," a "six-by-six," a "weapons carrier," a "'47 Ford car," and a "pickup." The "wrecker" was most likely a M-342 5-ton wrecker that was assigned to the Balloon Branch for launch and recovery operations.[117] Other vehicles described were also the type used to launch and recover anthropomorphic dummies. The "six-by-six" is a likely reference to a M-35 2 1/2-ton cargo truck; "weapons carriers" were the common name of a Dodge M-37 3/4-ton utility truck. References to "the pickup" and a "'47 Ford car," were likely descriptions of other civilian and military vehicles often present at high altitude balloon launch and recovery locations.

"Crash" Site 2

(Allegedly 175 miles Northwest of Roswell)

This purported flying saucer "crash" site is allegedly 175 miles northwest of Roswell in an area of New Mexico known as the San Agustin Plains.[118] The contention that a flying saucer crashed at this location and was recovered by the U.S. military is supported by three principal testimonies, two secondhand and one firsthand.

The Secondhand Accounts

These accounts were related by Mr. Vern Maltais and Ms. Alice Knight, who were acquainted with the alleged original eyewitness, Mr. Grady L. Barnett, who is deceased. Unless otherwise noted, the following statements appeared on footage used to prepare a video, *Recollections of Roswell Part II*, by the The Fund for UFO Research (see Appendix C).

Alice Knight

"I don't recall the date"[119]

"I don't remember whether it was before my husband and I were married or after, I don't recall the date. But he [the eyewitness] saw a UFO fall...and he got nearly to the site...but they got nearly up to the UFO but it was close enough that you could see some creatures. He said they didn't look like human beings out there. And along came government cars and trucks. I guess it was government. You know it was a long time ago...and they told him to go on back and forget that they ever saw anything, and that's all I recall."

Assessment

This brief testimony suggests that the witness did not know the date of this event. It also appears that the "creatures" were seen from a distance, as evidenced by the statement, "They got nearly up to the UFO but it was close enough that you could see some creatures." The testimony also seems consistent with a description of anthropomorphic dummies as the witness stated they "didn't look like human beings."

Vern Maltais

"Their heads were hairless...no eyebrows, no eyelashes, no hair"[120]

This secondhand witness alleged that the eyewitness told him he observed "beings" from a "flying saucer that had burst open" that were "about three and a half to four feet tall, very slim...their heads were hairless, with no eyebrows, no eyelashes, no hair" with "sort of a pear-shaped head." He also related that "the beings were...not exactly like human beings...similar but not exactly." He described that the hands of the beings "were not covered"...and [they] only had "four fingers." He also related that the clothing of the beings was "one-piece and gray in color"[121] The witness concluded that "As they [the witnesses] were just starting to look things over really closely, the military moved in and gave them a briefing to not say anything about it."

Assessment

This description of events also indicates that the eyewitness apparently did not closely examine the scene and was "just starting to look things over" when the military arrived. As with the previous testimony, from a distance the dummies were likely to look, as described by the witness, "not exactly like humans...similar but not exactly." The description of the flying saucer that had "burst open" is a likely description of the dummy suspension rack that was open on the sides (see figures 74, 75, 76). The detailed descriptions of the "beings" as "about three and a half to four feet tall, very slim in stature...their heads were hairless, with no eyebrows, no eyelashes,

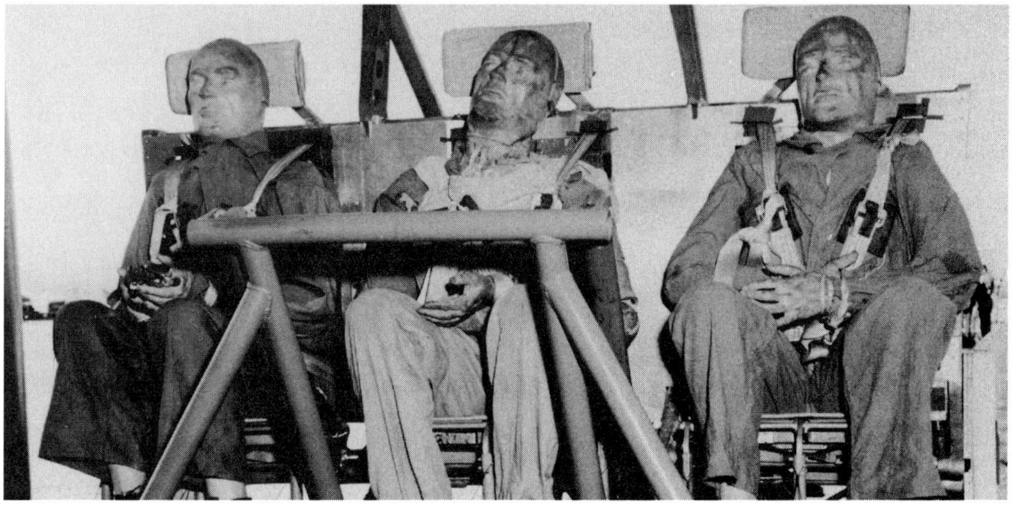

Fig. 72. "Their heads were hairless...no eyebrows, no eyelashes, no hair," a likely description of Alderson Laboratories type anthropomorphic dummy. These Alderson dummies, of the same type used for Projects HIGH DIVE/EXCELSIOR, were used to test NASAs APOLLO spacecraft three-man couch at Holloman AFB, N.M. in 1965. *(U.S. Air Force photo)*

no hair," with "hands that were not covered" and "had only four fingers," is a likely description of an Alderson Research Laboratories model anthropomorphic dummy. The head of the Alderson dummy was "bald" and the area of the eyebrows protruded but had no "hair" (see figure 72). Also, a distinguishing feature of the Alderson dummy, unlike the Sierra dummy, was that it had individual fingers not covered by gloves that were often damaged during the tests resulting in the loss of fingers (see figures 35, 73, 75).

Due to the secondhand nature of these accounts, even UFO theorists were not convinced that this "incident" actually occurred. Corroborating testimony of a firsthand witness was necessary to verify these claims. The firsthand testimony is examined next.

The Firsthand Account

This testimony became part of the Roswell Incident in 1990 following an episode of the television program *Unsolved Mysteries*.[122] Following a dramatized re-creation on the program, persons with information concerning this event were encouraged to call a special toll free telephone number.

From the outset, some UFO theorists were skeptical of this testimony due to the amount of detail provided from the witness who was only five years old in 1947. In fact, UFO organizations sponsored a conference in February 1992 to evaluate the testimony for authenticity.[123] The witness was asked to take a polygraph examination, which he passed.[124] Many UFO enthusiasts remained skeptical of the claims and denounced this testimony as "no more than a fabrication."[125]

Unless otherwise noted, two sources of testimony attributed to the witness have been used in this examination; interviews used to prepare the video *Recollections of Roswell Part II* by the Fund for UFO Research (see Appendix C) and *Crash at Corona* by Don Berliner and Stanton Friedman (passages from this book were used only when exact quotations of the witness were indicated).

Gerald Anderson

"I thought they were plastic dolls...I didn't think they were real" [126]

Anderson related that as a five-year-old boy on an outing with his family in west central New Mexico, they stumbled upon the crash of some type of aerial vehicle.[127] When he first saw the craft he thought it was a "blimp."[128] According to Anderson he "didn't really get very close,"[129] but thought he saw four bandaged crewmembers and at first he "thought they were plastic dolls."[130] He also described attempts by persons in his party to communicate with one of the "crewmembers."[131] Soon after, other civilians arrived (some wearing pith helmets) followed by military personnel in an assortment of vehicles and aircraft commanded by a "redheaded captain."[132] The military personnel, after "screaming and hollering" at the civilians "this is a military secret," started a recovery operation of the alien craft and crew.[133] Anderson also recalled that the military personnel threatened some of the civilians with imprisonment or death before escorting them out of the area.[134]

Assessment

Anderson's choice of the terms "blimp" to describe the crashed vehicle, and "dolls" to describe the "crew," strongly suggests that a balloon with an anthropomorphic dummy payload was the foundation for this testimony. He also provided an abundance of supporting details that accurately described vehicles, aircraft, equipment, and procedures used by the Holloman AFB Balloon Branch to launch and recover anthropomorphic dummies.

An aspect of this testimony that is not accurate is the alleged threats and intimidation of civilians by military personnel. The use of such heavy-handedness was not a tactic used by the Air Force. A careful review of official records and interviews with numerous persons who actively participated in and were responsible for the conduct of Air Force members on high altitude balloon recovery operations revealed that these allegations are untrue.[135] Additionally, the witness alleges that the military personnel were "screaming and hollering" "this is a military secret."[136] This statement might lead uninitiated persons to believe that the witness observed something highly classified and that by telling everyone present that it was a "military secret" would somehow help it to remain so. However, logic dictates that if something was classified "screaming and hollering" it was "secret," would compromise it and not serve to protect its classification. This application of logic, combined with the fact that the launch and recovery of anthropomorphic dummies was unclassified, widely publicized, and often observed by local civilians, indicates that the witness' recollections are in error. There was never a reason to disrespect, "scream," "holler," or forbid any person from talking about the launch or recovery of anthropomorphic dummies.

The "Crewmembers." The statement "I thought they were plastic dolls" seems an odd choice of words to describe an extraterrestrial being and is a likely reference to an anthropomorphic dummy whose skin was made of plastic.[137] This description is similar to that of the sole witness of the other crash site, north of Roswell, who described the "aliens" as "dummies."[138] Other references provided by this witness further indicate that anthropomorphic dummies were the basis for these descriptions. The heads of the "crewmembers" were described as "completely bald" with "no visible ears...just a rise...and then a hole."[139] This is an accurate description of Alderson Research Laboratories model dummies that did not have "hair" and had either plastic "ears" molded to the head or a circular opening where a "demountable ear" or additional instrumentation was attached (see figure 22).[140] The statement "they didn't have a little finger,"[141] a detail very similar to one provided by another witness, also appears to be a description of dummies manufactured by Alderson Laboratories that were often damaged during the balloon tests resulting in the loss of fingers.

The assertion that "they were all wearing one-piece suits...a shiny silverish-gray color," "trimmed in ...maroon-like cording"[142] is a likely reference to a standard issue, gray, Air Force flightsuit used to outfit the dummies and red duct-type tape used in the tests that prevented air from filling the flightsuit (see fig. 30).[143] The recollection that "crewmembers" had "bandages"[144] on their bodies were likely references to tape and nylon webbing used to prevent flailing

Fig. 73. "Some kind of container, a metal box," was described as laying on the ground near the alleged aliens. This appears to be a reference to boxes containing electrical components of the remote controlled systems positioned on the top of the dummy suspension rack. *(U.S. Air Force photo)*

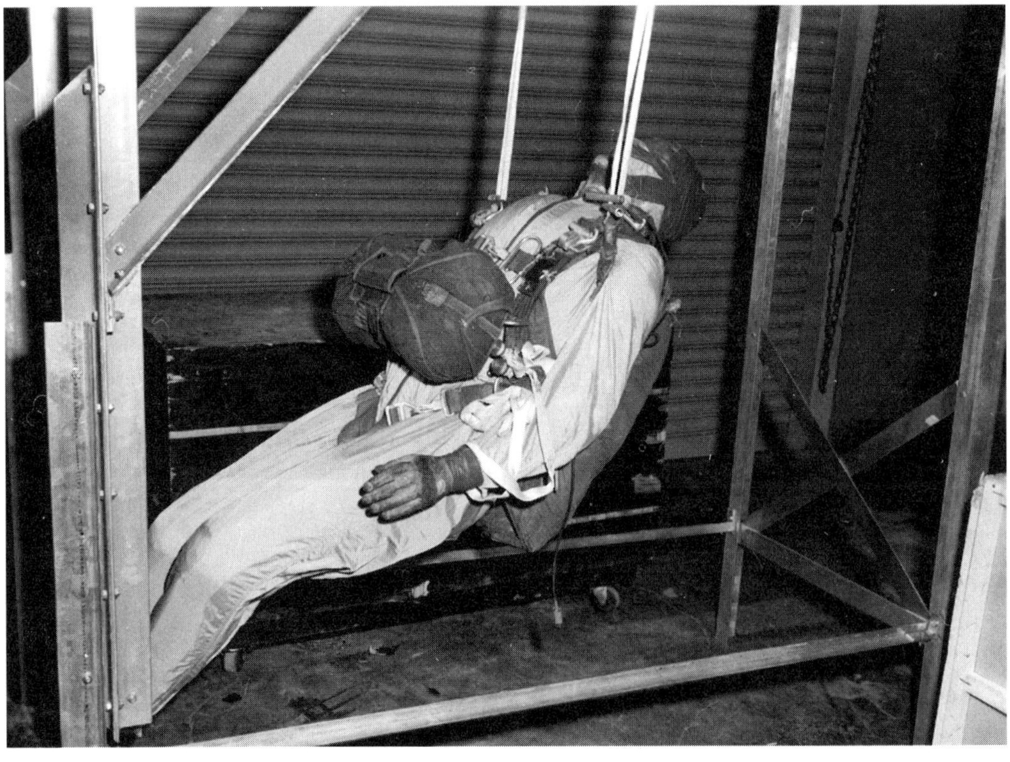

Fig. 74. "They looked like they had some sort of bandages on 'em...over his... arm... around his midsection and partially over his shoulder"—witness description of tape and nylon webbing used to prevent arms and legs from flailing, and parachute harness that had chest and shoulder straps. Tape was also used to secure the removable back plate of the head *(also see figs. 29, 30, 73,75). (U.S. Air Force photo)*

Fig. 75. "It's uniform was torn in a couple spots...their uniforms were in pretty sad shape"—witnesses description of secondhand flightsuits that were used repeatedly on tests; tears and other damage were common. In this photo, 1st Lt. Raymond A. Madson "rigs" a dummy to its suspension rack for project HIGH DIVE at Holloman AFB, N.M. *(U.S. Air Force photo)*

Fig. 76. A witness described at least one person at a "crash" site wearing a pith helmet. In the 1950s, the pith helmet was part of the Air Force uniform and was often worn on balloon launches and recoveries. In this publicity photo from *On the Threshold of Space*, Air Force members at Holloman AFB who were extras in the film can be seen wearing pith helmets. *(also see figure 49)*

of a dummy's arms and legs during tests.[145] A reference to a bandage "around his [the crewmember's] midsection and partially over his shoulder"[146] is a likely reference to the standard B-4 or B-5 parachute with chest and shoulder straps worn by the dummies.[147]

The "Craft." In what appears to be a clear reference to a balloon, was that when he saw the crashed vehicle he "thought it was a blimp."[148] Additional descriptions of cables that "went from one kind of a package of components to another kind of package" and a "metal box" were likely references to the balloon control package that was positioned on top of the dummy suspension rack.[149] A further reference to a balloon payload is the statement that on a hot New Mexico day the crashed vehicle was "ice cold, it felt like it just came out of the freezer."[150] This accurately describes a physical condition known as "cold soaking" common to high altitude payloads that had recently been exposed to sub-zero temperatures of the upper atmosphere.

Military Aircraft. The witness also described two aircraft of the same type used for anthropomorphic dummy recoveries as having been involved in the activity he witnessed. One aircraft was described as a "C-47" and another as an "observation aircraft...a high-winged aircraft."[151] These were a C-47 and a L-20 aircraft used extensively by the Balloon Branch during the mid 1950s for tracking and recovering anthropomorphic dummy

Fig. 77. "An observation aircraft...a high-winged aircraft"—a witness's probable reference to a U.S. Air Force L-20 aircraft used extensively by Holloman AFB crews to track and recover anthropomorphic dummies. *(U.S. Air Force photo)*

Fig. 78. Described as present at a flying saucer "crash" site was a C-47 aircraft. This is a probable reference to a U.S. Air Force C-47 transport aircraft used to move equipment to launch sites distant from Holloman AFB. These aircraft were also used for aerial tracking of high altitude balloon flights including those that flew anthropomorphic dummies. *(U.S. Air Force photo)*

balloon flights.[152] This testimony also described aircraft that were typically overhead during a recovery and an established procedure of landing on a rural road or in a field to reach isolated balloon launch or recovery locations.[153]

Military Vehicles. Numerous military vehicles, several of which were described by other witnesses as having been at the other crash site north of Roswell, were also described. Witnesses at the two different sites described a "wrecker" and a "six-by-six," both of the type used for anthropomorphic dummy recoveries.[154] The account also described two vehicles unique to the Balloon Branch that were used for the majority of high altitude balloon recoveries during the mid-to late-1950s.

The witness described a "jeep-like truck that had a bunch of radios in it"...There was a guy sittin' in there wearin' earphones and he was talking on the radio."[155] This is a likely description of a Dodge M-37 3/4-ton utility truck, known as a weapons carrier, that had been specially modified to carry radio equipment for balloon recovery operations. The Holloman AFB Balloon Branch modified these vehicles in 1953, ruling out the possibility that the witness observed them in 1947, when such vehicles were not available to organizations performing balloon operations.[156] The other vehicle described and used by the Balloon Branch were "military ambulances."[157] During the mid-1950s, the Balloon Branch modified three M-43 3/4-ton ambulances for use as balloon recovery and communications vehicles.[158] These vehicles were used for anthropomorphic dummy launch and recovery missions to relay messages to circling recovery aircraft and the balloon operations center at Holloman AFB.[159] The witness also described "a trailer with a motor on it, like a generator."[160] This is a likely description of a 1 1/2-ton cargo trailer with an MB-19 15 Kilowatt diesel generator. These generators were used primarily on balloon launch sites during the 1950s and 1960s (see fig. 71).

Balloon Branch Procedures. Descriptions of military personnel "stretching stuff out on the ground, dragging stuff out of trucks"[161] is a likely description of a balloon launch procedure that required the fragile

Fig. 79. "Stretching stuff out on the ground, dragging stuff out of trucks"—a likely witness reference to high altitude balloon inflation procedure that required the balloon to be stretched out on a protective ground cloth prior to inflation. *(U.S. Air Force photo)*

polyethylene balloon and its protective ground cloth to be removed from a launch vehicle and laid out on the ground prior to inflation. Another procedure described by the witness was an apparent reference to a balloon recovery practice of recording the names of civilians who observed high altitude balloon recoveries.[162] The witness stated that military personnel "took everybody's name and everything,"[163] which was a procedure to ensure payment of a $25 dollar reward to persons who assisted in the recovery. This procedure was also necessary to settle future claims of property damage caused by the balloon, payload, or recovery vehicles.[164]

Fig. 80. Witnesses described a "tanker," "military ambulances," a "6x6," and a "wrecker"—probable references to *(from left)* a helium tank trailer, a M-43 ambulance (converted to a communications vehicle), a M-35 cargo truck (partially obscured), and a M-342 wrecker. These vehicles were used for off-range launch and recovery operations of anthorpomorphic dummies for Project HIGH DIVE/EXCELSIOR. Shown here is a May 29, 1957 dummy launch near Hatch, N.M. *(also see figs. 23, 28, 64, 71, 81). (U.S. Air Force photo)*

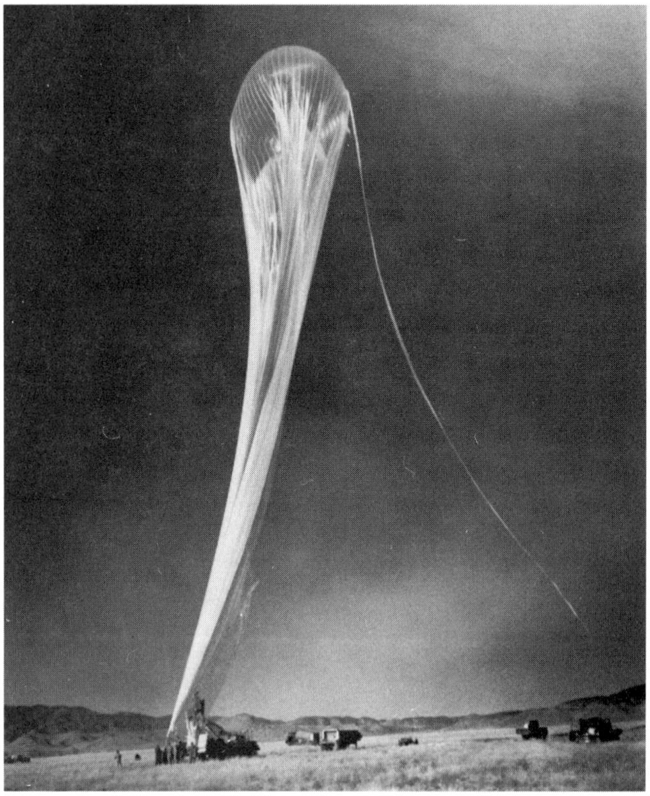

Fig. 81. Scene typical of a mid- to late 1950s off-range high altitude balloon launch. *(U.S. Air Force photo)*

Summary

When the claims offered by UFO theorists to prove that an extraterrestrial spaceship and crew crashed and were recovered by the U.S. Air Force are compared to documented Air Force activities, it is reasonable to conclude, with a high degree of certainty, that the two "crashes" were actually descriptions of a launch or recovery of a high altitude balloon and anthropomorphic dummies. This conclusion was based on the remarkable similarities and independent corroboration between the witnesses who described *both* of the "crash sites." Statements such as "they was using dummies in those damned things" and a characterization of the crashed vehicle as, "I thought it was a blimp" are two of the many similarities. The extensive detailed descriptions provided by the witnesses, too numerous to be coincidental, were of the equipment, vehicles, procedures, and personnel of the Air Force research organizations who conducted the scientific experiments HIGH DIVE and EXCELSIOR.

Though it is clear anthropomorphic dummies were responsible for these accounts, the specific locations of the events described was difficult, if not impossible, to determine since the witnesses were not specific. A witness to the "crash site" north of Roswell, Mr. James Ragsdale, was not certain of the actual location as evidenced by a change in his sworn testimony that moved the site many miles from its original location.[165]

However, since Ragsdale reportedly lived or worked in the Roswell, Artesia, and Carlsbad, N.M. areas during the period when the dummies were used, it is likely he described one or more of the nine documented dummy recoveries in areas near there.

Reports of the other crash site, allegedly 175 miles northwest of Roswell on the San Agustin Plains, is likely based on descriptions of more than one launch and recovery of anthropomorphic dummies. Since one witness, Gerald Anderson, described procedures consistent with the launch *and* recovery of high altitude balloons, it is likely that he witnessed both of these activities, with at least one that included an anthropomorphic dummy payload.

The two secondhand witnesses to this "crash," Vern Maltais and Alice Knight, could have related descriptions from any of the dummy launch or landing sites. However, Maltais and Knight repeatedly described the impact location of the flying saucer as on the San Agustin Plains. One possible explanation is that the witnesses, in the 30 or more years since they were told the story by the original eyewitness, Mr. Barney Barnett, a soil conservation engineer who reportedly traveled extensively throughout New Mexico, may have confused San Agustin Plains with San Agustin Pass or San Agustin Peak, an area in the San Agustin Mountains of New Mexico. These areas are just outside the boundary of the White Sands Missile Range and the adjacent Jornada Test Range. Numerous anthropomorphic dummy balloon flights terminated and were recovered in this area. Furthermore, if the civilians witnessed dummy landings on either the White Sands Missile Range or the Jornada Test Range, both test areas and restricted U.S.

Government reservations, then this explains why they may have been told to leave the landing site. In the popular Roswell scenarios, witnesses were allegedly instructed by military personnel to leave the area because they witnessed something of a highly classified nature. This would be unlikely since the witnesses described projects that utilized anthropomorphic dummies which were unclassified. It is likely, however, that if the witnesses ventured onto one of these ranges they were instructed to leave, not because of classified activities, but for their own safety.

These conclusions are supported by official files, technical reports, extensive photographic documentation, and the recollections of numerous former and retired Air Force members and civilian employees who conducted Projects HIGH DIVE and EXCELSIOR. The descriptions examined here, provided by UFO theorists themselves, were so remarkably—and redundantly— similar to these Air Force projects that the only reasonable conclusion can be that the witnesses described these activities. These many similarities are summarized in Table1.1.

The next section will examine the accounts of "aliens" at the hospital at Roswell Army Air Field. As previously stated, due to the lack of general or detailed similarities with testimony of the two rural "crash sites," the hospital account was determined not to be associated with these reports.

Fig. 82.

Table 1.1
Comparison of Testimony to Actual Air Force Equipment, Vehicles, and Procedures Used to Launch and Recover Anthropomorphic Dummies

Notes:
"Crash Site" 1 - Site North of Roswell
"Crash Site" 2 - Site 175 miles Northwest of Roswell
Shaded areas indicates corroboration between witnesses.
Boxed shaded areas indicates corroboration between witnesses at different "crash" sites.

Witness Description	Air Force Equipment/Procedure	"Crash Site"
The "Aliens"		
1. "They was using dummies in those damned things."[166] *Ragsdale*	Reference to anthropomorphic dummies (figs. 11, 14, 21-22, 29, 30-33, 35, 40, 72-75, 45).	Site 1
2. "I thought they were plastic dolls"[167] *Anderson*	Reference to anthropomorphic dummies that had plastic skin.	Site 2
3. "an experimental plane with dummies in it"[168] *Kaufman*	Reference to anthropomorphic dummies.	Site 1
4. "I'm sure that was bodies... either bodies or dummies."[169] *Ragsdale*	Reference to anthropomorphic dummies.	Site 1
5. "it was either dummies or bodies or something laying there." [170] *Ragsdale*	Reference to anthropomorphic dummies.	Site 1
6. "his eyes was open, staring blankly" [171] *Anderson*	Reference to anthropomorphic dummy.	Site 2
7. "not exactly like human beings...similar, but not exactly."[172] *Maltais*	Reference to anthropomorphic dummies.	Site 2
8. "didn't look like human beings"[173] *Knight*	Reference to anthropomorphic dummies.	Site 2
9. "they didn't have a little finger"[174] *Anderson*	Reference to Alderson Laboratories dummy that were reused many timesand were often damaged but remained in service. (figs. 35, 73, 75).	Site 2

Witness Description	Air Force Equipment/Procedure	"Crash Site"
10. "they had four fingers"[175] *Maltais*	Corroboration of description # 8. See above.	Site 2
11. [the beings were] "three and a half to four feet tall"[176] *Maltais*	Likely description of anthropomorphic dummy missing legs after fall from altitude.	Site 2
12. [the being were] "four foot tall, four and a half feet tall." [177] *Anderson*	Corroboration of description #11. See above.	Site 2
13. "they weren't over four or five foot long at the most." [178] *Ragsdale*	Corroboration of description #11. See above.	Site 1
14. "Their skin coloration... [was] a bluish tinted milky white"[179] *Anderson*	Probable description of a "Sierra Sam" dummy with pale white "skin" (fig. 21).	Site 2
15. "their heads were hairless...no eyebrows, no eyelashes, no hair" [180] *Maltais*	Anthropomorphic dummies did not have "hair" (figs. 21, 22, 36-38, 40).	Site 2
16. "no hair...completely bald" [181] *Anderson*	Corroboration of description # 15. See above.	Site 2
17. "no visible ears... just a rise there and then a hole"[182] *Anderson*	Dummies had ears that were molded to their heads with openings for placement of instruments (fig. 22).	Site 2
18. "The hands were not covered"[183] *Maltais*	Reference to Alderson dummy which did not have gloves on hands (figs. 35, 73-75).	Site 2
19. "they were all wearing one piece suits...a shiny silverish gray color"[184] *Anderson*	Reference to gray flight suits worn by the dummies for some of the tests (figs. 14, 29, 30).	Site 2
20. "Their clothing seemed to be one piece and gray in color."[185] *Maltais*	Corroboration of description #19. See above.	Site 2

Witness Description	Air Force Equipment/Procedure	"Crash Site"
21. "It's uniform was torn in a couple spots...their uniforms were in pretty sad shape."[186] *Anderson*	Dummy uniforms were often secondhand, rips and other defects were common but they remained in service (fig. 75).	Site 2
22. "Around the collar it [the suit] was trimmed in...maroon-like cording"[187] *Anderson*	Reference to red duct tape used to prevent air from filling the dummy's flightsuit (figs. 29, 30).	Site 2
23. "They looked like they had some sort of bandages on 'em...over his [the crewmember's] arm."[188] *Anderson*	Reference to tape and nylon webbing used to prevent arms and legs of dummy from flailing. Tape was also used to secure the removable back plate of head (figs. 29, 30, 35, 72-75).	Site 2
24. [bandages] "around his midsection and partially over his shoulder"[189] *Anderson*	Reference to parachute harness that had chest and shoulder straps.	Site 2
The "Craft"		
25. "It [the crewmember] felt dead when I touched it, it was very cold."[190] *Anderson*	Description of a high altitude balloon payload that was cold soaked at sub zero temperatures of the upper atmosphere.	Site 2
26. "it was a dirigible, a blimp that had crashed"[191] *Anderson*	Reference to a partially inflated or deflated high altitude balloon (figs. 23, 70).	Site 2
27. "a flying saucer that had burst open"[192] *Maltais*	Reference to the dummy suspension rack that did not have sides (figs. 35, 73-75).	Site 2
28. "clusters of thread like material in the form of a cable"[193] *Anderson*	Numerous cables and wires were used in the dummy instrumentation kits and balloon control package.	Site 2
29. "others of those [cables] went from one kind of package of components to another kind of package"[194] *Anderson*	Both balloon control package and dummy instrumentation kits were connected by cables (fig. 73).	Site 2
30. "some kind of container, a metal box"[195] *Anderson*	Reference to balloon control package or dummy instrumentation kit (fig. 73).	Site 2

Witness Description	Air Force Equipment/Procedure	"Crash Site"
31. "it was ice cold, it felt like it just came out of a freezer"[196] *Anderson*	Condition of a balloon payload after it has been "cold soaked" in the upper atmosphere at temperatures far below zero.	Site 2
Vehicles		
32. a "jeeplike truck that had a bunch of radios in it and two big antennas....There was a guy sittin' in there wearin' earphones and he was talking on the radio."[197] *Anderson*	Reference to a modified M-37 3/4-ton utility truck, commonly referred to as a weapons carrier, unique to the Balloon Branch. One of the primary vehicles used by recovery crews. Balloons were tracked by direction finding gear and required a radio operator to wear headphones (fig. 32).	Site 2
33. "weapons carriers"[198] *Ragsdale*	Corroboration of description #32. See above.	Site 1
34. "six by six Army trucks"[199] *Ragsdale*	Reference to M-35 21/2-ton cargo truck used to transport dummies and suspension racks for launch and recoveries (fig. 31).	Site 1
35. "six by [six]... military truck with canvas...wagon type...thing over it"[200] *Anderson*	Corroboration of description #34. See above.	Site 2
36. "wreckers [with] cranes on 'em"[201] *Anderson*	reference to M-246 wrecker used to launch and recover anthropomorphic dummy payloads (figs. 23, 28, 70).	Site 2
37. "a wrecker"[202] *Ragsdale*	Corroboration of description # 36. See above.	Site 1
38. "there was military ambulances"[203] *Anderson*	Reference to a converted M-43 ambulances used as balloon recovery communications vehicles (figs. 64, 71, 80).	Site 2
39. "the pick-up"[204] *Anderson*	Pick-up trucks were often used to recover anthropomorphic dummies (figs. 71, 79).	Site 2

Witness Description	Air Force Equipment/Procedure	"Crash Site"
40. "tankers, like, maybe had fuel or water in 'em"[205] *Anderson*	reference to M-49 fuel trucks used to refuel aircraft or helium trailer used to inflate balloon (figs. 23, 70, 80, 81).	Site 2
41. "a military car"[206] *Anderson*	A variety of military and civilian cars were often used for balloon recoveries and launches (Fig. 71).	Site 2
42. "'47 Ford car"[207] *Ragsdale*	Corroboration of description #41. See above.	Site 1
43. "there was a jeep that was pulling a trailer with a motor on it, like a generator."[208] *Anderson*	Reference to 1-ton trailer and MB-19 15 Kilowatt diesel generator that were used at balloon launch and recovery locations (fig. 71).	Site 2
Aircraft		
44. "observation aircraft...high winged aircraft"[209] *Anderson*	Reference to an L-20 aircraft, primary "chase" aircraft used for balloon recovery in the mid 1950s (fig. 77).	Site 2
45. "C-47 sittin there"[on the road][210] *Anderson*	C-47 aircraft were often used on dummy launch and recovery operations (fig. 78).	Site 2
Procedures		
46. "The federal government could have been doing something because they didn't want anyone to know what this was...they was using dummies in those damned things...they could use remote control"[211] *Ragsdale*	Reference to balloon borne anthropomorphic dummies that were dropped by remote control by balloon controllers at Holloman AFB	Site 1
47. "they took everybody's name and everything"[212] *Anderson*	Procedure used by balloon Branch to ensure payment of $25 reward and to settle claims of property damage.	Site 2
48. "they cleaned everything all up...I mean they cleaned everything"[213] *Ragsdale*	Balloon Branch personnel were required to remove as much debris as possible from balloon and payload landing areas to avoid complaints and legal actions.	Site 1

Witness Description	Air Force Equipment/Procedure	"Crash Site"
49. "they had the road barricaded off"[214] *Anderson*	Procedure used for aircraft operations.	Site 2
50. "they had the road sealed off"[215] *Ragsdale*	Corroboration of description #49. See above.	Site 1
51. "airplanes sitting there they had landed on the highway"[216] *Anderson*	Established procedure to refuel an aircraft, launch a balloon from an isolated location or recover a small payload near a rural road.	Site 2
52. "there was airplanes in the sky" [over the crash site].[217] *Anderson*	Reference to balloon "chase" aircraft used to direct ground recovery crews to balloon impact site.	Site 2
53. "stretching out cables of some kind...they were stretching stuff out on the ground, dragging stuff out of trucks"[218] *Anderson*	Reference to balloon inflation procedure that required the balloon and ground cloth to be removed from a vehicle and laid on the ground (fig. 79).	Site 2

SECTION TWO

Reports of Bodies at the Roswell AAF Hospital

This section examines the remaining portion of the Roswell Incident claims—the reports of "bodies" at the Roswell AAF hospital. Examinations of the various "crashed saucer" scenarios revealed references to the Roswell AAF hospital appeared in virtually all of them. Most of these were based on the account of one individual, W. Glenn Dennis. His undocumented and uncorroborated recollections, reportedly first related in 1989, over 42 years after the alleged Roswell Incident, are based on activities he allegedly encountered as a mortician providing contract services to the Roswell AAF hospital. Dennis' recollections have, in turn, been interpreted by UFO theorists as evidence that the U.S. Army Air Forces recovered "alien" bodies and autopsied them at the Roswell AAF hospital in July 1947.

Dennis has been described as the "star witness" and his claims as the most credible of the Roswell Incident.[1] This, even though his most sensational assertions were not based on his own experiences but on information allegedly related to him by unidentified mystery witnesses.

Fig. 1. The International UFO Museum and Research Center in Roswell, N.M.

The mystery witnesses were allegedly an Army Air Forces nurse and a pediatrician both assigned to the Roswell AAF hospital in 1947.[2] To casual observers, this account, which contains references to actual U.S. Army Air Forces and U.S. Air Force personnel and activities, appears to have a ring of authenticity. However, when examined closely by Air Force researchers, the dates of events, the events themselves, and the people described as having participated in them, were found to be grossly inaccurate and totally unrelated to activities of July 1947.

The Account

The following is a summary of information provided by W. Glenn Dennis, who claimed he was a 22-year-old mortician at the Ballard Funeral Home in Roswell in July 1947, when he alleged these events occurred.*

On July 7, 1947, Dennis alleged he received a series of phone calls at the Ballard Funeral Home, where he worked, from the Mortuary Affairs officer at Roswell Army Air Field. He recalled that the mortuary officer inquired as to the availability of child sized caskets and procedures for preserving bodies that had been "laying out in the elements."[3] Later that day he received an emergency ambulance call (the civilian mortuary for which he worked also provided an ambulance service) to respond to the site of a minor traffic accident in Roswell.[4] The accident victim was an "airman" stationed at Roswell AAF, and Dennis transported the airman to the hospital at the base.[5]

As Dennis walked into the hospital he noticed three military box-type ambulances, one or more of which contained what appeared to be "wreckage."[6] He described the wreckage as being inscribed with odd markings or symbols and bluish-purplish in color.[7] He recalled that some of this wreckage was resting against the inside wall of the rear compartment of the ambulance and two pieces of it "looked kind of like the bottom of a canoe."[8] He described other wreckage on the floor of the ambulance as being "all sharp" and as best he could tell "was like broken glass."[9] He also recalled observing Military Policemen (MPs) standing at the back of two of these ambulances.[10]

When he went inside the hospital, he encountered a military nurse who was assigned there and with whom he was previously acquainted.[11] The nurse, who looked upset, was covering her mouth with a cloth and told him that "you're going to get in a lot of trouble" and that he should "just get out of here."[12] Dennis also stated that he encountered a military doctor who was assigned to the hospital, a pediatrician, with whom he was "pretty good friends" but did not speak with at that time.[13]

---

* Excerpts of interviews contained in this summary were taken from audio or video recordings made by persons referenced in the appropriate endnote. The sole exception is the interview conducted by Stanton T. Friedman on August 5, 1989. Quotations from this interview were taken from a transcript which is reportedly an accurate representation of the interview. Friedman has not honored repeated requests for an audio recording.

Having seen the wreckage in the rear of the ambulance and believing there had been an accident, he asked another officer in the hospital if there had been a plane crash. The officer, whom Dennis had never seen before, asked him: "Who in the hell are you?" When he responded he was "from the funeral home," the officer summoned two MPs to escort him from the hospital.[14]

However, before Dennis and the two MPs had left the hospital, he heard someone say, "We're not through with that SOB, bring him back here."[15] When Dennis turned around, he observed a redheaded captain (in one version of these events Dennis is quoted as describing this person as a "big redheaded colonel"[16]) who said, "You did not see anything. There was no crash here. You don't go into town making any rumors that you saw anything or that there was any crash... you could get in a lot of trouble."[17]

Angry about being called an SOB, Dennis informed the redheaded officer that he was a civilian, not under his authority, and that he, the redheaded officer, "can't do a damn thing to me."[18] The redheaded officer was alleged to have threatened Dennis by responding "Oh yes we can"... "Somebody will be picking your bones out of the sand"..."We can do anything to you..." That we want to."[19] A black sergeant, whom Dennis recalled had accompanied the redheaded officer, allegedly stated he would "make real good dog food."[20] Following this exchange, Dennis claimed he was "picked up...arm and arm" and escorted back to his place of business by two MPs.[21]

The following day, July 8, 1947, Dennis attempted to telephone the nurse he had seen in the hall at the hospital to find out "what was going on."[22] He stated that he was unable to reach the nurse but did reach another nurse, a "Captain Wilson," who explained to him that the nurse he was trying to contact was not on duty, but "Wilson" would give her a message to call him.[23] The nurse called Dennis later that same day at the funeral home where he worked and agreed to meet with him at the officers' club at Roswell AAF that afternoon.[24]

When the two met, the nurse appeared disturbed and ill.[25] Dennis asked her to explain what was going on when they met in the hospital the day before. The nurse explained that, in the course of her normal duties, she entered an examining room to get some supplies and encountered two doctors whom she did not recognize that "supposedly were doing a preliminary autopsy" on "three," "very mangled," "black," "little bodies."[26] The doctors requested the nurse remain in the room because they needed her assistance.[27] She allegedly explained that there was a terrible odor in the room that made both her and the doctors ill.[28] Due to this terrible odor and inadequate ventilation, the nurse allegedly told Dennis that the autopsies were moved to another facility on the base and then "everything" was taken to "Wright Field" (now Wright-Patterson AFB, Ohio).[29]

The nurse described the little bodies in detail and even provided a diagram.[30] She described "little bodies" three to four feet in length that had large, "flexible," heads, and concave eyes and noses.[31]

After this meeting Dennis claimed he never saw the nurse again, and he was told she had been shipped out the same afternoon (July 8, 1947) or the next day (July 9, 1947).[32] However, some time later Dennis received a letter from the nurse that indicated she was in London, England.[33] Dennis stated that he tried to respond to the nurse, but his letter was returned stamped "return to sender" and "deceased."[34] After receiving this letter, he inquired at the base about the nurse and was told by "Captain Wilson" that she didn't know where the nurse was, but there was a rumor that she and several other nurses had been killed in a plane crash while on a training mission.[35]

Some years later, Dennis stated that he visited the unidentified military pediatrician he had seen at the hospital.[36] The pediatrician had since left the military and set up practice in Farmington, N.M.[37] Dennis said he and the pediatrician discussed the incident of years past but was stopped short when the pediatrician told him that he was consulted regarding this incident, but that "it was completely out of [his] field of medicine," then ended the discussion.[38]

Based on this account, UFO theorists have presented the following assertions:

> **a.** Dennis, the "missing" nurse, and the unidentified pediatrician inadvertently stumbled onto the highly classified autopsies of alien bodies at Roswell AAF hospital in July 1947.
>
> **b.** The two mysterious doctors at the hospital were sent to Roswell AAF from a higher headquarters to conduct the autopsies after which the bodies were transported to what is now Wright-Patterson AFB, Ohio.
>
> **c.** The bluish-purplish wreckage that looked like the bottom of a canoe in the rear of the ambulance, were "escape pods" from a flying saucer flown by the aliens that crashed in the Roswell area.
>
> **d.** Dennis was forcibly removed from the hospital and threatened with death by the redheaded officer because he had witnessed some of these activities.
>
> **e.** The nurse was kidnapped, possibly murdered, and all records that she ever existed were systematically destroyed by government agents, also because she witnessed these activities.

As in other accounts examined in this report, the episodes described here became part of the Roswell Incident only because the witness claimed they occurred at a very specific time, July 7-9, 1947. These dates coincide with an actual event: the retrieval of experimental Project Mogul research equipment that was erroneously reported as a flying disc (see Section One).[39] If the events described here occurred at any other time—years, months, weeks, or even days before or after July 7-9, 1947—they might be considered unusual to an uninformed person, but certainly not part of the Roswell Incident.

Air Force research revealed that the witness made serious errors in his recollections of events. When his account was compared with official records of the actual events he is believed to have described, extensive inaccuracies were indicated including a likely error in the date by as much as 12 years.

2.1
The "Missing" Nurse and the Pediatrician

To illustrate the errors in this account and to identify actual events, the following section will examine the accounts of the missing nurse and the unidentified pediatrician. Both of these persons were allegedly present at the Roswell AAF hospital when the events described by the witness occurred.

The "Missing" Nurse

Dennis recalled that the nurse was quickly and suspiciously shipped out either the same day or the day after he met with her in the Roswell AAF Officers' Club. If this allegation was true, it certainly seemed unusual—and verifiable. Therefore, the morning reports, the certified daily personnel accounting records required to be kept by all Army Air Forces units at that time, were obtained and reviewed. These reports did not indicate that a nurse or any other person was reassigned on the days alleged, July 8 or July 9, 1947. [40] The morning reports of the 427th Army Air Forces Base Unit (AAFBU) Squadron "M," the unit that all the medical personnel at Roswell AAF were assigned in July 1947, did not indicate a sudden or overseas transfer of a nurse or any other person. Records indicated that one nurse was reassigned on July 23, 1947, over two weeks after the purported events described by Dennis.[41] That nurse was transferred by normal personnel rotation procedures to Ft. Worth AAF (now Carswell AFB), Texas, where she remained on active duty until March 1949.[42] In fact, the Squadron "M" morning reports revealed the strength of the Army Nurse Corps (ANC) at Roswell AAF for July 1947 was only five nurses. Of these five nurses none were transferred overseas or killed in a plane crash—the "rumored" fate of the missing nurse.[43]

This review of the hospital morning reports also indicated that the name of the missing nurse provided by the witness was inaccurate. The witness stated in several interviews that he believed the nurse's name was Naomi Maria Selff.[44] A comprehensive search of morning reports and rosters from the Roswell AAF Station Hospital indicated that no person by this name, or a similar name, had ever served there. This finding was supported by a search of personnel records at the National Personnel Records Center (NPRC) in St. Louis, Mo., a part of the National Archives and Record Administration. NPRC is the depository for all U.S. military personnel records. The search at NPRC also did not find a record that a person named Naomi Maria Selff had ever served in any branch of the U.S. Armed Forces.

These findings were consistent with previous efforts of several pro-UFO researchers who have also attempted to locate this nurse or members of her family. They, likewise, were also unable to confirm her existence.[45] While some UFO theorists continue to allege that this absence of records regarding a nurse by this name is part of a conspiracy to withhold information, the most likely reason for the lack of records is that this name is inaccurate.*

Even though the name of the nurse is incorrect, it appears that a nurse assigned to the Roswell AAF Station Hospital in 1947 may have been the basis for the claims. Eileen Mae Fanton was the only nurse of the five assigned to Roswell AAF in July 1947, whose personal circumstances and physical attributes not only resembled those of the missing nurse, but appeared to be nearly an exact match.

The "Missing Nurse?"

Fig. 2. Eileen M. Fanton
(U.S. Air Force photo)

1st Lt. Eileen M. Fanton was assigned to the Roswell Army Air Field Station Hospital from December 26, 1946 until September 4, 1947.[46] Fanton, who is deceased, was retired from the U.S. Air Force at the rank of Captain on April 30, 1955, for a physical disability.[47]

In this account, the missing nurse is described as single, "real cute, like a small Audrey Hepburn, with short black hair, dark eyes and olive skin."[48] Lieutenant Fanton was single in 1947, 5'1" tall, weighed 100 pounds, had black hair, dark eyes, and was of Italian descent.[49] Dennis also stated that the nurse was of the Catholic faith, and had been "strictly raised" according to Catholic beliefs.[50] Fanton's personnel record listed her as Roman Catholic, a graduate of St. Catherine's Academy in Springfield, Ky. and as having received her nursing certification from St. Mary Elizabeth's Hospital in Louisville, Ky.[51]

The witness also recalled that the "missing nurse" was a lieutenant, was a general nurse at the hospital, and had sent him correspondence at a later date which stated she was in London, England with a New York, N.Y. APO number (military overseas mailing address) as the return address.[52] Records revealed that Fanton was a First Lieutenant (promoted from Second Lieutenant to First Lieutenant in June 1947), and she was classified as a "nurse, general duty."[53] Records also indicated that of the five nurses assigned to the Roswell AAF Station Hospital in July 1947, she was the only one that later served a tour of duty in England. Furthermore, she was assigned to the 7510th USAF Hospital, APO 240, New York, N.Y., where she served from June 1952 until April 1955.[54]

---

* Interestingly, an article published in the Fall 1995 edition of *Omni* magazine, a publication that in the past has published sensational "Roswell" claims, also independently accounted for all five of the nurses and expressed a decidedly skeptical opinion of the account of the "missing nurse."

The 7510th USAF Hospital was located approximately 45 miles north of London at Wimpole Park, Cambridge, England.

An additional similarity between Fanton and the "missing nurse" is that her personnel record indicated that she quickly departed Roswell AAF and it is probable that the hospital staff would not have provided information concerning her departure. Fanton's unannounced departure from Roswell AAF, on September 4, 1947 was to be admitted to Brooke General Hospital, Ft. Sam Houston, Texas, for a medical condition.[55] This condition was first diagnosed in January 1946 and ultimately led to her medical retirement in 1955.[56] Therefore, if someone other than a family member contacted the Station Hospital at Roswell AAF and inquired about Fanton, as Dennis stated he did, the staff was simply protecting her privacy as a patient. The staff was not participating in a sinister "cover-up" of information as alleged by UFO theorists.

The Pediatrician

In at least two interviews, the witness stated that a pediatrician stationed at the hospital was involved in the events he described.[57] When asked by an interviewer how he knew the pediatrician was involved, Dennis was quoted as replying, "I know he was involved because I saw him there."[58] Dennis is also quoted as saying that he and the pediatrician were "pretty good friends," and after the pediatrician left the military he [the pediatrician] set up a practice in Farmington, N.M. "I used to go fishing all the time up north and I visited him several times up there and he was involved," Dennis said. "I don't remember his name, I think he is still practicing in Farmington." [59]

A review of personnel files and interviews with former members of the Roswell AAF/Walker AFB hospital staff, revealed that only one physician ever relocated to Farmington, N.M. following his military service. The former Capt. Frank B. Nordstrom served at Walker AFB from June 1951 until June 1953.[60] Records also revealed that Nordstrom was indeed a pediatrician and while at Walker AFB, served as the Chief of Pediatric Services.[61] When Nordstrom, a resident of the small town of Aztec, N.M., was interviewed for this report, he stated that he did not recall ever meeting Dennis and could not recall any events that supported any of his claims (see signed sworn statement in Appendix B).[62]

Farmington (population 8,000 in 1954) is located in the primarily rural Four Corners region of New Mexico approximately 300 miles northwest of Roswell. According to Nordstrom, Farmington did not have a pediatrician before his arrival in 1954. From 1954 until approximately 1970, Nordstrom believes he was the only pediatrician in the area. His recollections were confirmed by a local Farmington pharmacist, Charles E. Clouthier.[63] Clouthier also served at the Walker AFB hospital, from 1955 to 1957, and following his military service returned to Farmington, his hometown, where he had lived since 1934. Clouthier has been employed by and co-owned a business, Farmington Drug, since 1957. He is familiar with most, if not all, of the doctors who practice in Farmington and the Four Corners region of New Mexico. Clouthier's confirmation that Nordstrom was the first pediatrician to practice in the Farmington area, was based on both his frequent professional contacts with local physicians and his experiences as a longtime Farmington resident.[64]

Although Nordstrom believed that he was the pediatrician described, he was at a loss to explain how Dennis gained information concerning his military and civilian employment history. In a signed sworn statement, Nordstrom stated that he did not recall ever meeting Dennis and had certainly never been visited by Dennis as he has claimed. One possible source of the information is that from approximately 1958 until approximately 1961 Dennis operated a drugstore in Aztec, N.M., a small town near Farmington where Nordstrom resides (interestingly Aztec is the location of the original "crashed flying saucer" story, see below). However, Nordstrom also did not recall any contact with Dennis in his capacity as a drugstore operator.

Behind the Roswell Incident?

The "Roswell Incident" story is hardly original. In 1948, a work of fiction reportedly appeared in the *Aztec* (N.M.) *Independent Review* describing the crash of a flying saucer with "little men" near Aztec, N.M. In 1950, Frank Scully, a columnist for the theatrical publication *Variety*, published a book, *Behind the Flying Saucers*, which proclaimed the story to be true.[65] Based on

"Doodlebuggers" deluxe, Silas M. Newton (left) and partner Leo A. GeBauer, conned an amazing flock of suckers into buying non-producing oil leases.

Maybe these con men didn't know a flying saucer from a hole in the ground. But they used both to sucker their victims. They were almost $400,000 ahead when TRUE's reporter broke the amazing case of the...

Flying Saucer Swindlers

By J. P. CAHN

DENVER

Back in 1952, the September issue of TRUE ran a story of mine titled *The Flying Saucers and the Mysterious Little Men*. It was an exposé of a best-selling book that maintained flying saucers from Venus, manned by 3-foot characters in blue suits, had landed on earth. Despite solemn prefaces by both the author and publisher, the book was a complete hoax. I rounded up proof that the little-men-from-Venus yarn was as phony as a headwaiter's bow and smile.

Digging into the story of the bogus flying saucers, I learned that two men—Silas M. Newton and Leo A. GeBauer—had manufactured the hoax and fobbed it off on a gullible author. When we broke the story, TRUE and I had some pretty good ideas why Newton and GeBauer had dreamed up their yarn, but we couldn't prove our suspicions. And what you can't prove you don't print. So we said what we could, and hoped for the rest. Thanks to TRUE's vast readership, we got the new leads we were hoping for, and now we can give you the wrap-up story on as slippery a pair of swindlers as ever came down the pike.

It happened like this:

As we had suspected, while chasing the flying saucer story to earth, Newton and GeBauer were more than a couple of fun-loving pranksters. Newton had a record that went back to 1931. It started with an arrest for conspiracy in Montclair, New Jersey, and worked its way through grand lar-

36 ☆ TRUE

Fig. 3. Story by J.P. Cahn, that appeared in the August 1956, *True* magazine.

the Aztec story, *Behind the Flying Saucers* bears many similarities to the Roswell Incident, most notably, descriptions of covert "flying saucer" and "little men" recoveries interspersed with doses of unsubstantiated accusations directed at the U.S. Air Force.[66]

In his book, Scully claimed he had information from two scientists, Silas M. Newton and a mysterious "Dr. Gee," who he claimed investigated the crash for the government.[67] In reality, Newton and Gee were con-men who convinced Scully of the story's authenticity.[68]

Intrigued by the sensational claims made in *Behind the Flying Saucers*, a reporter for the *San Francisco Chronicle*, J. P. Cahn, decided to look into the matter. What resulted from Cahn's research were articles in the September 1952 and August 1956 edition of *True* magazine which determined that the story was as "phony as a headwaiters bow and smile."[69]

Cahn, with the assistance of a magician, devised a plan to "sting" the two con-men.[70] To execute the sting, he used sleight of hand switching an "indestructible" metal disk, claimed to be from a flying saucer, with a slug of his own manufacture. After the switch, Cahn submitted the disk to a laboratory for analysis revealing that they were of earthly origin, in particular, a grade of aluminum used to manufacture pots and pans![71]

Even with the exposure of this obvious fraud, the Aztec story is still revered by UFO theorists. Elements of this story occasionally reemerge and are thought to be the catalyst for other crashed flying saucer stories, including the Roswell Incident.

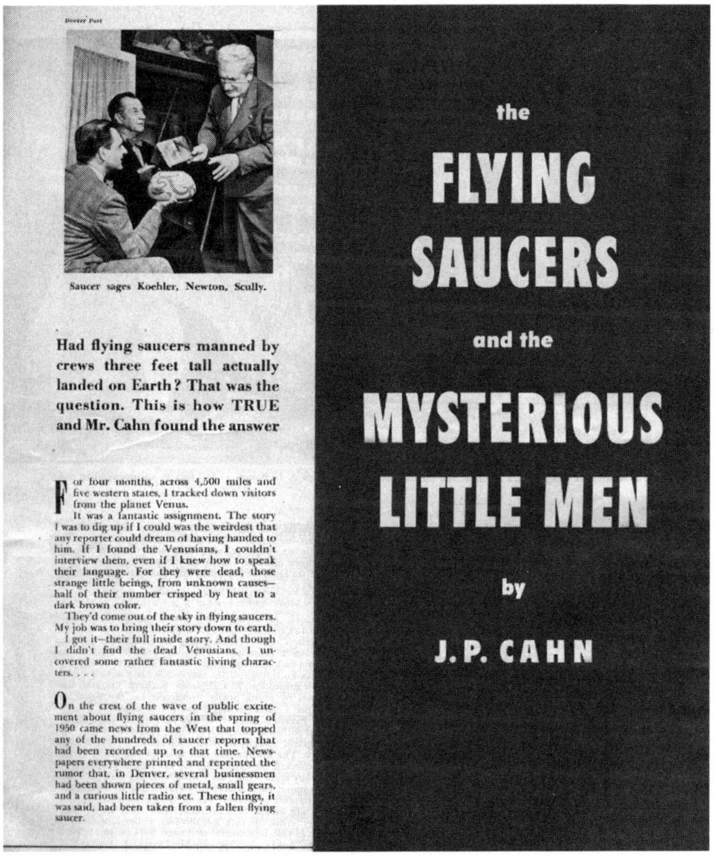

Saucer sages Koehler, Newton, Scully.

Had flying saucers manned by crews three feet tall actually landed on Earth? That was the question. This is how TRUE and Mr. Cahn found the answer

For four months, across 4,500 miles and five western states, I tracked down visitors from the planet Venus.

It was a fantastic assignment. The story I was to dig up if I could was the weirdest that any reporter could dream of having handed to him. If I found the Venusians, I couldn't interview them, even if I knew how to speak their language. For they were dead, those strange little beings, from unknown causes—half of their number crisped by heat to a dark brown color.

They'd come out of the sky in flying saucers. My job was to bring their story down to earth.

I got it—their full inside story. And though I didn't find the dead Venusians, I uncovered some rather fantastic living characters. . . .

On the crest of the wave of public excitement about flying saucers in the spring of 1950 came news from the West that topped any of the hundreds of saucer reports that had been recorded up to that time. Newspapers everywhere printed and reprinted the rumor that, in Denver, several businessmen had been shown pieces of metal, small gears, and a curious little radio set. These things, it was said, had been taken from a fallen flying saucer.

the

FLYING SAUCERS

and the

MYSTERIOUS LITTLE MEN

by

J.P. CAHN

Fig. 4. September 1952 *True* magazine story that exposed the Aztec, N.M. hoax.

Descriptions of Other Air Force Members

Since official records proved that none of the nurses at Roswell AAF in July 1947 were missing, and the nurse and pediatrician described in this account had been identified, major discrepancies between Dennis' recollections and official records were apparent. In an effort to provide for the fullest possible accounting of these claims, even though key aspects had already been proven false, Air Force researchers sought additional information to determine if there was validity to *any* portion of the account. Since the witness has never provided documentation to support his claims, the only source of additional information was the numerous interviews he had previously provided to private researchers and the media. His many statements, which have appeared in newspapers, videos, magazines, movies, books, lectures, journals and television programs, were reviewed for information that might further explain his testimony.

Examination of this large body of publicly available information immediately provided clues that the witness may have recalled incidents from a period other than July 1947. The first clue was that he repeatedly, in all of the interviews, referred to the injured military person he allegedly transported to the Roswell AAF hospital as an airman. The rank of airman was not in existence in 1947. It was implemented on April 1, 1952.[72] Prior to that date an airman in the Air Force was referred to by the U.S. Army equivalent, a private. Another possible indication that he recalled events from a different time was the description of an alleged "black sergeant" that accompanied the redheaded officer at the hospital. The pairing of a white officer with a black NCO seemed unlikely since in 1947 the U.S. Army Air Forces was racially segregated, as were all branches of the armed forces. The U.S. Air Force did not begin racial integration until the May 11, 1949 issuance of Air Force Letter 35-3 that formally ended segregation.[73] Though it was not impossible in 1947 for a black NCO to accompany and seem to be working with a white officer, it would be unlikely. These two discrepancies did not provide a firm time frame of actual events, if any occurred at all.

To approximate a time frame for actual events, the specific details of the information provided were examined. This examination was to determine if any military members were identified by name or by a combination of any other distinguishing characteristics such as rank, position, age, or physical attributes. If the testimony identified a military member as having been present for an event, then their personnel record could be used to affix an approximate date. Affixing a date of an event by referencing personnel records was possible since each military member's personnel file contains a physical description and chronological listing of duty stations, units of assignment, and work assignments for his/her entire military career.

This detailed examination revealed several likely references to specific individuals, which through their personnel files, were documented as having been assigned to the hospital at Roswell AAF or Walker AFB (Roswell AAF was renamed Walker AFB in January 1948).

The "Big Redheaded Colonel." An indication that Dennis might have mistaken the date of actual events was that he was quoted in at least one book as having said that the officer who threatened him in the hospital was a big redheaded colonel.[74] Research revealed that only one tall colonel with red hair was known to have been assigned to the Walker AFB hospital. Colonel Lee F. Ferrell was the hospital commander from October 1954 until June 1960.[75] Ferrell was 6'1" tall and had red hair.[76]

Fig. 5. Col. Lee F. Ferrell *(left)*, was commander of the Walker AFB hospital from 1954-1960. In this photo Ferrell escorts U.S. Senator Dennis Chavez (N.M.) on a tour of the new Walker AFB hospital in June 1960, which was named in honor of the senator. *(U.S. Air Force photo)*

"Captain 'Slatts' Wilson." In at least two interviews Dennis repeatedly made reference to a nurse named "Captain Wilson."[77] He recalled that "Captain Wilson", who he believed was the head nurse, was another nurse stationed at the Roswell AAF hospital in July 1947.[78] Dennis claims he spoke to "Captain Wilson" several times in reference to the alleged missing nurse.[79]

He claims that on the day after he met with the missing nurse at the Roswell AAF Officers' Club, he attempted to contact her by telephone at the hospital but was told that she wasn't on duty.[80] Instead, he spoke with "Captain Wilson." "I called the station I knew she [the missing nurse] always worked at," Dennis said, "She was a general nurse... I was informed that she wasn't working that day. [Dennis then telephoned] An old girl by the name of Wilson, Captain Wilson, and I asked her 'what happened'? She said, 'Glenn, I don't know what happened, she's not on duty.' She said she'd try to get word to her [the missing nurse] that you [Dennis] want to talk to her."[81] Later in the same interview Dennis further described Wilson. "We called her 'Slatts' Wilson who was a big tall nurse about six foot two or three—big tall skinny gal—and we called her 'Slatts'—everybody called her 'Slatts.' She's the one who told me she heard there was a plane crash and the nurses went down on a training mission."[82]

The testimony appeared to clearly identify by name, rank, position, physical attributes and by a distinctive nickname, "Slatts," another nurse present at the hospital in July 1947. But a review of the morning reports of the Roswell AAF hospital for July 1947 did not contain the name of a nurse, or anyone else, named Wilson.[83] The only female captain assigned to the Roswell AAF Hospital in July 1947 was the Chief Nurse Capt. Joyce Goddard.[84] Goddard, who was 5'6" tall, was transferred from Roswell AAF to Korea on August 21, 1947.[85]

Therefore, according to Dennis' recollection of events, this review of the morning reports indicated that there were two missing nurses, not one—"Lieutenant Naomi Selff" and "Captain 'Slatts' Wilson." Further scrutiny of personnel records of individuals assigned to the Roswell AAF/Walker AFB hospital indicated that Dennis'recollections of events were apparently inaccurate.

Examination of the August 1947 morning reports did not list a nurse named Wilson, but they *did* list a nurse named Slattery.[86] Captain Lucille C. Slattery, who retired as a Lieutenant Colonel and is now deceased, was reassigned from Ft. George Wright, Wash. to Roswell AAF on August 7, 1947.[87]

Fig. 6. Lt. Col. Lucille C. Slattery, the only Air Force nurse ever known as "Slatts," served as a captain at the Roswell AAF/Walker AFB hospital from August 1947 to September 1950. Records indicate that Slattery did not arrive at Roswell AAF until one month *after* the "Roswell Incident," in direct contradiction to statements made by the sole witness to this account.
(U.S. Air Force photo)

Slattery replaced Goddard as the Chief Nurse and was the only female captain assigned to the Roswell AAF hospital. Interviews of persons with longtime professional and personal associations with Slattery, revealed that she was known by the unusual nickname of Slatts.[88] Additionally, former associates of Slattery interviewed for this report, recalled that she was the only Air Force nurse that had ever been known as Slatts.[89] Persons interviewed were Air Force nurses who retired in the 1960s, each with more than 20 years of service, including retired Air Force Col. Ethel Kovatch-Scott, who served as Chief Nurse of the Air Force from 1963 to 1965.

Upon review of Slattery's personnel file it was learned that she was only 5'3" tall and therefore was most likely not the 6'2" or 6'3" "tall skinny" nurse described.[90] This discrepancy in physical description and the fact that she did not arrive at Roswell AAF until nearly one month *after* Dennis claims he spoke to her, led to the conclusion that perhaps he confused Slattery with some other tall thin nurse, possibly named Wilson, who was stationed at the Roswell AAF or Walker AFB hospital at some other time.

Consequently, a comprehensive review of the morning reports and rosters of the Roswell AAF/Walker AFB hospital revealed that only one nurse named Wilson had ever served there and she did not arrive until February 1956.[91*] Capt. Idabelle Miller, who became Maj. Idabelle Wilson in 1958 due to marriage and a promotion, was assigned to the Walker AFB hospital from February 1956 until May 1960.[92]

Upon review of Maj. Wilson's personnel file, it was learned that she was 5'9" tall and thin. Also, she served as the Head Nurse of the surgical ward at the Walker AFB hospital.[93] Therefore, Wilson's physical attributes, tall and thin, and position as Head Nurse matched Dennis' recollections of "Captain Wilson." When contacted by Air Force researchers, Wilson stated she had no recollection of Dennis, of ever having conversations with him, any of the events he described, or of a nurse that was missing.[94] She also made it abundantly clear that as an Air Force officer and medical professional she would not spread a rumor of a plane crash, as Dennis alleged "Captain Wilson" did in conversations with him.[95]

Results of Missing Nurse and Pediatrician Research

Examination of the missing nurse and the pediatrician stories, and other facts established by research, provide a foundation for further analysis to determine what actual event(s), if any, were responsible for these claims. Based on information developed, it appears this witness may be mistaken in

---

*Records were also searched for names similar to Wilson. Three nurses stationed at Roswell AAF/Walker AFB were identified; Martha Wasem, Carol Williams, and Chalma Walker. None of these nurses phyisical descriptions or personal/professional circumstances were similar to the descriptions of "Captain Wilson" described by the witness.

some of his statements, especially regarding the time frame of these events.

The following facts have been established:

a. The only physician who ever relocated to Farmington, N.M., following his military service at Roswell AAF/Walker AFB was the former Chief of Pediatric Services at the Walker AFB hospital, the former Capt. Frank B. Nordstrom. Further, he did not arrive at Walker AFB until June 1951, four years *after* the purported Roswell Incident, has no recollection of Dennis, the statements Dennis attributes to him, or of any actual events that explain his account.

b. The only nurse ever assigned to the Roswell AAF hospital (subsequently renamed Walker AFB) named Wilson, was Idabelle Wilson. She served at the Walker AFB hospital from 1956 until 1960 and had no recollection of ever meeting or speaking with Dennis or any of the activities he described.

c. Captain Lucille C. Slattery, the only Air Force nurse ever known by the distinctive nickname "Slatts," *was* stationed at the Roswell AAF hospital. However, she did not arrive until August 7, 1947. This was one month *after* the Roswell Incident, making it improbable that Dennis spoke with her in early July 1947.

d. There is no record that a nurse named Naomi Maria Selff, was ever assigned to Roswell AAF, Walker AFB, or was ever a member of the U.S. military.

e. All nurses assigned to the Roswell AAF hospital in July 1947, have been accounted for, thereby eliminating any possibility that there was ever a missing nurse.

Since actual Air Force members who served at Roswell AAF/ Walker AFB hospital were described in this account, the next step was to determine if actual events that occurred at the hospital were possibly the source of this story. As stated earlier in this report, a thorough examination of both classified and unclassified records from 1947 revealed no Army Air Forces or U.S. Air Force activities that explained the alleged events. Therefore records were reviewed from other time periods, based on personnel records of individuals believed to have been identified. These persons and the periods when they were assigned to Roswell AAF/Walker AFB are listed in Table 2.1.

Table 2.1
Persons Described and Periods of Service at Roswell AAF/Walker AFB

Witness Description	Actual Individual Described	Period of Service at Roswell AAF/Walker AFB
the "missing" nurse	1st Lt. Eileen M. Fanton	Dec. 1946 - Sept. 1947
"Capt. 'Slatts' Wilson" (composite of two individuals)	Capt. Lucille C. Slattery and Maj. Idabelle M.Wilson	Aug. 1947 - Sept. 1950 Feb. 1956 - May 1960
"the pediatrician"	Capt. Frank B. Nordstrom	June 1951 - June 1953
"big redheaded colonel"	Col. Lee F. Ferrell	Oct. 1954 - June 1960

The Research Profile

With the establishment of a possible time frame, research efforts paralleled the previous examination in Section One of this report that determined high altitude balloons with anthropomorphic dummy payloads were responsible for the reports of aliens at the two rural New Mexico "crashed saucer" locations. A further review of Air Force activities was then made to determine if any were significantly similar to the information provided. Based on the time period established by personnel records and statements contained in the witness' own account, the following profile of possible events was established:

An event involving the Walker AFB hospital that took place between 1947 and 1960;

a. that may have resulted in "very mangled," "black," "little bodies," that had a strong "odor" being placed in "body bags";

b. that may have resulted in two persons not normally assigned to the hospital, believed to be doctors, that were "supposedly doing preliminary autopsies" on the "little bodies";

c. that may have involved a body with a head that was much larger than normal which was transported to Wright-Patterson AFB, Ohio;

d. that may have involved a redheaded captain or a big red-headed colonel;

e. that may have resulted in an ambulance parked in the rear of the hospital containing wreckage with inscriptions, that were bluish-purplish which looked kind of like the bottom of a canoe; and,

f. that may have required a heightened state of security.

2.2
Aircraft Accidents

The examination of events that involved the Walker AFB hospital that may explain reports of bodies was begun by reviewing the most prominent possible source, which were aircraft accident(s).* A review of aircraft accidents from 1947 to 1960 revealed eight fatal accidents that involved Walker AFB.

Table 2.2
Fatal Aircraft Accidents by Year in the Vicinity of Walker AFB
1947-1960

Year	Aircraft Type	Location of Accident (distance from Walker AFB, N.M.)	Number of Fatalities
1947			
None			
1948			
8/12/48	B-29	4 miles South	13
1949			
5/16/49	C-47	6 miles Northeast	6
12/15/49	B-29	2 miles Northwest	7
1950			
6/1/50	KB-29	12 miles East/Southeast	3
1951			
None			
1952			
None			
1953			
None			
1954			
None			
1955			
6/16/55	T-33	On runway	2
10/3/55	B-47	34 miles West	2
1956			
6/26/56	KC-97	8.8 miles South	11
1957			
None			
1958			
None			
1959			
None			
1960			
2/3/60	KC-135	On runway and ramp	13

The following three basic criteria were used to narrow research efforts to specific accidents for more detailed examinations: were the victims burned, resulting in possible descriptions of "black" "little bodies"?; were the victims transported to the Walker AFB hospital?; and, were the victims

* Other possible explanations such as automobile accidents, house fires, etc., were also examined. However, none of these were determined to be responsible for this account of bodies.

autopsied? To facilitate this examination, researchers reviewed official accident reports, organizational and base histories, individual personnel records of victims, and contemporary newspaper accounts of the accidents. Interviews of persons who participated in the aftermath of these accidents were also conducted. As a result, only one accident met the three criteria, the June 1956 KC-97 accident.

Table 2.3
Analysis of Air Force Aircraft Accidents by Year in the Vicinity of Walker AFB
1947-1960

Date of Accident	Aircraft Type	Fatalities		
		Burned?	Taken to WAFB Hospital?	Autopsied?
8/12/48	B-29	Yes[96]	No[97]	No[98]
5/16/49	C-47	Yes[99]	No[100]	No[101]
12/15/49	B-29	No[102]	Yes[103]	Yes[104]
6/1/50	KB-29	No[105]	No[106]	No[107]
6/16/55	T-33	Yes[108]	No[109]	Yes[110]
10/3/55	B-47	Yes[111]	No[112]	No[113]
6/26/56	KC-97	Yes[114]	Yes[115]	Yes[116]
2/3/60	KC-135	Yes[117]	No[118]	No[119]

Upon detailed review of records of the 1956 accident and interviews with persons who participated in the recovery and identification of the victims, extensive similarities to the description the witness provided were apparent.

Fatal KC-97 Aircraft Mishap

In 1956, Walker AFB, N.M. was the home of Strategic Air Command's 6th and 509th Bombardment Wings.[120] Additionally, Walker was home of the 509th Aerial Refueling Squadron (509th ARS) equipped with the KC-97G aircraft.

Fig. 7. A KC-97 similar this of the 509th Aerial Refueling Squadron crashed 8.8 miles south of Walker AFB on June 26, 1956 with the loss of 11 lives. Descriptions of the aftermath of this tragedy are believed to be the basis for some of the reports of "bodies" at the Walker AFB hospital. *(U.S. Air Force photo)*

The accident occurred on June 26, 1956, 8.8 statute miles south of Walker AFB.[121] A KC-97G aircraft with 11 crewmen on board, while on a refueling training mission, experienced a propeller failure four and one half minutes after takeoff.[122] As a result of the propeller failure, a propeller blade was believed to have punctured the deck fuel tank of the fully loaded tanker causing an intense cabin fire.[123] The aircraft was quickly engulfed in flames, spun out of control, and was completely destroyed. All 11 Air Force members were killed instantly by the fire and impact explosion.[124] Due to the isolated rural impact location on property owned by the state of New Mexico, there was minimal collateral damage and no fatalities or injuries to persons on the ground.[125]

The remains of the crewmen were recovered from the crash site and transported by members of the 4036th USAF Hospital (numerical designation of the hospital at Walker AFB) to the hospital facility at Walker AFB for identification.[126]

On the day following the crash, an identification specialist from Wright-Patterson AFB, Ohio arrived at the hospital to assist in identifying the remains.[127] Part way through the identification process, conducted by both the identification specialist and Air Force members assigned to the Walker AFB hospital, the identification activities were moved to a refrigerated compartment at the Walker AFB commissary.[128] This was due to an overpowering odor emitted by the burned and fuel-soaked bodies and the lack of proper storage facilities at the small base hospital.[129] Also on the day following the crash, June 27, 1956, autopsies of three of the victims were accomplished by a local Roswell pathologist.[130] These examinations were performed at a local funeral home.[131] Upon completion of the identification procedures and the post-mortem examinations, the remains were shipped to the next of kin for burial.

Fig. 8. Main entrance of the 4036th USAF hospital at Walker AFB, 1956. Initial identification procedures of the 11 aircrewmen killed in the June 26, 1956 KC-97 accident were conducted here before being transferred to another facility on the base with refrigeration capability. *(U.S. Air Force photo)*

Comparison of the Account to the KC-97 Mishap

This series of actual events contains extensive similarities to the account provided by Dennis. The numerous and extensive similarities indicate that some elements of this actual event were most probably included in Dennis' account. This aircraft accident provides an explanation for the following elements of the research profile—the very mangled, black, little bodies in body bags, the odor, the two strange doctors, and the report of a redheaded colonel.

Aircraft Crashes and UFOs

Since the first flying saucer story in June 1947, persons have attempted to exploit actual military aircraft accidents to support UFO theories and propagate the flying saucer phenomenon.

One of the first exploitation attempts involved a fatal August 1, 1947 Army Air Forces B-25 accident near Kelso, Wash. Descriptions of this accident, which UFO theorists contend was caused because the aircraft carried parts of a flying saucer, were included in a poorly executed hoax. Nonetheless, it received a considerable amount of attention.

Another incidence was photographs of an "alien," supposedly from a 1948 crash of a flying saucer in Mexico. However, when the photographs were examined by Air Force officials, they noticed a pair of government issue, aviator style, sunglasses lying underneath the "alien" body.

Perhaps the most famous attempt to exploit an actual aircraft accident involved the fatal January 1948 crash of a Kentucky Air National Guard F-51 fighter near Franklin, Ky. Theorists contend the fighter was shot down by a UFO. However, it was determined that this aircraft most probably crashed while observing a newly invented high altitude research balloon thought to be a UFO. The large balloon, which matched eyewitnesses' descriptions at the time, was released the previous day, and its ground track placed it precisely in the area where the unidentified object was sighted the next day. Regardless, shameless attempts to exploit this event continued as recently as 1995, when the tabloid TV program, *Sightings,* aired and published (*Sightings*, Simon & Schuster, 1996, 170-176) a distorted interpretation of this tragedy.

The "Black" "Little Bodies." Review of the autopsy protocols of the victims of this accident revealed extensive similarities to the descriptions of the bodies allegedly described by the missing nurse. Dennis related in various interviews that the missing nurse described, "...three; very mangled; black; little bodies in body bags."[132] Records of this mishap confirmed that the victims suffered "injuries, extreme, multiple."[133] According to persons who assisted in the identification of the remains from this crash, and in compliance with Air Force directives in effect at that time, human remains pouches, commonly called body bags, were used to recover and transport victims' bodies.[134]

Statements made by Dennis described bodies that were "three-and-a-half to four feet tall," and "black" in color.[135] The autopsy protocols of two victims described extensive third degree burns and loss of the lower extremities.[136] Dennis also described a head of one of the bodies that was not rigid but "flexible" and tissues of a body in "strings" that looked as if they were "pulled" by predatory animals after the crash.[137] An autopsy protocol of a victim described "multiple fractures of all bones of the skull" and "partially cooked strands of bowel...over the abdomen and in the chest." [138] Additional similarities between the autopsy protocols and Dennis' statements were a detached hand and descriptions of the fingers and arms of the crash victims.[139]

The autopsy protocol of one victim also described remains with a "face completely missing."[140] This description corresponds with Dennis' recollections of a body with eyes and nose that were concave. Also, the drawing of the head of one of the "little bodies" Dennis claims is representative of a drawing given to him by the missing nurse is a reasonably accurate representation of a human body with its face completely missing.[141]

Another similarity to Dennis' account is that of the 11 victims of this accident, only three were autopsied—the same number of bodies that were allegedly autopsied in the missing nurse's account.[142] Finally, records revealed that due to limited facilities at the Walker AFB hospital, the autopsies were performed at the Ballard Funeral Home in Roswell.[143] This is the same funeral home where Dennis claimed to be employed in 1947 until 1962.[144*]

The Odor. Transportation of remains to a small base hospital was unusual since the hospital did not have the necessary facilities— a preparation room, refrigeration equipment or a morgue, to accommodate multiple deceased persons. Records of other crashes involving Walker AFB showed that the remains of crash victims were transported either to another facility on Walker AFB or directly to a local funeral home.[145]

Fig. 9. Three of the 11 Air Force members killed in the June 26, 1956 KC-97 accident were autopsied at the Ballard Funeral Home in Roswell. The actual descriptions of the remains (only three were autopsied), closely corresponds with Dennis' descriptions regarding the "little bodies." Additionally, this is the same funeral home where Dennis claimed to be employed from 1947 until 1962.

---

[*] It is unclear when Dennis worked at this funeral home since city and phone directories listed him as co-owning a different funeral home in Roswell, as vice-president of another funeral home in Roswell, and as having been employed as a drug store supervisor and oil field worker during the periods when he claims he worked at the Ballard Funeral Home.

In fact, the Air Force manual that prescribed the policies, standards and procedures relating to the care and disposition of deceased Air Force personnel in effect in 1956, Air Force Manual 143-1, *Mortuary Affairs*, did not direct that remains be brought to a hospital. It encouraged the local commander to "improvise facilities" and make use of "garages, warehouses, large tents, or other facilities for processing groups of remains."[146] Nonetheless, records of the June 1956 crash and interviews with the persons who processed the remains indicated that the victims were brought from the crash site to the Walker AFB hospital.[147] During the identification procedures, the odor became too strong and the bodies and the identification activities were moved to a refrigerated compartment at the base commissary.[148]

Interviewed for this report were the registrar of the hospital, 1st Lt. Jack Whenry (now a retired Major) and a medical administration specialist assigned to the registrar, SSgt. John Walter (now a retired Master Sergeant), both of whom assisted in the processing and identification of the deceased aircrewmen. Whenry and Walter both recalled the strong odor, that some persons became ill during the procedures (as did the alleged missing nurse), and the unusual transfer of the remains to the Walker AFB commissary (the nurse also allegedly described the transfer of remains to another building on the base). However, neither recalled that a nurse was missing or any of the other activities as described by Dennis.[149]

The "Big Redheaded Colonel." The big redheaded colonel is a likely reference to the hospital commander, Col. Lee F. Ferrell, who was 6'1" tall and had red hair. Ferrell served at the Walker AFB hospital from 1954 until 1960.[150] It would not be unusual for the hospital commander to be present at the hospital following a major aircraft accident.

The Two Mysterious "Doctors." The two doctors not assigned to the Walker AFB hospital who were allegedly observed at the hospital performing preliminary autopsies have been identified as an Air Force civilian identification specialist and a local Roswell pathologist.

Identification Specialist. In an aircraft mishap involving multiple fatalities, identification of victims can go beyond the capabilities of a small Air Force hospital such as the one at Walker AFB. Beginning in July 1951, the Air Force Memorial Affairs Branch, now called Air Force Mortuary Services, employed full-time civilian morticians and funeral directors, known as identification specialists, to assist Air Force installations in the identification of deceased persons.[151] When requested by the local commander, the identification specialists, on a 24-hour standby basis, responded from Wright-Patterson AFB to the location of an incident.[152] Records confirm that Walker AFB only requested an identification specialist on two occasions, in October 1955 and to identity the victims of the June 1956 crash.[153] For this accident the identification specialist arrived at Walker AFB on June 27, 1956 and made positive identifications of the 11 crewmen on June 28, 1956.[154]

When contacted for this report, the retired identification specialist who responded to this accident, Mr. George Schwaderer, did not have any recollections of Dennis, the nurse, the pediatrician, or any of the other unusual activities as alleged.[155] Schwaderer did recall that on identifications of group remains such as this, it was typical to wear standard hospital surgical gowns and masks and that he was often mistaken for a pathologist.[156]

Due to restrictions on the release of information concerning the identification process, uninformed individuals who may, by chance, have witnessed some portions of the identification, were often the source of a considerable amount of speculation. The identification procedures employed by the identification specialists were not classified, but AFM-143-1, *Mortuary Affairs*, directed that "no information will be divulged concerning identification or shipment of any remains until a final determination of identity has been resolved for all remains."[157]

For this accident, identification took approximately two days and any releases of information were restricted to individuals with an official requirement. These restrictions extended, not only to the general public, but also to Air Force members.

A possible reference to the identification specialist is found in one of Dennis' recitations of the account. Dennis, a mortician who might possess limited knowledge of Air Force mortuary procedures, stated that he was told the "doctors" might be pathologists from "Walter Reed Army Hospital."[158] Walter Reed Army Medical Center in Washington D.C. is a likely location that an unknown pathologist performing an autopsy on military personnel might have been based. Co-located at Walter Reed is the Armed Forces Institute of Pathology (AFIP) and beginning in 1955, AFIP sent pathologists into the field to examine aircraft accidents. A review of records at AFIP and interviews with persons involved with the identification procedures at Walker AFB do not indicate AFIP sent any personnel to assist in this accident.[159]

Pathology Consultant. In June 1956, the Walker AFB hospital did not have a pathologist on staff.[160] All autopsies and examinations of pathological specimens were conducted by a civilian consultant from Roswell.[161] The autopsy protocols of the deceased crewmen from the June 1956 crash indicated that Dr. Alfred S. Blauw of Roswell performed the three autopsies.[162] Obviously, neither the pathologist nor the identification specialist were normally assigned to the Walker AFB hospital and would not be expected to be present at the hospital, especially to an observer with limited knowledge of these activities.

Continuing Research

The focus of research was now shifted to other activities that might explain the remaining portions of the profile. The unexplained portions were:

a. the presence of a redheaded captain;

b. the wreckage in the rear of the ambulance outside the Walker AFB hospital;

c. the heightened state of security at the Walker AFB hospital; and,

d. the shipment of a body with a large head to Wright-Patterson AFB.

Based on previous research, this effort began by examining records of the other Air Force aerial vehicle known to have operated extensively in the Roswell area since the late 1940s—high altitude research balloons.

2.3
High Altitude Research Projects

By 1960, hundreds of high altitude research balloons, some that carried anthropomorphic dummies, descended and were recovered in areas surrounding Walker AFB and Roswell. But based on the descriptions of the bodies and the involvement of a hospital and medical personnel, it did not seem likely that high altitude research balloons with scientific instruments or anthropomorphic dummies could possibly account for this testimony. Therefore, the focal point of the research shifted to manned high altitude balloon flights conducted by the Air Force during the mid to late 1950s and early 1960s.

Manned Balloon Flights

Two manned balloon projects, MAN HIGH and EXCELSIOR, were conducted within the time period targeted for research: MAN HIGH from 1957 to 1958[163] and the manned portion of EXCELSIOR in 1959 and 1960. The only other manned high altitude balloon project in Air Force history, STARGAZER, did not fly until 1962.

It was discovered that only six manned flights were made for MAN HIGH and EXCELSIOR. These flights were determined unlikely as the source of the testimony since there were no injuries or deaths, all six flights had been the subject of intense media coverage, and none were flown in the vicinity of Roswell. Despite the apparent dead end these flights presented to explain this account, records were obtained and persons involved in MAN HIGH and EXCELSIOR were contacted and interviewed. These records and interviews confirmed that there were, in fact, only six USAF manned high altitude

Fig. 10. Maj. David G. Simons (MC) (*left*), balloon designer Otto C. Winzen (*center*) and Capt. Joseph W. Kittinger, Jr., examine a scale model of a low altitude balloon gondola used to train pilots for high altitude missions. *(photo courtesy of Mike Smith, Raven Industries)*

balloon flights, none with characteristics similar to the testimony. However, detailed examinations of the records revealed that, in addition to the six high altitude balloon flights, there were also numerous low altitude balloon flights made to train and qualify the high altitude balloon pilots.[164] Records of the training flights indicated that some of these were conducted at Holloman AFB, N.M., and several mishaps occurred resulting in injuries to the pilots.[165]

Further research revealed that one accident had taken place just northwest of Roswell.[166] The accident occurred on May 21, 1959, 10 miles northwest of Walker AFB, on a pilot training mission for the upcoming Project Excelsior and Stargazer flights scheduled to begin that fall. Analysis of the accident revealed actual events that closely resembled the remaining portions of the established profile.

U.S. Air Force Manned High Altitude Balloon Projects

In addition to unmanned high altitude balloon research flights, from 1957 to 1962 the U.S. Air Force conducted a series of seven manned high altitude flights. These forward-looking projects investigated the upper reaches of the earth's atmosphere and laid the foundation for manned spacefight. Most flights were conducted before rocket booster technology was available to propel a spacecraft into earth's orbit. In this interim period, to "bridge the gap" while awaiting developments in rocket technology, high altitude balloons were the only vehicles capable of reaching the altitudes required. All three of the USAF manned high altitude balloon projects, Man High, Excelsior, and Stargazer utilized Holloman AFB balloons to transport men to the very edge of space, above approximately 99 per cent of the earth's atmosphere, a region known as "near space."

Project Man High. In 1955, a combined effort by the U.S. Air Force Aeromedical Field Laboratory, Winzen Research International, and the Holloman Balloon Branch resulted in the first Air Force manned balloon program. Project Man High, officially known as the Biodynamics of Space Flight, directed by Lt. Col. David Simons (MC), was the first of the three

Fig. 11. *(Left)* Test pilot Capt. Joseph W. Kittinger, Jr. just before launch of Man High I at New Brighton, Minn. on June 2, 1957. Kittinger flew in all three USAF high altitude balloon projects and has accumulated more high altitude balloon flying hours than anyone else in the world. *(U.S. Air Force photo)*

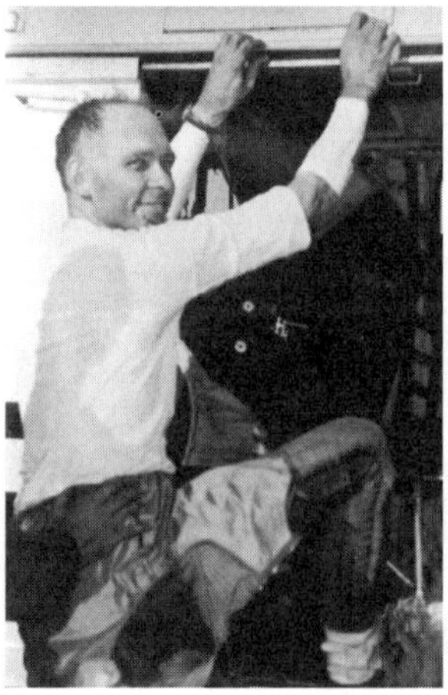

Fig. 12. *(Center)* Lt.Col. David G. Simons (MC), a physician and pilot of the Man High II high altitude balloon mission, is shown here boarding the recovery helicopter near Frederick, S.D. following the successful flight on August 19, 1957. This flight lasted 33 hours and 10 minutes attaining a peak altitude of 101,500 feet. *(U.S. Air Force photo)*

Fig. 13. (Right) Holloman AFB Balloon Branch Meteorologist and Engineer, Bernard D. Gildenberg, instructs high altitude balloon pilot 1st Lt. Clifton McClure, pilot of Man High III, in the operation of a low altitude training balloon on May 12, 1959 at Holloman AFB, N.M. *(U.S. Air Force photo)*

widely publicized manned high altitude balloon programs. The objective of Project MAN HIGH was to measure the physiological and psychological capabilities of a human in a space equivalent environment. Many developments of this successful project were later incorporated into the first phase of the U.S. Air Force Man in Space Program nicknamed MAN IN SPACE SOONEST (MISS). Technology developed for MISS was transferred to NASA in 1959 and became part of Project MERCURY, the initial series of U.S. space missions.[167]

Fig. 14. Project officer and pilot, Capt. Joseph W. Kittinger, Jr., standing beside the EXCELSIOR gondola at Holloman AFB, N.M. On his third and final high altitude parachute jump, from 102,800 feet, he established world records for highest parachute jump and length of free-fall which still stand today. *(U.S. Air Force photo)*

Project EXCELSIOR. In 1959 and 1960 the U.S. Air Force Aero Medical Laboratory collaborated with the Holloman Balloon Branch for Project EXCELSIOR, the second Air Force manned high altitude balloon program. EXCELSIOR was the dramatic climax of the high altitude free-fall studies that began as Project HIGH DIVE in 1953 using anthropomorphic dummies. As the test director for Project EXCELSIOR, Capt. Joseph W. Kittinger, Jr. made three parachute jumps from balloons, EXCELSIOR I, II, and III, from 76,000, 75,000, and a still standing record altitude of 102,800 feet. EXCELSIOR's scientific objective was to develop a parachute system and techniques required to return a pilot or astronaut to earth following an emergency high altitude escape.

Project STARGAZER. Project STARGAZER was the third Air Force manned high altitude balloon program. Capt. Joseph W. Kittinger, Jr., the veteran high altitude balloon pilot of MAN HIGH and EXCELSIOR, was both the pilot and project engineer. On December 13, 1962, Kittinger and U.S. Navy civilian astronomer William C. White rose to 86,000 feet to make astronomical observations with a gyro-stabilized telescope. A joint U.S. Air Force, U.S. Navy, Smithsonian Institution, and Massachusetts Institute of Technology program, STARGAZER made only one of a scheduled four flights due to budget shortfalls and equipment difficulties.

Fig. 15. Project STARGAZER pilot and project engineer, Capt. Joseph W. Kittinger, Jr. *(left)*, after landing near Lordsburg, N.M. on December 13, 1962 with U.S. Navy civilian astronomer William C. White. Kittinger and White ascended to 86,000 feet to make astronomical observations in the seventh, and final, U.S. Air Force manned high altitude balloon flight. *(U.S. Air Force photo)*

Table 2.4
U.S. Air Force Manned High Altitude Balloon Flights

Date	Project/Flight	Altitude (feet)	Pilot
6/2/57	MAN HIGH I	96,200	Capt. Joseph W. Kittinger, Jr.
8/19/57	MAN HIGH II	101,500	Lt. Col. David G. Simons (MC)
10/8/58	MAN HIGH III	99,700	1st Lt. Clifton McClure
11/16/59	EXCELSIOR I	76,400	Capt. Joseph W. Kittinger, Jr.
12/11/59	EXCELSIOR II	74,700	Capt. Joseph W. Kittinger, Jr.
8/16/60	EXCELSIOR III	102,800	Capt. Joseph W. Kittinger, Jr.
12/13/62	STARGAZER	86,000	Capt. Joseph W. Kittinger, Jr.

With the completion of Project STARGAZER and the success of NASA's Project MERCURY space flights, future investigations were accomplished by space vehicles. This signaled the end of an era of manned high altitude balloon flight; however, these projects had indeed "bridged the gap," and manned space flight was now safely possible.

Low Altitude Balloon Training Missions

Background. In April 1958, Col. John P. Stapp, commander of the U.S. Air Force Aero Medical Laboratory at Wright-Patterson AFB, appointed a new project officer for Project EXCELSIOR, Capt. Joseph W. Kittinger, Jr.. EXCELSIOR was part of an ongoing program to examine high altitude aircraft escape procedures and equipment.[168] Kittinger was an experienced fighter test pilot who was the pilot of the first Air Force manned high altitude balloon project, MAN HIGH I, in June 1957.[169] In addition to being the

EXCELSIOR project officer, Kittinger was the pilot and project engineer of STARGAZER which also utilized high altitude balloons.

By 1959, Kittinger was an integral part of both EXCELSIOR and STARGAZER and one of only three individuals in the Air Force with high altitude balloon pilot experience. Due to the hazardous nature of these important projects, Stapp was concerned that an injury to Kittinger might result in the cancellation of one or both of them. Therefore, Stapp determined there was a need for backup pilots. Selected as backup pilots were Captains Dan D. Fulgham and William C. Kaufman. Both men were rated aircraft pilots, parachutists, and research and development officers assigned to the Aero Medical Laboratory at Wright-Patterson AFB.

During the third week of May 1959, a series of low altitude manned balloon flights were flown to train Fulgham and Kaufman.[170] These flights were launched by the Holloman AFB Balloon Branch. To satisfy safety requirements, the flights were closely monitored by medical personnel at all times. A helicopter with medical personnel followed the flights during daylight hours, a C-131 aircraft followed during hours of darkness, and at all times medical personnel followed in an ambulance.[171] Balloon recovery and communications technicians also followed the missions on the ground in a communications vehicle and a balloon recovery vehicle.[172] The safety requirements were a result of several recent balloon mishaps that resulted in serious injuries to the pilots.

To meet the training schedule, Kittinger, Kaufman and Fulgham were assigned temporary duty (TDY) from the Aero Medical Laboratory at Wright-Patterson AFB to the Balloon Branch at Holloman AFB, N.M.

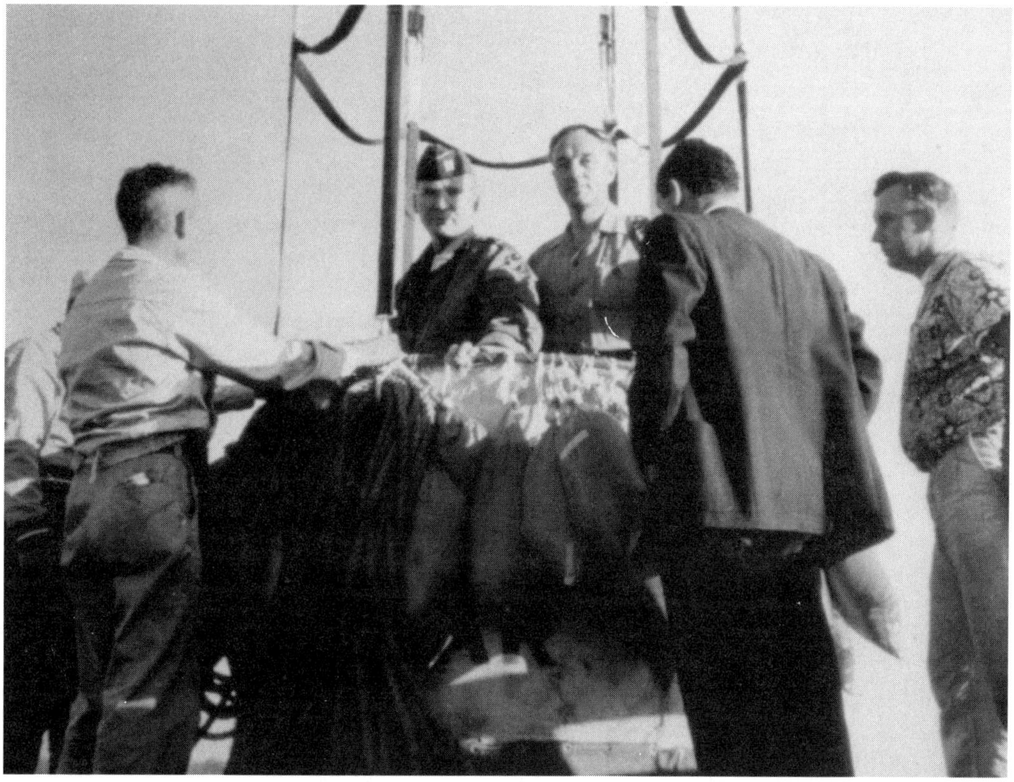

Fig. 16. In 1958 while training for the upcoming U.S. Air Force Aero Medical Laboratory high altitude MAN HIGH III balloon flight, balloon designer Otto C. Winzen (*right*) and space physiologist Capt. Grover Schock *(left)*, were seriously injured in a balloon accident near Ashland, Wisc. Additionally, two training flights at Holloman AFB also resulted in injuries to pilots. These injuries prompted Air Force officials to require close medical supervision during future training flights. *(photo courtesy of Mike Smith, Raven Industries)*

The three pilots, Kittinger, Kaufman and Fulgham, flew training missions together. Kaufman and Fulgham alternately flew the balloon while Kittinger instructed. The missions were flown at night to take advantage of light winds and avoid the effects of diurnal heating on the helium (the lifting gas that filled the balloon). Used for these missions were 30-foot diameter polyethylene balloons and an aluminum gondola especially designed for low altitude training.

The first training mission scheduled for May 19, 1959 was canceled due to equipment problems.[173] Problems overcome, the next day at 1:30 a.m. the mission launched from White Sands Proving Ground.[174] The objective of this flight was to practice gas valving and ballasting techniques necessary for balloon control and to practice landings. After a five-hour flight, the balloon landed without incident just after sunrise northwest of El Paso, Texas.[175]

The second training flight, launched at 2:41 a.m. on May 21, 1959, from behind the Balloon Branch building, Bldg. 850 at Holloman AFB.[176] Near the end of another successful training mission with the same objectives as the previous flight, a mishap occurred resulting in injuries to two of the pilots, Fulgham and Kittinger.[177]

Fig. 17. In May 1959, Capt. Dan D. Fulgham *(left)* and Capt. William C. Kaufman, pilots and Aero Medical Research officers from Wright-Patterson AFB, Ohio were assigned temporary duty to Holloman AFB, N.M. to train as high altitude balloon pilots. Fulgham and Kaufman were trained by Capt. Joseph W. Kittinger, Jr. *(photo collection of Dan D. Fulgham)*

The Mishap. Just after sunrise on May 21, 1959, following a successful low level training flight east of Holloman AFB over the Sacramento Mountains, Kittinger, the instructor pilot, determined the balloon should be landed in a small field approximately 10 miles northwest of Roswell.[178] This was necessary because of approaching bad weather and the field was the last suitable landing site before overflying the city of Roswell.[179] When the balloon touched down, a higher than normal forward velocity for landing caused the gondola to overturn.[180] The three pilots, Kittinger, Fulgham, and Kaufman, were spilled from the gondola pinning Fulgham's head between the edge of the gondola and the ground.[181] The impact shattered his helmet and he sustained a head injury.[182] When the three pilots climbed out from under the gondola, Fulgham noticed that his "head seemed to be protruding outward from underneath [his] helmet."[183] Kittinger also received an injury, a minor facial laceration. The crew of the nearby chase helicopter and personnel in the ground tracking vehicles rushed to the scene.[184] For medical treatment, the pilots were transported by the helicopter to nearby Walker AFB.[185]

When the helicopter landed at Walker AFB, it was met by armed security personnel who sought to verify the purpose of the unannounced arrival.[186] The security personnel escorted the balloon pilots to the hospital.[187] The balloon recovery and communications crew, after retrieving the gondola and balloon, drove to Walker AFB to check on the injured crew and to inform the Balloon Branch at Holloman AFB of the accident.[188]

At the Walker AFB hospital, Fulgham and Kittinger received treatment for their injuries and neither required admission. Meanwhile, the Walker AFB security officials continued to escort the unannounced visitors while verifying their identities.[189] The pilot's identities and purpose for their visit were confirmed via phone by Colonel Stapp, Aero Medical Laboratory commander at Wright-Patterson AFB (the pilots and Project EXCELSIOR were assigned to this organization).[190]

Kittinger, the EXCELSIOR project officer, wanted to leave the hospital as quickly as possible after he and Fulgham received medical attention.[191] The quick departure was to avoid unwanted scrutiny by Walker AFB flying safety officials.[192] When released by the flight surgeon, the three pilots boarded the chase helicopter and returned to Holloman AFB approximately 100 miles to the west.

Fig. 18. The balloon training missions flown from Holloman AFB, N.M. in May 1959, were made in an open gondola suspended beneath a 30-foot diameter polyethelyne balloon. This photo was taken on May 21, 1959 by Balloon Branch communications technician, A2C Ole Jorgeson just prior to the mishap which resulted in injuries to two of the pilots. *(photo collection of Ole Jorgeson)*

2.4
Comparison of the Hospital Account to the Balloon Mishap

The balloon mishap near Roswell on May 21,1959 provides the probable explanation for some of the remaining elements of the incident profile—the redheaded captain, the unusual security at the hospital, the wreckage in the rear of an ambulance, and one portion of the accounts of "aliens" at the Roswell AAF hospital.

The "Redheaded Captain"

It is highly probable that the descriptions of a redheaded captain are those of Capt. Joseph W. Kittinger, Jr., now a retired Colonel. Kittinger, who has red hair, was present at the Walker AFB hospital the entire time the events involving the balloon mishap took place. This is the second Roswell account that describes a captain with red hair. As related in Section One of this report (see page 77 and Appendix C, page 194), a redheaded captain was also allegedly present at the "crashed saucer" site on the San Agustin Plains.[193] That account was consistent with Kittinger's responsibilities as the Excelsior and Stargazer pilot and project officer. As project officer of two research programs that utilized high altitude balloons and as a chase pilot on many other high altitude balloon missions, Kittinger often accompanied balloon launch and recovery crews. He was present both on the ground and in the air at balloon launch and recovery locations throughout New Mexico and the Southwest United States to launch and retrieve anthropomorphic dummies used for Project Excelsior and unmanned test gondolas used for Project Stargazer.[194]

Following the accident, when the balloon pilots were transported to the Walker AFB hospital for medical treatment, Kittinger wanted to leave as soon as possible.[195] He recalled in a recent interview that his desire to quickly leave Walker AFB was to avoid the initiation of a formal accident investigation. He believed that an accident investigation might bring unwanted scrutiny to Project Excelsior and delay or even cancel the controversial project.[196] The controversy surrounding Project Excelsior was due principally to the hazardous nature of the high altitude escape research. Some senior research and development officials within the Air Force were reluctant to support a project that required a human subject to parachute from a balloon gondola at over 100,000 feet. An accident investigation at this juncture would most likely delay the human high altitude free-fall tests scheduled for the fall of 1959 and may have resulted in cancellation of the project.[197]

While at the hospital, Kittinger consulted by phone with his commander, Colonel Stapp.[198] Stapp agreed with Kittinger's assessment that a quick departure from the Walker AFB hospital, after receiving appropriate medical attention, was in the best interest of the project.[199]

The statements attributed to the redheaded captain, "You did not see anything. There was no crash here. You don't go into town making any rumors that you saw anything or that there was any crash,"[200] were consistent with Kittinger's desire to avoid an accident investigation. However, when interviewed for this report, neither Kittinger nor any of the other persons documented as having been present in the hospital that day recalled encountering Dennis.[201]

What may have led an uninformed person, such as Dennis, to believe they were witnessing, or were told of, an unusual or classified event, was that when the injured balloon pilots arrived at the Walker AFB hospital, even though Project Excelsior was unclassified, Kittinger sought to limit disclosure of negative information and publicity.[202]

By 1959, having been the subject of intense media scrutiny following his June 1957 Man High I high altitude balloon flight, Kittinger was aware of both the positive and negative aspects of publicity. In his 1961 book, *The Long, Lonely Leap,* Kittinger described this self-imposed secrecy regarding Project Excelsior, "The secrecy imposed upon Excelsior was of our own choosing. We believed...that any unnecessary conversation about our activities...would simply be premature."[203] When interviewed for this report, Kittinger further explained of Project Excelsior and the visit to the hospital at Walker AFB: "We didn't want publicity... about anything we were doing. So it would have appeared to someone not conversant with the project that we were 'hush-hush,' that we were secretive... it might look like we were trying to cover up a classified mission."[204]

The allegations that the redheaded captain, an apparent reference to Kittinger, threatened anyone while he was at the Walker AFB hospital are untrue. When interviewed for this report and in signed statements obtained from Kittinger, the two other balloon pilots, the doctor who treated them, the medic aboard the helicopter, and the Balloon Branch communications technician who were present at the hospital that day (see Appendix B), none of them recalled that Kittinger was involved in an altercation or made threatening remarks to anyone.[205] Involvement in an altercation with a civilian would have highlighted the presence of the balloon crew and possibly brought the type of negative publicity Kittinger sought to avoid. This would not only have violated Kittinger's policy of maintaining a low profile in regard to Excelsior, but would be completely out of character for the seasoned test pilot.

Throughout his career, Kittinger was renowned for his ability to maintain his composure in difficult, often life threatening, situations. He faced these situations as a test pilot, as a combat pilot and squadron commander in Southeast Asia, and as a Prisoner of War while subjected to severe torture at the hands of the North Vietnamese. In *The Pre-Astronauts,* which chronicles many of Kittinger's accomplishments in the field of aeronautics, including Project Excelsior and Stargazer, the author offered the following description of him:

Kittinger was not Buck Rogers, nor was he a daredevil or thrill-seeker. He was a modern day test pilot: intense, focused, usually quiet, and always polite with firm religious convictions and a powerful sense of loyalty. If he was often stubborn, uncompromising, and demanding he also dealt fairly and respectfully with those who came into contact with him. He was a straight arrow and a straight shooter. [206]

Fig. 19. Maj. Joseph W. Kittinger, Jr. in 1963 as a member of the 1st Air Commando Wing, Ben Hoa, Republic of Vietnam. *(U.S. Air Force photo)*

Colonel Joseph W. Kittinger, Jr., USAF (Ret)

Colonel Joseph W. Kittinger, Jr.'s career in the U.S. Air Force and in aviation has spanned the spectrum of experiences: test pilot, balloon pilot, test parachutist, combat fighter pilot, MiG killer, combat squadron commander, and prisoner of war. He has demonstrated, during a nearly 30-year military career and beyond, that he is among the very best in the U.S. Air Force and the field of aeronautics.

Kittinger began his career in 1949 as a U.S. Air Force aviation cadet. After earning his wings at Las Vegas AFB, Nev. in March 1950, he was assigned to fighter squadrons in Germany and then as a test pilot for NATO. In 1953, Kittinger received an assignment as a test pilot to Holloman AFB, N.M. While at Holloman, he began a many year collaboration with the legendary Air Force scientist and physician, Col. John P. Stapp. In association with Stapp on numerous aero medical projects, Kittinger became the first pilot to fly zero-gravity experiments, now commonly used for astronaut training. For project Man High on June 2, 1957, Kittinger piloted a high altitude balloon to 96,000 feet to examine the physiological and psychological effects on man in a space equivalent environment. This flight marked the origins of the manned U.S. space program with the experience gained from Man High being incorporated in NASA's Project Mercury.

After Man High, and again in association with Stapp, Kittinger directed Project Excelsior, a study of human free-fall characteristics following aircraft escape at extremely high altitudes. After extensive testing with anthropomorphic dummies, Kittinger made three parachute jumps from high altitude balloons: 76,400 feet on November 16, 1959; 74,700 feet on December 11, 1959; and 102,800 feet on August 16, 1960. For these courageous scientific achievements Kittinger was awarded the Distinguished Flying Cross, the Harmon Trophy by President Eisenhower, the still-standing world records for highest parachute jump and length of a free-fall—and the distinction of being the only living person to exceed the speed of sound without an aircraft or spacecraft!

With the completion of Excelsior, Kittinger became the pilot, project officer, and project engineer for Stargazer, an astronomical observation experiment. This was the third and final Air Force manned high altitude balloon project, Kittinger had flown in all three.

In 1963, he was assigned to the Air Commandos (now Special Operations) and flew two combat tours in Southeast Asia in B-26 and A-26 aircraft. After a tour in Germany as a liaison officer with the U.S. Army Special Forces, Kittinger returned to Southeast Asia in 1971, flying F-4 aircraft and commanding the famous 555th "Triple Nickel" Tactical Fighter Squadron at Udorn AB, Thailand. On March 1, 1972 Kittinger engaged and destroyed a MiG-21 over North Vietnam and is credited with an aerial victory. On May 11, 1972, after 483 combat missions and more than 1,000 combat flying hours, Kittinger was shot down over Hanoi and spent 11 months as a POW in the infamous "Hanoi Hilton." When placed with other POWs following solitary confinement and severe torture, Kittinger was moved repeatedly by his North Vietnamese captors due to his effectiveness in motivating other prisoners to maintain strong resistance postures.

Kittinger retired from the Air Force in 1978 and became involved in both sport aircraft flying and gas ballooning. He operated Rosie O' Grady's Flying Circus in his hometown of Orlando, Fla., performing skywriting, banner towing, and hot air and helium balloon demonstrations at nearby Walt Disney World. He also captured the coveted Gordon Bennett Gas Balloon Championship an unprecedented four times (three consecutive), entitling him to retire the trophy.

In September 1984, Kittinger made history again, when, in the tradition of Lindbergh, he became the first person to make a solo crossing of the Atlantic Ocean by balloon.

Kittinger's military decorations include the Silver Star with one oak leaf cluster, Legion of Merit with one oak leaf cluster, Distinguished Flying Cross with five oak leaf clusters, Bronze Star Medal with "V" device and two oak leaf clusters, Air Medal with 23 oak leaf clusters, Purple Heart with one oak leaf cluster, POW medal, and the Republic of Vietnam Cross of Gallantry with Palm.

Kittinger's indomitable spirit, personal courage and dedication to duty are legendary. His ability to achieve seemingly unattainable objectives while earning the respect and absolute loyalty of those who served with him defines this rare breed of warrior-leader.

In October 1995, he received yet another honor and was named a recipient of the prestigious "Elder Statesman of Aviation" award by the National Aeronautics Association. This honor is bestowed upon an individual who over a period of years, has made "significant contributions to aeronautics" and for "reflecting credit upon himself and America." Without a doubt, there are few that exemplify these virtues more than this truly distinctive American, Joseph W. Kittinger, Jr.

The "Wreckage" in the Rear of the Ambulance

The various types of wreckage described in the rear of an ambulance at the Walker AFB hospital also appear to be related to the 1959 balloon accident. Some of this wreckage allegedly had odd inscriptions, touted by UFO theorists as "alien" hieroglyphics.

A requirement of balloon pilot training missions were that they be closely monitored by balloon recovery and medical personnel.[207] Ground crews from Holloman AFB followed the balloon flight from its launch site there to its landing site 10 miles northwest of Roswell.[208] Two of the vehicles that followed the balloon were Dodge M-43 3/4-ton field ambulances and a third was an M-37 3/4-ton utility vehicle or "weapons carrier."[209] One ambulance was assigned to this mission for its standard use—a medical response vehicle. The other ambulance had been converted by the Holloman AFB Balloon Branch and served as a communications vehicle on balloon recovery missions.[210] The additional communications equipment, mounted in the rear compartment of the ambulance, drastically altered what someone expected to see in an ambulance of this type.

Dennis related that he was walking fast when he observed what he thought was wreckage in the rear of an ambulance.[211] This quick glance apparently resulted in descriptions of two pieces of wreckage leaning against the interior of the rear compartment of the ambulance that "was kind of like the bottom of a canoe...like stainless steel...with kind of a bluish-purplish tinge to it."[212] UFO theorists have suggested that these objects were alien spaceship "escape pods" recovered by the Army Air Forces. However, this appears to be a remarkably accurate description of two steel panels painted Air Force blue on a converted ambulance used by the Balloon Branch for this mission.

Fig. 20. Balloon Branch Communications Technician, A2C Ole Jorgeson, now a retired Master Sergeant, in the rear compartment of an M-43 ambulance. Ambulances of this type were converted by the Balloon Branch to communications vehicles in the late 1950s. It appears the witness described the two panels painted Air Force blue *(lower right and left of ambulance)* as "bluish-purplish" "wreckage" that looked "kinda like the bottom of a canoe" and the stenciled writing above them as "hieroglyphics"—See figs. 21 and 22 on next page. *(photo collection of Ole Jorgeson)*

Fig. 21. *(Above)* Enlargement of stenciled writing from photograph below. This lettering was apparently later described as "hieroglyphics."

Fig. 22. *(Below)* Steel panels painted Air Force blue *(lower right and left)* described as "bluish-purplish" "wreckage" that looked "kinda like the bottom of a canoe." *(U.S. Air Force photo)*

The "inscription or something,"[213] the so called "hieroglyphics," were a probable reference to the lettering painted on the equipment support rack above the panels. The lettering on the rack would be visible, but probably not readable, to an observer that quickly walked past the ambulance. Other wreckage "all over the floor" that was "like broken glass,"[214] was a probable reference to the clear plastic 30-foot polyethylene balloon that was recovered following the balloon training mission and placed in the back of the converted ambulance or the weapons carrier for later disposal.

Dennis also recalled that he parked the vehicle he was driving near three field ambulances and then walked up the ramp into the hospital.[215] The description of ambulances near a "ramp" is consistent with the recollections of the Balloon Branch Communication Technician who drove the converted ambulance to the Walker AFB hospital following the balloon accident. While waiting for the injured pilots, A2C Ole Jorgeson, now a retired Master Sergeant, recalled in a recent interview that he parked the converted ambulance near a ramp at the hospital.[216] A review of Walker AFB hospital records revealed that there was only one ramp. The ramp was attached to the hospital dispensary, Walker AFB Bldg. 317.[217] The other ambulances described by the witness were either the other ambulance from Holloman

AFB that provided medical support of the balloon flight or the two "standby" ambulances, that in May 1959, were routinely positioned adjacent to the ramp behind the dispensary at Walker AFB.[218]

Fig. 23. "It was all sharp... like broken glass," a witness' description of debris in the rear of an ambulance at Walker AFB. The debris described was most probably the remnants of the polyethylene balloon, similar to the one in this photo, recovered by Balloon Branch personnel following the mishap in May 1959.
(U.S. Air Force photo)

Additional Security at the Walker AFB Hospital

The witness described what appeared to be a heightened state of security at the hospital when he allegedly took the injured airman there for treatment. UFO theorists contend the heightened security at the hospital was because alien remains were being autopsied. However, it appears that the witness described the security measures taken by Walker AFB personnel due to the unusual circumstances of the arrival of the balloon crew.

In 1959, Walker AFB was a part of the 47th Air Division of Strategic Air Command (SAC). It was home of the 6th Bombardment Wing (6th BW), equipped with the nuclear capable B-52 Stratofortress bomber (the 509th BW was reassigned to Pease AFB, NH on July 1, 1958).[219] The mission of the 6th BW, to strike the enemy with nuclear weapons anywhere in the world at a moment's notice, demanded a heightened state of security at all times. One of the methods instituted during this period to maintain the high standards of security and effectiveness of SAC units, was unannounced "surprise" visits of Headquarters SAC inspection teams. A favored method of transportation for these surprise visits was a helicopter. When a SAC inspection team landed at a base, often the first evaluation they made was of the security response to their unannounced arrival. Failure of security personnel to properly challenge unidentified visitors, regardless of their method of arrival, was considered a serious breach of security.

When transported to Walker AFB for medical treatment, unexpected and at an early hour, the balloon crew, not surprisingly, was met by armed security personnel.[220] The security personnel escorted them to the hospital and remained with them until their identities and purpose of their visit were verified. Kaufman, one of the balloon pilots, recalled that their presence at Walker AFB was initially met with skepticism.

"The [helicopter] pilot called the tower and said... having come from an experimental base, it was nothing unusual for him to have a balloon accident. 'We've got an injured pilot on board. There's been a balloon accident and we would like the flight surgeon and an ambulance to meet us at the tower.' The tower established the fact that yes, we were an Air Force chopper and that we seemed to have somebody injured and what had we been doing? We had been shooting touch and go landings in a balloon?...We got clearance to land...right in front of the tower, and we were met by an ambulance and several MPs with machine guns."[221]

Fig. 24. Walker AFB Building 317, hospital dispensary with attached ramp, as it appeared in June 1954. It is in this building that UFO theorists allege that "alien autopsies" were accomplished in July 1947. However, this was the same building that Capt. Fulgham received treatment following the balloon accident on May 21, 1959. Persons apparently observed him and later related the unusual circumstances surrounding the balloon mishap as part of the "Roswell Incident." *(U.S. Air Force photo)*

Fig. 25. Main gate at Walker AFB, N.M., formerly Roswell AAF, as it appeared in 1954. During the 1950s, the highly secure base was the home of the nuclear capable 509th and 6th Bombardment Wings of Strategic Air Command. *(U.S. Air Force photo)*

According to the medical technician who arrived on the helicopter with the pilots, he had difficulty persuading a flight surgeon to attend to the injured pilots. SSgt. Roland H. "Hap" Lutz, now a retired Chief Master Sergeant, recalled when he first contacted the Walker AFB hospital explaining that he had three persons injured in a "gondola accident," the flight surgeon told him to "Go home and sleep it off."[222] Fulgham, the injured pilot, recalled that when they got to the hospital, "there was this controversy going on in the hospital about who in the hell we were...we weren't supposed to be there and nobody knew anything about Air Force officers flying balloons...we could have been…[trying] to penetrate the security."[223] Walker AFB security officials were satisfied of the pilots' identities when they spoke to Colonel Stapp, commander of the Aero Medical Laboratory at Wright-Patterson AFB, Ohio.

Fig. 26. Capt. Joseph W. Kittinger, Jr. *(right)*, is shown here in 1962 with Dr. J. Allen Hynek while preparing for the project STARGAZER high altitude balloon flight. *(U.S. Air Force photo)*

The "Red-headed Captain" and Dr. J. Allen Hynek

Captain Kittinger, the STARGAZER high altitude balloon pilot and project engineer, had extensive professional contact with Dr. J. Allen Hynek, an astronomer and STARGAZER project scientist. Additionally, Hynek was also one of the scientific consultants in the Air Force study of UFOs, Project BLUEBOOK. Hynek is best known, however, for his apparent endorsement of extraterrestrial theories concerning UFOs after concluding his associations with the Air Force.

When asked about his recollections of Hynek, Kittinger stated that when they were associated, from 1958 to 1963, they discussed UFOs at length.[224]

At that time, Hynek was steadfast in his opinion that most, if not all, UFO sightings could be resolved by applying known scientific analysis.[225] Kittinger said he was "flabbergasted" when, years later, Hynek appeared to reverse his opinion and endorse extraterrestrial explanations.[226] Hynek's reversal in philosophies led to numerous commercial endeavors, most notably as a technical advisor for the science-fiction film *Close Encounters of the Third Kind.*

Also, based on his experience with project STARGAZER, Hynek was familiar with balloon operations at Holloman AFB, visiting the Holloman Balloon Branch several times.[227] Interestingly, there is no record that Hynek, who died in 1986, ever endorsed what is now presented as the "best evidence" of UFOs, the so-called Roswell Incident, which was actually a conglomeration of numerous events, some with origins in Holloman AFB launched balloons.

The Alien at the Hospital

In at least one account of the Roswell Incident, a witness claimed he observed a "creature" walk under its own power into the hospital.[228] While the specifics of this particular sighting cannot be verified, the injury that caused Fulgham's head to swell, resembling the classic science-fiction alien head, makes this account (and some others) that at first appeared to be the work of over-active imaginations, seem possible.

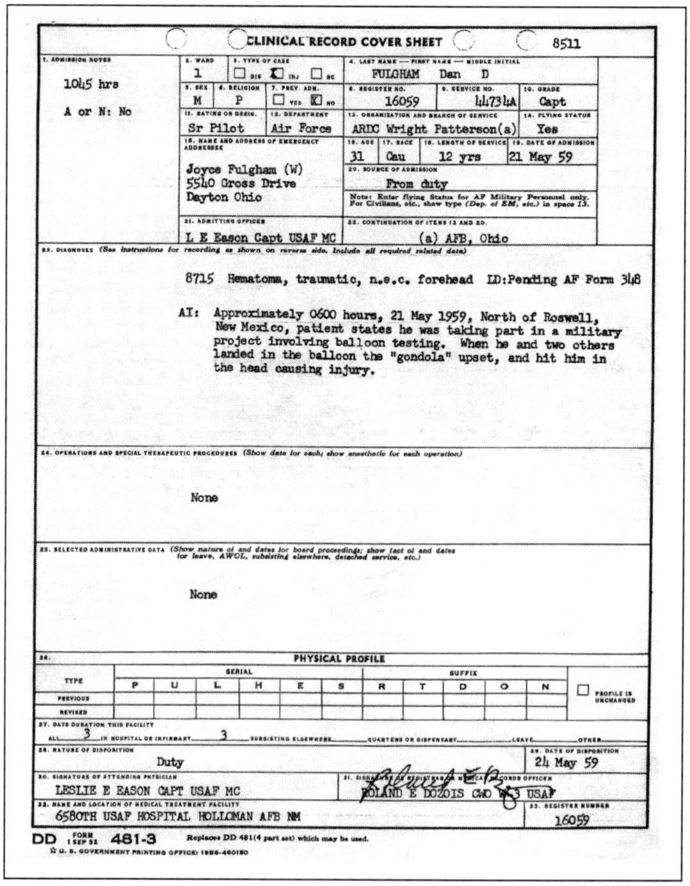

CLINICAL RECORD COVER SHEET 8511

1. ADMISSION NOTES: 1045 hrs
A or N: No

2. WARD: 1
3. TYPE OF CASE: ☐ DIS ☒ INJ ☐ SC
4. LAST NAME — FIRST NAME — MIDDLE INITIAL: FULGHAM Dan D
5. SEX: M
6. RELIGION: P
7. PREV. ADM.: ☐ YES ☒ NO
8. REGISTER NO.: 16059
9. SERVICE NO.: 44734A
10. GRADE: Capt
11. RATING OR DESIG.: Sr Pilot
12. DEPARTMENT: Air Force
13. ORGANIZATION AND BRANCH OF SERVICE: ARDC Wright Patterson(a)
14. FLYING STATUS: Yes
15. NAME AND ADDRESS OF EMERGENCY ADDRESSEE: Joyce Fulgham (W) 5540 Gross Drive Dayton Ohio
16. AGE: 31
17. RACE: Cau
18. LENGTH OF SERVICE: 12 yrs
19. DATE OF ADMISSION: 21 May 59
20. SOURCE OF ADMISSION: From duty
Note: Enter flying Status for AF Military Personnel only. For Civilians, etc., show type (Dep. of EM, etc.) in space 13.
21. ADMITTING OFFICER: L E Eason Capt USAF MC
22. CONTINUATION OF ITEMS 13 AND 20.: (a) AFB, Ohio

23. DIAGNOSES (See instructions for recording as shown on reverse side. Include all required related data)

8715 Hematoma, traumatic, n.e.c. forehead LD:Pending AF Form 348

AI: Approximately 0600 hours, 21 May 1959, North of Roswell, New Mexico, patient states he was taking part in a military project involving balloon testing. When he and two others landed in the balloon the "gondola" upset, and hit him in the head causing injury.

24. OPERATIONS AND SPECIAL THERAPEUTIC PROCEDURES (Show date for each; show anesthetic for each operation)

None

25. SELECTED ADMINISTRATIVE DATA (Show nature of and dates for board proceedings; show fact of and dates for leave, AWOL, subsisting elsewhere, detached service, etc.)

None

26. PHYSICAL PROFILE

TYPE	P	U	L	H	E	S	R	T	D	O	N	☐ PROFILE IS UNCHANGED
PREVIOUS												
REVISED												

27. DAYS DURATION THIS FACILITY: ALL 3 IN HOSPITAL OR INFIRMARY 3 SUBSISTING ELSEWHERE ___ QUARTERS OR DISPENSARY ___ LEAVE ___ OTHER ___
28. NATURE OF DISPOSITION: Duty
29. DATE OF DISPOSITION: 24 May 59
30. SIGNATURE OF ATTENDING PHYSICIAN: LESLIE E EASON CAPT USAF MC
31. SIGNATURE OF REGISTRAR OR MEDICAL RECORDS OFFICER: ROLAND E DOZOIS CWO W-3 USAF
32. NAME AND LOCATION OF MEDICAL TREATMENT FACILITY: 6580TH USAF HOSPITAL HOLLOMAN AFB NM
33. REGISTER NUMBER: 16059

DD FORM 1 SEP 52 481-3 Replaces DD 481(4 part set) which may be used.
U. S. GOVERNMENT PRINTING OFFICE: 1956-460150

Fig. 27. Clinical Record Cover Sheet from medical records of Capt. Dan D. Fulgham describing injuries he received in the balloon accident on May 21, 1959.

When the balloon gondola struck Fulgham's head, he received, according to his clinical record from May 21, 1959, an "Extensive hematoma forehead and ant [anterior] scalp."[229] A hematoma is a localized blood-filled swelling, that in this instance was on the forehead. The hematoma resulted in immediate facial swelling, two black eyes and later caused his skin to turn yellow.[230]

The rapid onset of the swelling caused both of Fulgham's eyes to close. As it progressed, according to Kittinger who accompanied Fulgham at the hospital, "His whole face had swollen up and his nose barely protruded."[231] This appearance lead Kittinger to characterize Fulgham's appearance at the time as "just a big blob" and "grotesque."[232]

When interviewed, Fulgham remembered that even though he didn't feel bad, "I didn't know how bad I looked." There was no attempt to hide or limit Fulgham's exposure to persons in the hospital that day. In fact, when he arrived at the hospital Fulgham recalled that he stopped outside the building to smoke a cigarette. Kaufman also recalled that the injured pilots, Fulgham and Kittinger, waited for treatment on a bench in the hallway of the hospital. Kaufman added that a number of military wives were present in the hospital that day for prenatal care, and there was no effort to keep Fulgham from their view.[233]

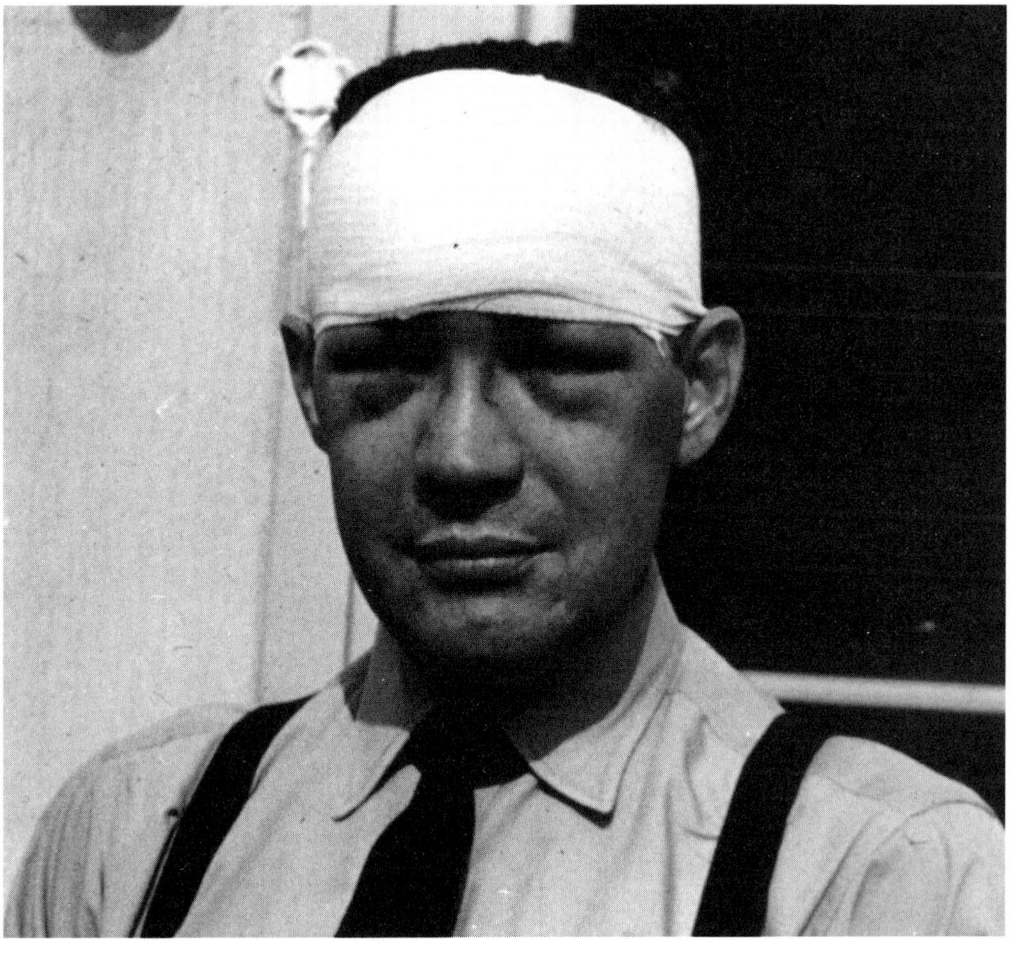

Fig 28. Capt. Dan D. Fulgham at Wright-Patterson AFB, Ohio several days after the balloon accident with a "traumatic hematoma" on his forehead. This photo shows Fulgham after blood had been aspirated from under his scalp and a substantial amount of swelling had dissipated. Concerns that Fulgham's odd appearance might startle uninformed persons was why he was returned to Wright-Patterson AFB aboard a specially arranged flight from Holloman AFB, N.M. *(photo collection of Dan D. Fulgham)*

"Bodies" with Large Heads and Wright-Patterson AFB, Ohio

UFO theorists contend that the U.S. Army Air Forces secretly shipped the alien bodies with large heads to Wright-Patterson AFB for further processing and deep-freeze storage. However, it is likely that, in this account, this is a reference to Fulgham's return to Wright-Patterson AFB following the balloon mishap.

Although Fulgham did not require hospitalization at Walker AFB, upon his return to Holloman AFB he was admitted to the base hospital for observation. Three days later on May 24, 1959, the balloon pilots were flown from Holloman to Wright-Patterson AFB on a specially arranged flight aboard a C-131 hospital aircraft.[234]

The return to Wright-Patterson AFB was directed by Stapp and coordinated by Kittinger.[235] The preliminary arrangements for this flight were made by Kittinger while at the Walker AFB hospital.[236] Kittinger recalled that conversations with Stapp regarding their return to Wright-Patterson AFB were made by phone in busy areas of the hospital and these conversations could have been overheard by nearly anyone present.[237]

Upon their arrival at Wright-Patterson, Fulgham, who Kittinger did not want to transport on a commercial flight due to his odd appearance, still could not open his eyes and had to be led down the steps of the aircraft. Kittinger recalled that Fulgham's wife was waiting at the bottom of the aircraft steps when they arrived.

"They dropped the ramp and I looked down at the bottom and there was Dan Fulgham's wife," Kittinger said. "Dan couldn't see...so I grabbed him by the arm...Dan's wife sees me leading this blob down the staircase... and she looks right at me and says, 'Where's my husband?' I said, 'Ma'am, this is your husband'. I presented her this blob that I was leading down the ramp. And she let out this scream you could hear a mile away. He was such a horrendous looking thing that she had no idea that the thing I was leading down that ramp was her husband."[238]

Fig. 29. As a physiologist for the space program, Fulgham *(third from left)* discusses Project GEMINI emergency escape systems at the U.S. Navy Aerospace Recovery facility at El Centro, Calif. on January 28, 1965. Shown with Fulgham *(from left)* are NASA astronaut Jim Lovell, NASA project engineer Hilary Ray, and NASA astronaut Alan Bean. *(U.S. Navy photo)*

Fig. 30. A veteran of 100 combat missions during the Korean conflict, Fulgham flew 133 combat missions in F-4 aircraft (shown here) in 1966-67 as a member of the 555th "Triple Nickel" Tactical Fighter Squadron at Ubon Air Base, Thailand. *(photo collection of Dan D. Fulgham)*

Fulgham recalled that upon his return to work at the Aero Medical Laboratory he received reactions of "immediate compassionate sympathy" from persons he encountered, including his secretary, who cried when she saw him.[239] Within several weeks, Fulgham returned to flying status with no permanent effects. Fulgham went on to complete a distinguished career in the Air Force and retired as a colonel in 1978. Fulgham's assignments included combat tours in fighter aircraft in both Korea and Vietnam, as well as an assignment as an experimental parachutist and physiologist for the space program.

Summary

In this section, documented research revealed that the reports of "bodies" at the Roswell AAF hospital were grossly inaccurate and most probably had origins in actual Air Force mishaps. Examinations of official records of the alleged primary witnesses revealed that the "missing nurse" was never missing, and the pediatrician did not arrive at the Walker AFB hospital until 1951—four years *after* the alleged incident. The many fundamental errors in the story, combined with the substantial similarities to the actual mishaps, show that the most credible account associated with the "Roswell Incident" is certainly not extraterrestrial and is unrelated to any events that occurred in July 1947.

Conclusion

When critically examined, the claims that the U.S. Army Air Forces recovered a flying saucer and alien crew in 1947, were found to be a compilation of many verifiable events. For the most part, the descriptions collected by UFO theorists were of actual operations and tests carried out by the U.S. Air Force in the 1950s. Despite the usual unsavory accusations by UFO proponents of cover-up, conspiracy, intimidation, etc., documented research revealed that many of the activities were actually historic scientific achievements of which the Air Force is very proud. However, other descriptions are believed to be distorted references to Air Force members who were killed or injured in the line of duty. The incomplete and inaccurate intermingling of these actual events were grounded in just enough fact to weave a sensational story, but cannot withstand close scrutiny when compared to official records.

To analyze reports of alien bodies that at first appeared to be so offbeat as to not be remotely based in fact, it was necessary to evaluate a wide range of books, interviews, videos, etc., that a less objective review might have rejected out of hand. Only through an inclusive evaluation of these sources were Air Force researchers able to understand the interconnectivity of the widely separated events believed responsible for this "incident." And, in opposition to critics who believe Air Force research involving this subject is anything but objective, this research relied almost exclusively on the descriptions ***provided by the UFO proponents themselves.*** When collected and examined, the actual statements of the witnesses—not the extraterrestrial interpretations of UFO proponents—indicated that something was very wrong. When these descriptions were compared to documented Air Force activities, they were much too similar to be a coincidence. Soon, it became apparent that the witnesses or the UFO proponents who liberally interpreted their statements were either 1) confused, or 2) attempting to perpetrate a hoax, believing that no serious efforts would ever be taken to verify their stories.

In preparing this report, attempts were made not to only explain *what* conclusions were reached, but *how* they were reached. This undertaking was to try to de-mystify the research process by outlining the simple and logical research techniques that identified the underlying actual events. In regard to statements of witnesses that were clearly descriptions of Air Force activities, such as those that described anthropomorphic dummies, these could be generously viewed as situational misunderstandings or even honest mistakes.

Fig. 31. Plaque placed at Holloman AFB honoring three Balloon Branch members killed during a high altitude balloon recovery when their L-20 balloon chase plane crashed in the rugged Gila Mountains near Stafford, Ariz. *(U.S. Air Force photo)*

Fig. 32. *(Left)* The balloon launch facility at Holloman AFB, N.M. was named in honor of Maj. Richard L. Nenninger who died of injuries received in an aircraft crash during a balloon recovery mission on April 7, 1970 in the Sacramento Mountains near Ruidoso, N.M. *(U.S. Air Force photo)*

Fig. 33. *(Right)* A semi-conscious Capt. Joseph W. Kittinger, Jr., following the EXCELSIOR I parachute jump from 76,000 feet. With his parachute wrapped around his neck and body and hopelessly out of control, his life was saved by an ingeniously designed reserve parachute system that opened just moments before contacting the desert floor; White Sands Proving Ground, November 16, 1959. *(U.S. Air Force photo)*

Other descriptions, particularly those believed to be thinly veiled references to deceased or injured Air Force members, are difficult to view as naive misunderstandings. Any attempt to misrepresent or capitalize on tragic incidents in which Air Force members died or were injured in service to their country significantly alters what would otherwise be viewed as simple misinterpretations or honest mistakes.

Finally, after reviewing this report, some persons may legitimately ask why the Air Force expended time and effort to respond to mythical, if not comedic, allegations of recoveries of "flying saucers" and "space aliens." The answer to those persons is:

- Initially the Air Force was required to respond to an official request from the General Accounting Office.
- High altitude balloon research, aircraft escape systems, and other technologies that were misrepresented as part of the Roswell Incident, accounted for significant contributions to the knowledge of the atmosphere, to the quest for space flight, and to the defense of this nation. The U.S. Air Force is exceedingly proud of these accomplishments. Distorted and incomplete descriptions of these activities do not pay tribute to these important exploits or to the individuals who, often at great personal risk, boldly carried them out.
- A sobering reality of the mission of the U.S. Air Force, as evidenced by the aircraft mishaps described in this report, is that defending this nation is a dangerous profession. On a daily basis, members of the U.S. Air Force perform hazardous missions in many locations throughout the world. Unfortunately, these missions sometimes result in injuries or deaths. It is the right—and indeed the duty—of the Air Force to challenge those who attempt to exploit these human tragedies wherever, and whenever, they are discovered.
- The misrepresentations of Air Force activities as an extraterrestrial "incident" is misleading to the public and is simply an affront to the truth.

This comprehensive further examination of the so-called "Roswell Incident" found no evidence whatsoever of flying saucers, space aliens, or sinister government cover-ups. But, even if unintentionally, it did serve to highlight a series of events that embody the proud history of the finest air force in the world—the U.S. Air Force. The actual events examined here, rich in human and scientific triumph, tempered by the stark realities of the dangers of the Air Force mission, are but one small portion of that history. The many Air Force activities cobbled together in the ever changing collage that has become the "Roswell Incident," when examined in the clear light of historical research, revealed a remarkable chapter of the Air Force story. In the final analysis, this examination simply illustrates once again, that fact is indeed stranger, and often much more fascinating, than fiction.

Notes - Section One

1. Headquarters United States Air Force, *The Roswell Report: Fact vs. Fiction in the New Mexico Desert* (Washington, D.C.: U.S. Government Printing Office, 1995), 20-22.
2. ibid.
3. Don Berliner and Stanton T. Friedman, *Crash at Corona* (New York: Paragon House, 1992), 14.
4. Headquarters United States Air Force, *The Roswell Report: Fact vs. Fiction in the New Mexico Desert* (Washington, D.C.: U.S. Government Printing Office, 1995), 20-22.
5. Ted Bloecher, *Report of the UFO Wave of 1947* (Washington D.C.: author, 1967), I-13-14.
6. Combined History, 509th Bomb Group and Roswell Army Airfield, 1 July-31 July 1947, 39, Air Force Historical Research Agency, Maxwell AFB, AL.
7. *Roswell Daily Record*, July 9, 1947, 1.
8. *Socorro* (N.M.) *Defensor Chieftan*, November 4, 1992.
9. Don Berliner, *A Rebuttal of the Air Force Project Mogul Explanation for the 1947 Roswell, New Mexico, UFO Crash* (Mount Ranier, Md.: The Fund for UFO Research, 1995), 2.
10. Headquarters United States Air Force, *The Roswell Report: Fact vs. Fiction in the New Mexico Desert* (Washington D.C.: U.S. Government Printing Office, 1995), Attachment 32, *Synopsis of Balloon Research Findings*, by 1st Lt. James McAndrew, 9.
11. Don Berliner and Stanton T. Friedman, *Crash at Corona* (New York: Paragon House, 1992), 14.
12. Video, *Recollections of Roswell, Part II,* Gerald Anderson interview (Washington, D.C.: Fund for UFO Research, 1993) (hereafter *Recollections of Roswell, Part II*).
13. James Ragsdale, transcript of interview with Donald R. Schmitt, January 26, 1994.
14. Frank J. Kaufman, interview with Kevin Randle and Donald Schmitt, January 27, 1990.

Notes - Section One

15. *Recollections of Roswell, Part II,* Maltais interview.

16. ibid., Anderson interview.

17. ibid.

18. ibid., Maltais interview.

19. *Recollections of Roswell, Part II,* Anderson interview.

20. Charles Berlitz and William L. Moore, *The Roswell Incident* (New York: Berkley, 1980), 61.

21. ibid.

22. *Recollections of Roswell, Part II,* Alice Knight interview.

23. Ragsdale and *Recollections of Roswell, Part II,* Anderson interview.

24. ibid.

25. *Recollections of Roswell, Part II*, Anderson interview.

26. Ragsdale.

27. James M. Grimwood, *Project Mercury: A Chronology,* Report No. SP4001 (Wash. D.C.: NASA, 1963) 2–3, and Lloyd Mallan, *Men, Rockets and Space Rats*, (New York: Julian Messier Inc., 1955) 84–98.

28. Research Division, College of Engineering, New York University, *Technical Report No. 93.02, Constant Level Balloons,* Section 3, *Summary of Flights,* July 15, 1949.

29. Capt. Vincent Mazza and Capt. Richard V. Wheeler, *High Altitude Bailouts*, MCREXD-695-66M (Wright-Patterson AFB, OH: USAF Air Materiel Command, September 18, 1950), 10-11.

30. A. M. Jacobs, "The Flier's SOS," *St. Nicholas Magazine*, Vol. LII, No. 10 (August 1925), 1034-1039.

31. ibid.

32. Memo, Major H.H. Arnold, Chief Field Service Section, to Commanding Officer, San Antonio Air Depot, subj: Drop Testing of Parachutes, November 2, 1929. National Air and Space Museum Archives, Paul E. Garber Facility, Silver Hill, Md., file no. 452.031, Parachutes- (Dummies) 1927-1929.

33. J. Allen Neal, *History: Development of Methods for Escape from High Speed Aircraft, Vol. 1,* (Wright-Patterson AFB, OH: Air Research and Development Command, 1958), U.S. Air Force Museum Archives, Wright-Patterson AFB, OH.

Notes - Section One

34. Memo, Ted Smith, to W.A. Daler, subj: Bid for Purchase Request No. 301200, September 17, 1954, National Archives and Records Administration, Accession No. 342-67E-2954, box 5/15, file 28.

35. H.T. E. Hertzberg, *Anthropology of Anthropomorphic Dummies*, Air Force Medical Research Laboratory, AMRL-TR-69-61, February 1970, 3.

36. Maj. John P. Stapp, *Human Tolerance to Linear Deceleration, Part I. Preliminary Survey of the Aft Facing Seated Position,* Air Force Technical Report 5915, (Wright Patterson AFB, OH: Wright Air Development Center, 1949) and Maj. John P. Stapp, *Part II. The Aft Facing Position and the Development of a Crash Harness*, Air Force Technical Report 5915 (Wright Patterson AFB, OH: Wright Air Development Center, 1951).

37. H.T. E. Hertzberg, *Anthropology of Anthropomorphic Dummies*, Air Force Medical Research Laboratory, AMRL-TR-69-61, February 1970, 3.

38. ibid.

39. ltr., H.L. Daulton, Vice President and Secretary-Treasurer, Sierra Engineering Company, to W.A. Daler, Headquarters Air Materiel Command, subject: Proposal, Purchase Request No. 301200, September 16, 1954, National Archives and Records Administration, Accession No. 342-67E-2954, box 5/15, file 28.

40. Joseph Smrcka, Senior Design Engineer, First Technology Safety Systems, "Dummies - Past and Present," 2 (unpublished manuscript).

41. Sierra Engineering Co., "Sierra Sam," 1955, National Archives and Records Administration, Accession No. 342-67E-2954, box 5/15, file 28.

42. 1st Lt. Raymond A. Madson, *High Altitude Balloon Dummy Drops, Part I. The Unstabilized Dummy Drops*, WADC Technical Report 57-477, (Wright Patterson AFB, OH: Wright Air Development Center, Oct 1957) (hereafter *High Altitude Balloon Dummy Drops Part I*), 27, and 1st Lt. Raymond A. Madson, *High Altitude Balloon Dummy Drops, II. The Stabilized Dummy Drops*, WADC Technical Report 57-477 (II) (Wright Patterson AFB, OH: Aeronautical Systems Division, Air Force Systems Command, August 1961) (hereafter *High Altitude Balloon Dummy Drops Part II*), 18.

43. *High Altitude Balloon Dummy Drops Part I*, 1.

44. *High Altitude Balloon Dummy Drops Part I,* and *High Altitude Balloon Dummy Drops Part II,* and Holloman Air Development Center, Weekly Test Status Reports, Project MX-1450B (Manned Balloon), National Archives and Records Administration, National Personnel Records Center, St. Louis, MO, Accession No. 342-62A-A-641, box 115/248, folder; R-695-61D, "High Altitude Escape Studies, Gen B-1, Manned Balloon Flights."

Notes - Section One

45. ibid.

46. *High Altitude Balloon Dummy Drops Part I,* 1, and *High Altitude Balloon Dummy Drops Part II,* 18.

47. Capt. Joseph W. Kittinger, Jr., *The Long, Lonely Leap*, (New York: E.P. Dutton & Co., Inc., 1961), and Lt. Col. David G. Simons, *Man High,* (New York: Doubleday & Company, Inc., 1960), and Capt. Joseph W. Kittinger, Jr., "The Long, Lonely Leap," *National Geographic* 118, no. 6 (December 1960): 854-873, "Fantastic Catch in the Sky, Record Leap towards Earth," *Life* 49, no. 9 (August 29,1960): 20-25, *Popular Mechanics Magazine*, January 1951: 118, *Collier's,* June 25, 1954, *Time*, September 12, 1955, "The Fastest Man on Earth".

48. Don Reilly, "MAD Salutes an Unsung Hero," *MAD,* no. 61, (March 1961), 46.

49. *High Altitude Balloon Dummy Drops Part I,* and *High Altitude Balloon Dummy Drops Part II.*

50. *High Altitude Balloon Dummy Drops Part II,* 11-12.

51. Signed, sworn statement of Raymond A. Madson, Lt. Col., USAF (Ret) and *High Altitude Balloon Dummy Drops, Part I*, 16.

52. *High Altitude Balloon Dummy Drops, Part I*, 5.

53. *High Altitude Balloon Dummy Drops, Part I,* 17.

54. ibid., and Memorandum, subj: Balloon Tracking and Recovery Equipment, n.d., National Archives and Records Administration, Accession No. 342-67B-2133, box 65/249, file 2, "Biophysics Branch-Escape Section, High Altitude Escape Studies, 7218-71719," and Robert Blankenship, retired Balloon Branch Recovery Supervisor, telephone interview with 1st Lt. James McAndrew, July 14, 1995.

55. Signed, sworn statement of Raymond A. Madson, Lt. Col., USAF (Ret).

56. Blankenship, and Balloon Tracking and Recovery Equipment, n.d., and Bernard D. Gildenberg, *Meteorological Aspects of Constant-Level Balloon Operations in the Southwestern United States* (hereafter *Meteorological Aspects of Constant-Level Balloon Operations in the Southwestern United States)*, AFCRL-66-706 (L.G. Hanscom Field, Bedford, MA: Air Force Cambridge Research Laboratories, October 1966), 27.

57. Historical Branch, Office of Information Services, Air Force Missile Development Center, *Contributions of Balloon Operations to Research and Development at the Air Force Missile Development Center Holloman AFB, N. Mex. 1947-1958* (Holloman AFB, NM: Air Research and Development Command, 1958) (hereafter *Contributions of Balloon Operations to Research and Development at the Air Force Missile Development Center, 1947-1958*), 90.

Notes - Section One

58. *High Altitude Balloon Dummy Drops, Part I,* 16.

59. ibid., 17.

60. *High Altitude Balloon Dummy Drops, Part I,* 17.

61. Maj. John P. Stapp, *Human Tolerance to Linear Deceleration, Part I. Preliminary Survey of the Aft Facing Seated Position,* Air Force Technical Report 5915, (Wright Patterson AFB, OH: Wright Air Development Center, 1949) and Maj. John P. Stapp, *Part II. The Aft Facing Position and the Development of a Crash Harness*, Air Force Technical Report 5915 (Wright Patterson AFB, OH: Wright Air Development Center, 1951).

62. *High Altitude Balloon Dummy Drops, Part II*, 6.

63. Signed, sworn statement of Joseph W. Kittinger, Jr., Col., USAF (Ret).

64. ibid.

65. Alderson Research Laboratories, Inc., "Instructions for Operation and Maintenance, Model F-95 Anthropomorphic Test Dummies," May 3, 1956, 1, and Glenn Richards, retired Balloon Branch Instrumentation Specialist, telephone interview with Capt. James McAndrew, September 5, 1995.

66. Alderson Research Laboratories, Inc., "Instructions for Operation and Maintenance, Model F-95 Anthropomorphic Test Dummies," May 3, 1956, 1, and Ronald G. Hansen, Lt. Col. USAR, (Ret), Balloon Recovery Helicopter Pilot, telephone interview with 1st Lt. James McAndrew, May 1, 1995.

67. *High Altitude Balloon Dummy Drops, Part I*, 7-8.

68. Blankenship.

69. ibid.

70. *The Beverly Hills Citizen,* March 12, 1956,7.

71. Research Division, College of Engineering, New York University, *Special Report No. 1, Constant Level Balloon*, May 1947, 20-22.

72. Research Division, College of Engineering, New York University, Technical Report No. 93.03, *Constant Level Balloons, Operations*, March 1, 1951, 105.

73. U.S. Air Force Phillips Laboratory, "Phillips Laboratory Space Experiments Directorate, Balloon, Rocket, and Satellite Capabilities," n.d., 33.

74. Bernard D. Gildenberg, Balloon Branch Meteorologist and Engineer, interviewed by 1st Lt. James McAndrew, May 28, 1995, and *Contributions of Balloon Operations 1947-1958,* 73.

75. ibid.

Notes - Section One

76. ibid.

77. *Contributions of Balloon Operations 1947-1958,* 73.

78. "Flight Summary, Non-Extensible Balloon Operations, 6580th Test Squadron (Special), June 1950 to October 1954," 22-24.

79. *Contributions of Balloon Operations 1947-1958,* 73-74.

80. Lt. Col. David G. Simons (MC), *Stratosphere Balloon Techniques for Exposing Living Specimens to Primary Cosmic Ray Particles*, Holloman Air Development Center TR 54-16, November 1954, 10-11.

81. "Flight Summary Non-Extensible Balloon Operations 6580th Test Squadron (Special), June 1950 to October 1954," 1-31, and *Contributions of Balloon Operations 1947-1958,* 24.

82. "Flight Summary Non-Extensible Balloon Operations 6580th Test Squadron (Special), June 1950 to October 1954," 4.

83. Research Division, College of Engineering, New York University, *Technical Report No. 93.02, Constant Level Balloons,* Section 3, *Summary of Flights,* July 15, 1949, 32, in Headquarters United States Air Force, *The Roswell Report: Fact vs. Fiction in the New Mexico Desert* (Washington, D.C.: U.S. Government Printing Office, 1995), Appendix 12.

84. Holloman Air Development Center, "Test Report on Radar Target Balloons", October 31, 1955, Air Force Historical Research Agency, Maxwell, AFB, AL, Reel # 31811, Frame 1139, and *Contributions of Balloon Operations 1947-1958,* 40-45.

85. Kevin C. Ruffner, ed., *Corona: America's First Satellite Program* (Washington, D.C.: Center for the Study of Intelligence, Central Intelligence Agency, 1995), 22.

86. ibid., 21-22.

87. Air Force Missile Development Center, "Chronology of Events," Sept. 1, 1957- Aug 10, 1962, Air Force Historical Research Agency, Maxwell, AFB, AL, Reel # 31731, Frame 561, and Flight Records of Bernard D. Gildenberg, Meteorologist, Holloman AFB Balloon Branch, October 12, 1956 - March 14, 1961.

88. Flight Summary, DISCOVERER Balloon Flights, March 31, 1960-April 22, 1960, Air Force Historical Research Agency, Maxwell, AFB, AL, Reel# 31811, frame 569.

89. ibid.

90. ibid.

Notes - Section One

91. Kevin C. Ruffner, ed., *Corona: America's First Satellite Program* (Washington, D.C.: Center for the Study of Intelligence, Central Intelligence Agency, 1995), 21-22.

92. ibid.

93. ibid.

94. Martin Marietta Corporation, "Viking '75, Balloon Launched Decelerator Test Program Post Flight Report, BLDT Vehicle AV-3," TR 3720293, 1972, IV-I and Edward J. Kirschner, *Aerospace Balloons; From Montgolfiere to Space* (Blue Ridge Summit, Pa.: Aero Publishers, 1985), 64-66.

95. Martin Marietta Corporation, "Viking '75, Balloon Launched Decelerator Test Program Post Flight Report, BLDT Vehicle AV-3," TR 3720293, 1972, IV-I.

96. Kevin D. Randle and Donald R. Schmitt, *The Truth About the UFO Crash at Roswell* (New York: Avon Books, 1994), photograph section.

97. Air Force Cambridge Research Laboratories, "Report on Research, for the Period July 1965 - June 1967", AFCRL TR-68-0039, November 1967, 150-151.

98. Gildenberg.

99. Database of high altitude balloon operations on file at SAF/AAZD compiled from the following sources: Research Division, College of Engineering, New York University, *Technical Report No. 93.02, Constant Level Balloons,* Section 3, *Summary of Flights,* July 15, 1949; "Flight Summary Non-Extensible Balloon Operations 6580th Test Squadron (Special), June 1950 to October 1954," National Archives and Records Administration, National Personnel Records Center, St. Louis, Mo., Accession No. 342-62A-181, box 14/18; Flight Records of Bernard D. Gildenberg, Meteorologist, Holloman AFB Balloon Branch., October 12, 1956 - March 14, 1961; "Summary of Balloon Flights Launched from Holloman AFB, N.M., 1962 thru 1987", Space and Missile Command, Test and Evaluation Unit (SMC/TE, OL-AC) files, Holloman AFB, N.M. Additional flight data on file (microfilm), U.S. Air Force Phillips Laboratory, Geophysics Directorate, Hanscom AFB, Mass.

100. Bernard D. Gildenberg, *Meteorological Aspects of Constant-Level Balloon Operations in the Southwestern United States*, AFCRL-66-706 (L.G. Hanscom Field, Bedford, MA: Air Force Cambridge Research Laboratories, October 1966), and Bernard D. Gildenberg, *General Philosophy and Techniques of Balloon Control,* in Lewis A. Grass, ed., *Proceedings, Sixth AFCRL Scientific Balloon Symposium*, AFCRL-70-0543, (L.G. Hanscom Field, Bedford, Mass.: Air Force Cambridge Research Laboratories, October 1970).

Notes - Section One

101. Blankenship.
102. ibid.
103. ibid.
104. ibid.
105. ibid.
106. Joseph Longshore, Balloon Branch Supervisor, telephone interview with Capt. James McAndrew, August 16, 1995.
107. Signed sworn statement of James Ragsdale in Ragsdale Productions Inc., *The Jim Ragsdale Story: A Closer Look at the Roswell Incident* (Hall Poorbough Press, Inc., 1996), 10-11, and signed sworn statement of James Ragsdale in Karl T. Pflock, *Roswell in Perspective* (Washington, D.C.: Fund for UFO Research, 1994), 167.
108. James Ragsdale, interview with Donald R. Schmitt, January 26, 1993.
109. *High Altitude Balloon Dummy Drops, Part II*, 17.
110. *High Altitude Balloon Dummy Drops Part I,* 27-30 and *High Altitude Balloon Dummy Drops, Part II,* 6, 10-12, 17.
111. Joseph W. Kittinger, Jr., Col., USAF (Ret), interview with 1st Lt. James McAndrew, June 23, 1995.
112. *Contributions of Balloon Operations to Research and Development at the Air Force Missile Development Center,1947-1958*, 90, and *Meteorological Aspects of Constant-Level Balloon Operations in the Southwestern United States*, 1.
113. *High Altitude Balloon Dummy Drops Part I,* 24.
114. Blankenship and Kittinger.
115. ibid.
116. Memorandum, subj: Balloon Tracking and Recovery Equipment, n.d., National Archives and Records Administration, National Personnel Records Center, St. Louis, Mo., Accession No. 342-67B-2133, box 65/249, file 2, "Biophysics Branch-Escape Section, High Altitude Escape Studies, 7218-71719."
117. ibid., and Blankenship.
118. Charles Berlitz and William L. Moore, *The Roswell Incident* (New York: Berkley, 1980), 64, and Don Berliner and Stanton Friedman, *Crash at Corona* (New York: Paragon House, 1992), 88.
119. *Recollections of Roswell, Part II,* Knight interview.
120. *Recollections of Roswell, Part II,* Maltais interview.

Notes - Section One

121. Charles Berlitz and William L. Moore, *The Roswell Incident* (New York: Berkley, 1980), 64, and Don Berliner and Stanton Friedman, *Crash at Corona* (New York: Paragon House, 1992), 88.

122. Berliner and Friedman, 89.

123. Mark Rodeghier and Fred Whiting, *The Plains of San Agustin Controversy, July, 1947: Gerald Anderson, Barney Barnett, and the Archaeologists,* Introduction (Chicago, IL, Washington, D.C.: J. Allen Hynek Center for UFO Studies and The Fund for UFO Research, June 1992), 2.

124. ibid.

125. Kevin D. Randle, Donald R. Schmitt, and Thomas J. Carey, *Gerald Anderson and the Plains of San Agustin,* in *The Plains of San Agustin Controversy, July, 1947: Gerald Anderson, Barney Barnett, and the Archaeologists* (Chicago, IL, Washington, D.C.: J. Allen Hynek Center for UFO Studies, and The Fund for UFO Research, June 1992), 19.

126. *Recollections of Roswell, Part II,* Anderson interview.

127. Berliner and Friedman, 90.

128. ibid., 91.

129. Gerald F. Anderson, interview with Kevin D. Randle, February 4, 1990, in *The Plains of San Agustin Controversy, July, 1947: Gerald Anderson, Barney Barnett, and the Archaeologists* (Chicago, IL, Washington, D.C.: J. Allen Hynek Center for UFO Studies and The Fund for UFO Research, June 1992), 59.

130. *Recollections of Roswell, Part II,* Anderson interview.

131. ibid.

132. ibid.

133. ibid.

134. ibid.

135. Blankenship and Kittinger.

136. *Recollections of Roswell, Part II,* Anderson interview.

137. "Sierra Sam: Scientific Whipping Boy," *Machine Design,* December 22, 1960 and "Dummy Takes a Beating for Science's Sake," *Aviation Week*, January 12, 1953.

138. Ragsdale.

139. *Recollections of Roswell, Part II,* Anderson interview.

140. Alderson Research Laboratories Inc., "Modular Series Anthropomorphic Test Dummies," Alderson Research Laboratories Inc., June 1955), 5.

Notes - Section One

141. *Recollections of Roswell, Part II,* Anderson interview.

142. ibid.

143. Signed, sworn statement of Raymond A. Madson, Lt. Col., USAF (Ret).

144. *Recollections of Roswell, Part II,* Anderson interview.

145. *High Altitude Balloon Dummy Drops, Part I,* 22.

146. *Recollections of Roswell, Part II,* Anderson interview.

147. *High Altitude Balloon Dummy Drops, Part I,* 9, and *High Altitude Balloon Dummy Drops, Part II,* 8.

148. Berliner and Friedman, 91.

149. ibid., 92-94.

150. *Recollections of Roswell, Part II,* Anderson interview.

151. ibid.

152. Memorandum, subject: Balloon Tracking and Recovery Equipment, n.d., National Archives and Records Administration, National Personnel Records Center, St. Louis, Mo., Accession No. 342-67B-2133, box 65/249, file 2, "Biophysics Branch-Escape Section, High Altitude Escape Studies, 7218-71719," and *High Altitude Balloon Dummy Drops, Part I,* 17, and "Weekly Test Status Report on Project 7218, Manned Balloon Flights, (MX-1450B)", for Week Ending 28 February 1955, National Archives and Records Administration, National Personnel Records Center, St. Louis, Mo., Accession No. 342-66A-181, Box 14/18.

153. Kittinger and Historical Branch, Office of Information Services, Air Research and Development Command, *History of Flight Support Holloman Air Development Center 1946-1957* (Holloman AFB, N.M.: Holloman Air Development Center, 1957), 101.

154. Blankenship.

155. Berliner and Friedman, 106.

156. Bernard D. Gildenberg, *Techniques Developed for Heavy Load Non-Extensible Balloon Flights*, Report No. HADC-TN-54-3 (Holloman AFB, NM: Holloman Air Development Center, March 1954), 7.

157. *Recollections of Roswell, Part II,* Anderson interview.

158. Blankenship and Ole Jorgeson, MSgt., USAF, (Ret), Balloon Branch Communications Supervisor, interview with 1st Lt. James McAndrew, May 28, 1995.

159. ibid.

160. Berliner and Friedman, 107.

161. ibid.

Notes - Section One

162. Blankenship.

163. Berliner and Friedman, 106.

164. Blankenship.

165. Signed sworn statement of James Ragsdale in, Ragsdale Productions Inc., *The Jim Ragsdale Story: A Closer Look at the Roswell Incident* (Hall Poorbough Press, Inc., 1996), 10-11, and signed sworn statement of James Ragsdale in Karl T. Pflock, *Roswell in Perspective* (Washington, D.C.: Fund for UFO Research, 1994), 167.

166. Ragsdale.

167. Frank J. Kaufman, interview with Kevin Randle and Donald Schmitt, January 27, 1990.

168. *Recollections of Roswell, Part II,* Anderson interview.

169. Ragsdale.

170. ibid.

171. Berliner and Friedman, 92.

172. *Recollections of Roswell, Part II,* Maltais interview.

173. ibid., Knight interview.

174. ibid., Anderson interview.

175. ibid., Maltais interview.

176. ibid.

177. ibid., Anderson interview.

178. Ragsdale.

179. *Recollections of Roswell, Part II,* Anderson interview.

180. ibid., Maltais interview.

181. ibid., Anderson interview.

182. ibid.

183. ibid., Maltais interview.

184. ibid., Anderson interview.

185. Charles Berlitz and William L. Moore, *The Roswell Incident* (New York: Berkley, 1980), 61.

186. Berliner and Friedman, 92.

187. *Recollections of Roswell, Part II,* Anderson interview.

188. Berliner and Friedman, 91.

189. ibid.

Notes - Section One

190. ibid., 92.
191. ibid., 91.
192. *Recollections of Roswell, Part II,* Maltais interview.
193. Berliner and Friedman, 93.
194. ibid., 93-94.
195. ibid., 92.
196. *Recollections of Roswell, Part II*, Anderson interview.
197. Berliner and Friedman, 106.
198. Ragsdale.
199. ibid.
200. *Recollections of Roswell, Part II*, Anderson interview.
201. ibid.
202. Ragsdale.
203. *Recollections of Roswell, Part II*, Anderson interview.
204. ibid.
205. ibid.
206. Berliner and Friedman, 106.
207. Ragsdale.
208. Berliner and Friedman, 107.
209. *Recollections of Roswell, Part II*, Anderson interview.
210. ibid.
211. Ragsdale.
212. *Recollections of Roswell, Part II*, Anderson interview.
213. Ragsdale.
214. *Recollections of Roswell, Part II*, Anderson interview.
215. Ragsdale.
216. *Recollections of Roswell, Part II*, Anderson interview.
217. ibid.
218. Berliner and Friedman, 107.

Notes - Section Two

1. Karl T. Pflock, "Star Witness: The Mortician of Roswell Breaks His Code of Silence," *Omni*, Fall 1995, 103.
2. Don Berliner and Stanton T. Friedman, *Crash at Corona* (New York: Paragon House, 1992), 117, 120, and W. Glenn Dennis, interview with Karl T. Pflock, November 2, 1992, 18-19.
3. Video, *Recollections of Roswell, Part II,* W. Glenn Dennis interview (Washington, D.C.: Fund for UFO Research, 1993) (hereafter *Recollections of Roswell, Part II*).
4. *Recollections of Roswell, Part II,* W. Glenn Dennis interview.
5. ibid.
6. ibid.
7. ibid.
8. ibid., and W. Glenn Dennis, interview with Karl T. Pflock, November 2, 1992, and Karl T. Pflock, "Star Witness: The Mortician of Roswell Breaks His Code of Silence," *Omni*, Fall 1995, 103.
9. Karl T. Pflock, "Star Witness: The Mortician of Roswell Breaks His Code of Silence," *Omni*, Fall 1995, 103.
10. *Recollections of Roswell, Part II,* W. Glenn Dennis interview.
11. ibid.
12. ibid.
13. Don Berliner and Stanton T. Friedman, *Crash at Corona* (New York: Paragon House, 1992), 120, and W. Glenn Dennis, interview with Karl T. Pflock, November 2, 1992.
14. Karl T. Pflock, "Star Witness: The Mortician of Roswell Breaks His Code of Silence," *Omni*, Fall 1995, 103.
15. *Recollections of Roswell, Part II,* W. Glenn Dennis interview.
16. Don Berliner and Stanton T. Friedman, *Crash at Corona* (New York: Paragon House, 1992), 117.
17. *Recollections of Roswell, Part II,* W. Glenn Dennis interview.
18. ibid.
19. ibid.
20. ibid.

Notes - Section Two

21. W. Glenn Dennis, interview with Stanton T. Friedman, August 5, 1989.

22. *Recollections of Roswell, Part II,* W. Glenn Dennis interview.

23. W. Glenn Dennis, interview with Karl T. Pflock, November 2, 1992.

24. *Recollections of Roswell, Part II,* W. Glenn Dennis interview.

25. W. Glenn Dennis, interview with Karl T. Pflock, November 2, 1992.

26. *Recollections of Roswell, Part II,* W. Glenn Dennis interview.

27. ibid.

28. ibid.

29. Don Berliner and Stanton T. Friedman, *Crash at Corona* (New York: Paragon House, 1992), 119, and Karl T. Pflock, "Star Witness: The Mortician of Roswell Breaks His Code of Silence," *Omni*, Fall 1995, 105.

30. *Recollections of Roswell, Part II,* W. Glenn Dennis interview.

31. ibid.

32. W. Glenn Dennis, interview with Karl T. Pflock, November 2, 1992.

33. ibid.

34. Karl T. Pflock, "Star Witness: The Mortician of Roswell Breaks His Code of Silence," *Omni*, Fall 1995, 105, and W. Glenn Dennis, interview with Karl T. Pflock, November 2, 1992.

35. Karl T. Pflock, "Star Witness: The Mortician of Roswell Breaks His Code of Silence," *Omni*, Fall 1995, 105.

36 W. Glenn Dennis, interview with Stanton T. Friedman, August 5, 1989.

37. ibid.

38. Don Berliner and Stanton T. Friedman, *Crash at Corona* (New York: Paragon House, 1992), 119.

39. Headquarters United States Air Force, *The Roswell Report: Fact vs. Fiction in the New Mexico Desert* (Washington, D.C.: U.S. Government Printing Office, 1995), Attachment 32, "Synopsis of Balloon Research Findings by 1st Lt. James McAndrew".

40. 427th AAFBU Sq "M" Morning Reports, July 8-9 1947, National Archives and Records Administration, National Personnel Records Center, St. Louis, Mo.

41. Personnel record of 1st Lt. Angele A. (LaRue) Thèssing, National Archives and Records Administration, National Personnel Records Center, St. Louis, Mo.

Notes - Section Two

42. ibid.

43. Personnel records of Capt. Joyce Goddard, 1st Lt. Rosemary J. Brown, 1st Lt. Eileen M. Fanton, 1st Lt. Angele A. LaRue, 1st Lt. Claudia Uebele, National Archives and Records Administration, National Personnel Records Center, St. Louis, Mo.

44. Karl T. Pflock, "Star Witness: The Mortician of Roswell Breaks His Code of Silence," *Omni*, Fall 1995, 132, and W. Glenn Dennis, interview with Stanton T. Friedman, August 5, 1989.

45. Paul McCarthy, "The Case of the Vanishing Nurses," *Omni*, Fall 1995, 107-114.

46. WD AGO FORM 66, "Officer's Qualification Record," Personnel Record of Capt. Eileen M. Fanton, National Archives and Records Administration, National Personnel Records Center, St. Louis, Mo.

47. DD Form 214, "Armed Forces of the United States Report of Transfer or Discharge", April 30, 1958, Personnel file of Capt. Eileen M. Fanton, National Archives and Records Administration, National Personnel Records Center, St. Louis, Mo.

48. Karl T. Pflock, "Star Witness: The Mortician of Roswell Breaks His Code of Silence," *Omni,* Fall 1995, 132.

49. WD AGO FORM 66, "Officer's Qualification Record," and WD AGO FORM 66-3, "AAF Medical Dep't Officer's Qualification Record," Personnel Record of Capt. Eileen M. Fanton, National Archives and Records Administration, National Personnel Records Center, St. Louis, Mo.

50. W. Glenn Dennis, interview with Karl T. Pflock, November 2, 1992.

51. WD AGO FORM 66-3, "AAF Medical Dep't Officer's Qualification Record," Personnel Record of Capt. Eileen M. Fanton, National Archives and Records Administration, National Personnel Records Center, St. Louis, Mo.

52. Karl T. Pflock, "Star Witness: The Mortician of Roswell Breaks His Code of Silence," *Omni*, Fall 1995, 104 and W. Glenn Dennis, interview with Karl T. Pflock, November 2, 1992, 11, 15.

53. WD AGO FORM 66, "Officer's Qualification Record," Personnel Record of Capt. Eileen M. Fanton, National Archives and Records Administration, National Personnel Records Center, St. Louis, Mo.

54. ibid.

Notes - Section Two

55. WD MD FORM 55A, "Clinical Record Brief," September 5, 1947, and WD AGO FORM 8-38, " Special Examination or Additional Data," September 11, 1947, Personnel Record of Capt. Eileen M. Fanton, National Archives and Records Administration, National Personnel Records Center, St. Louis, Mo.

56. ibid, and Physical Examination Board Proceedings, Capt. Eileen M. Fanton, August 24, 1955, Personnel Record of Capt. Eileen M. Fanton, National Archives and Records Administration, National Personnel Records Center, St. Louis, Mo.

57. W. Glenn Dennis, interview with Stanton T. Friedman, August 5, 1989, and W. Glenn Dennis, interview with Karl T. Pflock, November 2, 1992.

58. W. Glenn Dennis, interview with Stanton T. Friedman, August 5, 1989.

59. ibid.

60. Roster of Officers, 6th Bomb Wing, Walker AFB, N.M., December 30, 1952, "History of the 6th Bomb Wing, December 1952," Air Force Historical Research Center, Maxwell AFB, AL.

61. ibid.

62. Dr. Frank B. Nordstrom, interview with Capt. James McAndrew, April 25, 1996, and Dr. Frank B. Nordstrom, Signed Sworn Statement, April 25, 1996.

63. Charles E. Clouthier, Signed Sworn Statement, April 26, 1996.

64. ibid.

65. J.P. Cahn, "Flying Saucers and the Mysterious Little Green Men," *True* 31, No. 184, (September 1952), 19.

66. ibid., 103.

67. ibid., 19.

68. J.P. Cahn, "Flying Saucer Swindlers," *True* 36, No. 231, (August 1956), 36.

69. ibid., 36.

70. J.P. Cahn, " Flying Saucers and the Mysterious Little Green Men," *True* 31, No. 184, (September 1952), 110.

71. ibid.

72. "4 Rank Titles Change," *Air Force Times,* March 29, 1952, 1, 22.

73. Alan L. Gropman, *The Air Force Integrates, 1945-1964* (Washington, D.C.: Office of Air Force History, 1985), 243.

Notes - Section Two

74. Don Berliner and Stanton T. Friedman, *Crash at Corona* (New York: Paragon House, 1992), 117.

75. WD AGO FORM 66, "Officer's Qualification Record," and AF FORM 11, "Officer Military Record," Personnel Record of Col. Lee F. Ferrell, National Archives and Records Administration, National Personnel Records Center, St. Louis, Mo.

76. ibid.

77. Karl T. Pflock, "Star Witness: The Mortician of Roswell Breaks His Code of Silence," *Omni*, Fall 1995, 105, and W. Glenn Dennis, interview with Karl T. Pflock, November 2, 1992.

78. Karl T. Pflock, "Star Witness: The Mortician of Roswell Breaks His Code of Silence," *Omni*, Fall 1995, 105.

79. Karl T. Pflock, "Star Witness: The Mortician of Roswell Breaks His Code of Silence," *Omni*, Fall 1995, 105, and W. Glenn Dennis, interview with Karl T. Pflock, November 2, 1992.

80. W. Glenn Dennis, interview with Karl T. Pflock, November 2, 1992.

81. ibid.

82. ibid.

83. 427th AAFBU Sq. "M" Morning Reports, July 1-31,1947, National Archives and Records Administration, National Personnel Records Center, St. Louis, Mo.

84. WD AGO FORM 1, "Morning Report," 427th AAFBU Sq. "M," April 1, 1947 through October 1, 1947, and WD AGO FORM 66, "Officer's Qualification Record," Personnel Record of Capt. Joyce Goddard, National Archives and Records Administration, National Personnel Records Center, St. Louis, Mo.

85. WD AGO FORM 66, "Officer's Qualification Record," Personnel Record of Capt. Joyce Goddard, National Archives and Records Administration, National Personnel Records Center, St. Louis, Mo.

86. WD AGO FORM 1, "Morning Report," 427th AAFBU, Sq. "M," August 7, 1947, National Archives and Records Administration, National Personnel Records Center, St. Louis, Mo.

87. ibid., and WD AGO FORM 66, "Officer's Qualification Record," Personnel Record of Capt. Lucille C. Slattery, National Archives and Records Administration, National Personnel Records Center, St. Louis, Mo.

Notes - Section Two

88. Ethel Kovatch-Scott, Col., USAF (Ret), telephone interview with Capt. James McAndrew, May 5, 1995 and July 3, 1996, and Mary Hoadley, Lt. Col., USAF (Ret), telephone interview with 1st Lt. James McAndrew, May 5, 1995, and Mary L. Wiggins, Maj., USAF (Ret), telephone interview with 1st Lt. James McAndrew, May 5, 1995.
89. ibid.
90. WD AGO FORM 66, "Officer's Qualification Record," Personnel Record of Capt. Lucille C. Slattery, National Archives and Records Administration, National Personnel Records Center, St. Louis, Mo.
91. WD AGO FORM 1, "Morning Report," 427th AAFBU, Sq. "M," 509th Station Medical Group, 509th Medical Group, 509th Medical Squadron, January 1947 through February 1952, National Archives and Records Administration, National Personnel Records Center, St. Louis, Mo. and Rosters of Officers, 509th Bomb Wing- February 1952 through July 1958, 6th Bomb Wing- February 1952 through March 1967, and AF FORM 11, "Officer Military Record," Personnel Record of Maj. Idabelle M. Wilson, National Archives and Records Administration, National Personnel Records Center, St. Louis, Mo.
92. AF FORM 11, "Officer Military Record," Personnel Record of Maj. Idabelle M. Wilson, National Archives and Records Administration, National Personnel Records Center, St. Louis, Mo.
93. ibid.
94. Idabelle M. Wilson, Maj., USAF, (Ret), telephone interview with 1st Lt. James McAndrew, April 28, 1995.
95. ibid.
96. Memo: Jack A. Comstock, Maj. (MC), Surgeon, 509th Station Medical Group, to Major Robert W. Schick, Investigating Officer, Headquarters, USAF, subj: Investigation of B-29 Crash, 18 August 1948, Aircraft Accident No. 48-8-12, Aircraft #44-86383, Air Force Historical Research Agency, Maxwell AFB, AL. and WD AGO Form 8-33, "Clinical Record Brief," 12 August 1948, Personnel records of Air Force members, service numbers AF 18041408 and AF 16191866, National Archives and Records Administration, National Personnel Records Center, St. Louis, Mo.
97. ibid.
98. ibid.
99. WD AGO Form 8-33, "Clinical Record Brief," 16 May 1949, Personnel records of Air Force members, service numbers AO 827137 and AF 42050093, National Archives and Records Administration, National Personnel Records Center, St. Louis, Mo.

Notes - Section Two

100. WD AGO Form 5-4, "Individual Crash Fire Report," 20 May 1949, Aircraft Accident No. 49-5-16, Aircraft #43-48401, Air Force Historical Research Agency, Maxwell AFB, AL.
101. WD AGO Form 8-33, "Clinical Record Brief," 16 May 1949, Personnel records of Air Force members, service numbers AO 827137 and AF 42050093, National Archives and Records Administration, National Personnel Records Center, St. Louis, Mo.
102. WD AGO Form 5-4, "Individual Crash Fire Report," 19 December 1949, Aircraft Accident No. 49-12-15-2, Air Force Historical Research Agency, Maxwell AFB, AL.
103. WD AGO Form 8-33, "Clinical Record Brief," 19 December 1949, and "Autopsy Report," Personnel records of Air Force members, service numbers 17343A, AF 11101085, and 15239923, National Archives and Records Administration, National Personnel Records Center, St. Louis, Mo.
104. ibid.
105. WD AGO Form 8-33, "Clinical Record Brief," 1 June 1950, Personnel records of Air Force members, service numbers AO 685565 and AF 32668639, National Archives and Records Administration, National Personnel Records Center, St. Louis, Mo.
106. ibid.
107. ibid.
108. Standard form 503, "Autopsy Protocol," June 16, 1955 of Air Force members, service numbers AO 3006516 and AO 3004607, Aircraft Accident No. 55-6-16-6, Air Force Historical Research Agency, Maxwell AFB, AL.
109. DD Form 481-3, "Clinical Record Cover Sheet," June 16, 1955, Personnel Records of Air Force members, service numbers AO 3006516 and AO 3004607, National Archives and Records Administration, National Personnel Records Center, St. Louis, Mo.
110. Standard form 503, "Autopsy Protocol," June 16, 1955, of Air Force members, service numbers AO 3006516 and AO 3004607, Aircraft Accident No. 55-6-16-6, Air Force Historical Research Agency, Maxwell AFB, AL.
111. Air Force Form 14b, "Medical Report of an Individual Involved in AF Aircraft Accident," 3 October 1955, Aircraft Accident No. 55-10-3-6, Air Force Historical Research Agency, Maxwell AFB, AL.
112. Official Trip Report Walker AFB, N.M. October 4, thru October 7, 1955, George Schwaderer, Identification Specialist to MCTSG,

Notes - Section Two

October 12, 1955, Accession No. 342-65A-6025, Box 25/28, folder Trip Rpts., Search & Ident: Mar 56 to Dec 56. Trip #198 to 234, National Archives and Records Administration, National Personnel Records Center, St. Louis, Mo., and AF Form 715, "Preparation Room History," 4 October 1955, Personnel Record of Air Force member, service number 1521B/ 2009467, National Archives and Records Administration, National Personnel Records Center, St. Louis, Mo.

113. Air Force Form 14b, "Medical Report of an Individual Involved in AF Aircraft Accident," 3 October 1955, Aircraft Accident No. 55-10-3-6, Air Force Historical Research Agency, Maxwell AFB, AL.

114. Standard form 503, "Autopsy Protocol," June 27, 1956, Personnel Record of Air Force members, service numbers AO 2223861 and AF 37578524, National Archives and Records Administration, National ersonnel Records Center, St. Louis, Mo.

115. Official Trip Report Walker AFB, N.M. 27 June through 30 June 1956, George Schwaderer, Identification Specialist to Thomas W. Toy, Chief Memorial Affairs Branch, Air Force Services Division, Accession No. 342-65A-6025, Box 25/28, folder Trip Rpts., Search & Ident: Mar 56 to Dec 56. Trip #198 to 234, National Archives and Records Administration, National Personnel Records Center, St. Louis, Mo.

116. Standard form 503, "Autopsy Protocol," June 27, 1956, Personnel Record of Air Force members, service numbers AO 2223861and AF 37578524, National Archives and Records Administration, National Personnel Records Center, St. Louis, Mo., and Air Force Form 14b, "Medical Report of an Individual Involved in AF Aircraft Accident," June 26, 1956, Headquarters Air Force Safety Agency, Kirtland AFB, N.M.

117. AF Form 697, "Identification Findings and Conclusions," 3 Feb 1960, Personnel Records of Air Force members, service numbers AO 794152 and 1046844, National Archives and Records Administration, National Personnel Records Center, St. Louis, Mo.

118. ibid.

119. ibid.

120. Charles A. Ravenstein, *Air Force Combat Wings; Lineage and Honors Histories, 1947-1977* (Washington D.C.: U.S. Government Printing Office, 1984), 16, 275-276.

121. Air Force Form 14, "Report of Air Force Aircraft Accident," June 26, 1956, Headquarters Air Force Safety Agency, Kirtland AFB, N.M.

122. ibid.

123. ibid.

Notes - Section Two

124. ibid.

125. ibid.

126. Official Trip Report Walker AFB, N.M. 27 June through 30 June 1956, George Schwaderer, Identification Specialist to Thomas W. Toy, Chief Memorial Affairs Branch, Air Force Services Division, Accession No. 342-65A-6025, Box 25/28, folder Trip Rpts., Search & Ident: Mar 56 to Dec 56. Trip #198 to 234, National Archives and Records Administration, National Personnel Records Center, St. Louis, Mo.

127. ibid.

128. Jack L. Whenry, Maj., USAF, (Ret), telephone interview with 1st Lt. James McAndrew, January 26, 1995, and John C. Walter, MSgt., USAF (Ret), telephone interview with Capt. James McAndrew, June 29, 1995 and July 12, 1996.

129. ibid.

130. Official Trip Report Walker AFB, N.M. 27 June through 30 June 1956, George Schwaderer, Identification Specialist to Thomas W. Toy, Chief Memorial Affairs Branch, Air Force Services Division, Accession No. 342-65A-6025, Box 25/28, folder Trip Rpts., Search & Ident: Mar 56 to Dec 56. Trip #198 to 234, National Archives and Records Administration, National Personnel Records Center, St. Louis, Mo.

131. ibid.

132. *Recollections of Roswell, Part II,* W. Glenn Dennis interview, and Karl T. Pflock, "Star Witness: The Mortician of Roswell Breaks His Code of Silence," *Omni*, Fall 1995, 104.

133. DD Form 481-3, "Clinical Record Cover Sheet," June 26, 1956, Personnel Record of AF 37578524, National Archives and Records Administration, National Personnel Records Center, St. Louis, Mo.

134. Whenry, Walters, and Air Force Manual 143-1, 1 November 1953, "Mortuary Affairs," 28, Record Group 341, Entry 36, Box 13, Microfilm Reel 167, National Archives and Record Administration, College Park, Md.

135. *Recollections of Roswell, Part II*, W. Glenn Dennis interview.

136. Standard form 503, "Autopsy Protocol," June 27, 1956, Personnel Record of Air Force members, service numbers AO 2223861and AF 37578524, National Archives and Records Administration, National Personnel Records Center, St. Louis, Mo.

137. *Recollections of Roswell, Part II,* W. Glenn Dennis interview.

138. Standard form 503, "Autopsy Protocol," June 27, 1956, Personnel Record of Air Force member, service number AF 37578524, National

Archives and Records Administration, National Personnel Records Center, St. Louis, Mo.

139. ibid.

140. ibid.

141. *Recollections of Roswell, Part II,* W. Glenn Dennis interview.

142. Standard form 503, "Autopsy Protocol," June 27, 1956, Personnel Record of Air Force members, service numbers AO 2223861 and AF 37578524, National Archives and Records Administration, National Personnel Records Center, St. Louis, Mo., and Air Force Form 14b, "Medical Report of an Individual Involved in AF Aircraft Accident," June 26, 1956, Headquarters Air Force Safety Agency, Kirtland AFB, N.M.

143. DD Form 481-3, "Clinical Record Cover Sheet," June 26, 1956, Personnel Record of Air Force members, service numbers AO 2223861and AF 37578524, National Archives and Records Administration, National Personnel Records Center, St. Louis, Mo.

144. Karl T. Pflock, "Star Witness: The Mortician of Roswell Breaks His Code of Silence," *Omni*, Fall 1995, 108.

145. Official Trip Report Walker AFB, N.M. October 4, thru October 7, 1955, George Schwaderer, Identification Specialist to MCTSG, October 12, 1955, Accession No. 342-65A-6025, Box 25/28, folder Trip Rpts., Search & Ident: Mar 56 to Dec 56. Trip #198 to 234, National Archives and Records Administration, National Personnel Records Center, St. Louis, Mo., and AF Form 697, "Identification Findings and Conclusions," 3 Feb 1960, Personnel Records of Air Force members, service numbers AO 794152 and 1046844, National Archives and Records Administration, National Personnel Records Center, St. Louis, Mo.

146. Air Force Manual 143-1, 1 November 1953, "Mortuary Affairs," 28-29, Accession No. 341, Entry 36, Box 13, Microfilm Reel 167, National Archives and Record Administration, College Park, Md.

147. Official Trip Report- Walker AFB, N.M. 27 June through 30 June 1956, George J. Schwaderer, Identification Specialist, to Thomas W. Toy, Chief Memorial Affairs Branch, July 5, 1956, Accession No. 342-65A-6025, Box 25/28, folder Trip Rpts., Search & Ident: Mar 56 to Dec 56. Trip #198 to 234, National Archives and Records Administration, National Personnel Records Center, St. Louis, Mo., and Jack L. Whenry, Maj., USAF, (Ret), telephone interview with 1st Lt. James McAndrew, January 26, 1995, and John C. Walter, MSgt., USAF (Ret), telephone interview with Capt. James McAndrew, June 29, 1995 and July 12, 1996.

148. Walter and Whenry.

Notes - Section Two

149. ibid.

150. WD AGO FORM 66, "Officer's Qualification Record," and AF FORM 11, "Officer Military Record," Personnel Record of Col. Lee F. Ferrell, National Archives and Records Administration, National Personnel Records Center, St. Louis, Mo.

151. "Air Force Care of Deceased Personnel (1951-1959), Volume I: Text", Historical Study No. 236, Call No. K 201-326, Air Force Historical Research Agency, Maxwell AFB, AL.

152. Air Force Manual 143-1, 1 November 1953, "Mortuary Affairs," 27, Accession No. 341, Entry 36, Box 13, Microfilm Reel 167, National Archives and Record Administration, College Park, Md.

153. Official Trip Report Walker AFB, N.M. 27 June through 30 June 1956, George Schwaderer, Identification Specialist to Thomas W. Toy, Chief Memorial Affairs Branch, Air Force Services Division, July 5, 1956 and Official Trip Report Walker AFB, N.M. October 4, thru October 7, 1955, George Schwaderer, Identification Specialist to MCTSG, October 12, 1955, Accession No. 342-65A-6025, Box 25/28, folder Trip Rpts., Search & Ident: Mar 56 to Dec 56. Trip #198 to 234, National Archives and Records Administration, National Personnel Records Center, St. Louis, Mo.

154. Official Trip Report Walker AFB, N.M. 27 June through 30 June 1956, George Schwaderer, Identification Specialist to Thomas W. Toy, Chief Memorial Affairs Branch, Air Force Services Division, July 5, 1956, Accession No. 342-65A-6025, Box 25/28, folder Trip Rpts., Search & Ident: Mar 56 to Dec 56. Trip #198 to 234, National Archives and Records Administration, National Personnel Records Center, St. Louis, Mo.

155. George J. Schwaderer, telephone interview with Capt. James McAndrew, June 28, 1996.

156. ibid.

157. Air Force Manual 143-1, 1 November 1953, "Mortuary Affairs," 27, Accession No. 341, Entry 36, Box 13, Microfilm Reel 167, National Archives and Record Administration, College Park, Md.

158. Karl T. Pflock, "Star Witness: The Mortician of Roswell Breaks His Code of Silence," *Omni,* Fall 1995, 104.

159. Memo, Charles J. Stahl, M.D., Armed Forces Medical Examiner, to Capt. James McAndrew, SAF/AAZD, subj: Request for Information on Aircraft Crash Fatalities, October 13, 1995.

160. Unit history, 4036 USAF Hospital, Walker AFB, N.M., June 1956, 6, Air Force Historical Research Agency, Maxwell AFB, AL.

Notes - Section Two

161. ibid.

162. Standard form 503, "Autopsy Protocol," June 27, 1956, Personnel Record of of Air Force members, service numbers AO 2223861and AF 37578524, National Archives and Records Administration, National Personnel Records Center, St. Louis, Mo.

163. Air Force Missile Development Center, *MAN-HIGH I*, MDC-TR-59-24, 1959, and Lt. Col. David G. Simons, *MAN HIGH II*, Air Force Missile Development Center, Holloman AFB, N.M., AFMDC-TR-59-28, June 1959, 1, and Air Force Missile Development Center, *MAN HIGH III*, MDC-TR-60-16, 1961.

164. Historical Branch, Office of Information Services, Air Force Missile Development Center, Air Research and Development Command, Holloman AFB, N.M., *Contributions of Balloon Operations to Research and Development at the Air Force Missile Development Center Holloman Air Force Base, N. Mex. 1947-1958* (hereafter *Contributions of Balloon Operations 1947-1958*), 11.

165. ibid., and Air Force Missile Development Center FORM 597, Schedule Request- Project 7222/4.2- "Manned Gondola Flight," May 19, 20, 22, 1959, Accession No. 342-65B-3185, Box 4/22, National Archives and Records Administration, National Personnel Records Center, St. Louis, Mo.

166. DD FORM 481-3, "Clinical Record Cover Sheet," May 21, 1959, Personnel Record of Capt. Dan D. Fulgham, National Archives and Records Administration, National Personnel Records Center, St. Louis, Mo., and Air Force Missile Development Center FORM 597, Schedule Request- Project 7222/4.2- "Manned Gondola Flight," May 20, 1959, Accession No. 342-65B-3185, Box 4/22, National Archives and Records Administration, National Personnel Records Center, St. Louis, Mo.

167. DD Form 613, R&D Progress Card, Project 7164, "Physiology of Flight," Task 71840, "Life Supporting Systems for Advanced Vehicles," February 24, 1959, 30-31, National Archives and Record Administration Accession No. 342-75-095, Box 93/100, folder 1, and Technical "R&D" Record Book, Aeromedical Laboratory, Physiology Branch, "Life Support System for Orbital Flight," Project 7164, Task 71840, 13-16, National Archives and Record Administration, National Personnel Records Center, St. Louis, Mo. Accession No. 342-75-095, Box 93/100, folder 2.

168. Air Force Form 77, "USAF Officer Effectiveness Report, 1 Feb 58 to 31 Jan 59, Personnel Record of Capt. Joseph W. Kittinger, Jr., National Archives and Records Administration, National Personnel Records Center, St. Louis, Mo., and Capt. Joseph W. Kittinger, Jr., *The Long, Lonely Leap*, (New York: E.P. Dutton & Co., Inc., 1961) 131.

Notes - Section Two

169. Air Force Missile Development Center, *Man-High I*, MDC-TR-59-24, 1959.

170. Schedule Request- Project 7222/4.2- "Manned Gondola Flight," May 19, 20, 22, 1959, Accession No. 342-65B-3185, Box 4/22, National Archives and Records Administration, National Personnel Records Center, St. Louis, Mo.

171. ibid.

172. Ole Jorgeson, MSgt., USAF, (Ret), interview with 1st Lt. James McAndrew, May 28, 1995.

173. Air Force Missile Development Center FORM 597, Schedule Request- Project 7222/4.2- "Manned Gondola Flight," May 19, 1959, Accession No. 342-65B-3185, Box 4/22, National Archives and Records Administration, National Personnel Records Center, St. Louis, Mo.

174. Air Force Missile Development Center FORM 597, Schedule Request- Project 7222/4.2- "Manned Gondola Flight," May 20, 1959, Accession No. 342-65B-3185, Box 4/22.

175. ibid.

176. ibid.

177. ibid., and Joseph W. Kittinger, Jr., Col., USAF (Ret), interview with 1st Lt. James McAndrew, June 23, 1995.

178. Kittinger

179. ibid.

180. ibid.

181. Dan D. Fulgham, Col., USAF, (Ret), interview with 1st Lt. James McAndrew, May 26, 1995.

182. ibid. and Standard Form 539, "Abbreviated Clinical Record," May 21,1959, Personnel Record of Col. Dan D. Fulgham, National Archives and Records Administration, National Personnel Records Center, St. Louis, Mo.

183. ibid.

184. Jorgeson and Roland H. Lutz, CMSgt., USAF (Ret), interview with 1st Lt. James McAndrew, May 31, 1995.

185. ibid.

186. Fulgham and William C. Kaufman, Lt. Col., USAF, (Ret), interview with 1st Lt. James McAndrew, May 24, 1995.

187. ibid.

Notes - Section Two

188. Jorgeson.

189. Kaufman.

190. Signed, sworn statement of Dan D. Fulgham, Col., USAF, (Ret), May 25, 1995.

191. Kittinger.

192. ibid.

193. Video, *Recollections of Roswell, Part II,* Gerald Anderson interview, (Washington, D.C.: Fund for UFO Research, 1993).

194. Kittinger and Air Force Form 77, "USAF Officer Effectiveness Report," 1 Feb 58 to 31 Jan 59, Personnel Record of Col. Joseph W. Kittinger, Jr., National Archives and Records Administration, National Personnel Records Center, St. Louis, Mo.

195. Kittinger.

196. ibid., and Kaufman.

197. Kittinger.

198. ibid.

199. ibid.

200. *Recollections of Roswell, Part II,* W. Glenn Dennis interview.

201. Signed, sworn statements of Charles A. Coltman, Col. (MC), USAF, (Ret), Dan D. Fulgham, Col., USAF, (Ret), Joseph W. Kittinger, Jr., Col., USAF, (Ret), Roland H. Lutz, CMSgt., USAF, (Ret), Ole Jorgeson, MSgt., USAF, (Ret), and statement of William C. Kaufman, Lt. Col., USAF, (Ret).

202. Kittinger.

203. Capt. Joseph W. Kittinger, Jr., *The Long, Lonely Leap*, (New York: E.P. Dutton & Co., Inc., 1961) 130.

204. Kittinger.

205. Signed, sworn statements of Charles A. Coltman, Col. (MC), USAF, (Ret), Dan D. Fulgham, Col., USAF, (Ret), Joseph W. Kittinger, Jr., Col., USAF, (Ret), Roland H. Lutz, CMSgt., USAF, (Ret), Ole Jorgeson, MSgt., USAF, (Ret), and statement of William C. Kaufman, Lt. Col., USAF, (Ret).

206. Craig D. Ryan, *The Pre-Astronauts*, (Annapolis: Naval Institute Press, 1995), 200.

Notes - Section Two

207. Air Force Missile Development Center FORM 597, Schedule Request- Project 7222/4.2- "Manned Gondola Flight," May 19, 1959, Accession No. 342-65B-3185, Box 4/22, National Archives and Records Administration, National Personnel Records Center, St. Louis, Mo., and Memo: Maj. Lawrence M. Bogard, Chief, Balloon Branch, to MDWXB, subj: Project 7222, 8 May 1959.
208. ibid., and Jorgeson.
209. Jorgeson.
210. ibid.
211. *Recollections of Roswell, Part II,* W. Glenn Dennis interview.
212. ibid.
213. ibid.
214. Karl T. Pflock, "Star Witness: The Mortician of Roswell Breaks His Code of Silence," *Omni*, Fall 1995, 103.
215. *Recollections of Roswell, Part II,* W. Glenn Dennis interview.
216. Jorgeson.
217. Unit History, 47th Air Division, June 1954, photo section, Air Force Historical Research Agency, Maxwell AFB, AL.
218. Unit History, 6th Bomb Wing, June 1959, Annex "N," "Base Support Plan, Medical," June 1, 1959.
219. Charles A. Ravenstein, *Air Force Combat Wings; Lineage and Honors Histories, 1947-1977* (Washington D.C.: U.S. Government Printing Office, 1984), 16.
220. Kaufman.
221. ibid.
222. Roland H. Lutz, CMSgt., USAF, (Ret), interview with 1st Lt. James McAndrew, May 31, 1995.
223. Fulgham.
224. Kittinger.
225. ibid.
226. ibid.
227. ibid., and ltr., Dr. J. Allen Hynek, Director, Dearborn Observatory, Northwestern University, to Maj. Hector Quintanilla, Chief Aerial Phenomena Branch, December 6, 1965, National Air Intelligence Center historical files, Wright-Patterson AFB, OH.

Notes - Section Two

228. Kevin D. Randle and Donald R. Schmitt, *The Truth About the UFO Crash at Roswell* (New York: Avon Books, 1994), 22.
229. Standard Form 539, "Abbreviated Clinical Record," May 21, 1959, Personnel Record of Col. Dan D. Fulgham, National Archives and Records Administration, National Personnel Records Center, St. Louis, Mo.
230. Fulgham.
231. Kittinger.
232. ibid.
233. Kaufman.
234. DD Form 640, "Nursing Notes," May 24, 1959, and DD Form 728, "Doctor's Orders," May 22, 1959, Personnel Record of Col. Dan D. Fulgham, National Archives and Records Administration, National Personnel Records Center, St. Louis, Mo.
235. Kittinger, Kaufman, and DD Form 728 "Doctor's Orders," May 22, 1959, Personnel Record of Col. Dan D. Fulgham, National Archives and Records Administration, National Personnel Records Center, St. Louis, Mo.
236. ibid.
237. Kittinger.
238. ibid.
239. Fulgham.

Appendix A

Anthropormorphic Dummy Launch and Landing Locations

Source: Test records of U.S. Air Force aeromedical project no. 7218, task 71719 (HIGH DIVE) and project no. 7222, task 71748 (EXCELSIOR).

High Altitude Balloon Dummy Drops

Number	Date	Launch Site	Landing Site
1	6/23/54	Holloman AFB, N.M.	Holloman AFB, N.M.
2	6/28/54	Holloman AFB, N.M.	Dunkin, N.M.
3	6/30/54	Holloman AFB, N.M.	10 miles Southwest of Holloman AFB, N.M.
4	12/1/54	Holloman AFB, N.M.	Holloman AFB, N.M.
5	12/2/54	Holloman AFB, N.M.	12 miles South of Artesia, N.M.
6	12/6/54	Holloman AFB, N.M.	Near Twin Buttes, N.M.
7	12/9/54	Holloman AFB, N.M.	3 miles West of Twin Buttes, N.M.
8	2/23/55	Holloman AFB, N.M.	28 miles East of Roswell, N.M.
9	3/1/55	Holloman AFB, N.M.	25 miles South of Caprock, N.M.
10	3/3/55	Holloman AFB, N.M.	25 miles East/Northeast of Roswell, N.M.
11	6/15/55	Holloman AFB, N.M.	5 miles Northwest of Dunkin, N.M.
12	6/23/55	Holloman AFB, N.M.	35 miles Southwest of Holloman AFB, N.M.
13	6/29/55	Holloman AFB, N.M.	25 miles West of Three Rivers, N.M.
14	7/7/55	Holloman AFB, N.M.	13 miles West of Tularosa Peak, N.M.
15	7/15/55	Holloman AFB, N.M.	15 miles Northeast of Hatch, N.M.
16	11/17/55	Holloman AFB, N.M.	8 miles Northwest of Roswell, N.M.
17	11/21/55	Holloman AFB, N.M.	Holloman AFB, N.M.
18	1/25/56	Holloman AFB, N.M.	Holloman AFB, N.M.
19	2/8/56	Holloman AFB, N.M.	20 miles South of Roswell, N.M.
20	2/21/56	Holloman AFB, N.M.	20 miles East of Dunkin, N.M.
21	2/21/56	Holloman AFB, N.M.	Holloman AFB, N.M.
22	5/18/56	Holloman AFB, N.M.	Data Not Available
23	5/22/56	Holloman AFB, N.M.	Data Not Available

Number	Date	Launch Site	Landing Site
24	8/21/56	Holloman AFB, N.M.	Holloman AFB, N.M.
25	5/16/57	Truth or Consequences, N.M.	White Sands Proving Ground, N.M.
26	5/29/57	Hatch, N.M.	25 miles Northwest of Las Cruces, N.M.
27	6/4/57	Holloman AFB, N.M.	11 miles North of Las Cruces, N.M.
28	6/6/57	Holloman AFB, N.M.	17 miles South of Holloman AFB, N.M.
29	6/7/57	Holloman AFB, N.M.	Holloman AFB, N.M.
30	6/11/57	Hatch, N.M.	West of San Agustin Pass, N.M.
31	6/13/57	Holloman AFB, N.M.	Holloman AFB, N.M.
32	9/27/57	White Sands Natl MonumentPicnic Area	Orogrande, N.M.
33	10/8/57	White Sands Proving Ground	10 miles East of Picacho, N.M.
34	1/29/58	Data Not Available	20 miles South of Alamogordo, N.M.
35	1/9/59	Holloman AFB, N.M.	White Sands Proving Ground, N.M.
36	1/14/59	Las Palomas, N.M.	30 miles East/Southeast of Roswell, N.M.
37	1/30/59	Nutt, N.M.	White Sands Proving Ground, N.M.
38	2/4/59	Holloman AFB, N.M.	1 mile North of Bent, N.M.
39	2/6/59	Lake Valley, N.M.	Data Not Available
40	2/10/59	Caballo Dam, N.M.	White Sands Proving Ground, N.M.
41	2/11/59	Hatch, N.M.	Data Not Available
42	2/14/59	Data Not Available	30 miles West of Holloman AFB, N.M.
43	2/16/59	Ft. Craig, N.M.	Mescalero Apache Reservation (N.M.)

Appendix B

STATEMENT OF WITNESS

Date: 26 April 1996 Place: Farmington, NM

I Charles E. Clouthier, hereby state that James McAndrew, was identified as a Captain, USAFR on this date at my place of employment do hereby, voluntarily and of my own free will, make the following statement. This was done without having been subjected to any coercion, unlawful influence or unlawful inducement.

I was on active duty in the US Air Force and stationed at Walker AFB, Roswell, NM, from February 1955 until October 1956. During that time I was a pharmacist assigned to the base hospital. Following my tour of duty with the Air Force, I returned to my hometown, Farmington, NM, where I became an employee and eventually a co-owner of Farmington Drug.

With the exception of the two years in the US Air Force, I have been a resident of Farmington, NM since 1934. It is my recollection that Dr Frank B. Nordstrom was the first pediatrician to practice in the Farmington area and he remained the only pediatrician in Farmington until approximately 1970. I base these recollections on extensive professional and personal contacts with physicians in the Farmington area and as a father of two children who were patients of Dr Nordstrom's.

Also based on nearly 40 years of contact with physicians in the Farmington area, I believe that Dr Nordstrom is the only physician who served a tour of duty at Walker AFB. During the 1960s, I became aware that Dr Nordstrom had also served at the Walker AFB hospital. At various times in the ensuing years, Dr Nordstrom and I reminisced about our service at Walker AFB. During these conversations Dr Nordstrom never mentioned any activities during his tour of duty I considered unusual or that might explain reports of bodies or aliens. During the time I was stationed at Walker AFB, I did not witness, nor did I hear rumors, of anything that involved flying saucers, aliens, or anything else of an extraterrestrial nature.

I am not part of a conspiracy to withhold information from either the US government or the American public. There is no classified information that I am withholding related to this inquiry, and I have not been threatened by US government persons concerning not talking about this matter.

SIGNED:

Charles E. Clouthier

WITNESS:

Subscribed and sworn before a person authorized to administer oaths this 26th day of April 1996 at Farmington, NM

James McAndrew, Capt, USAFR

STATEMENT OF WITNESS

Place Date: 25 May 95

I, Charles A. Coltman, Jr., Col, USAF, MC (Ret), hereby state that James McAndrew was identified as a Lieutenant, USAFR, on this date at my place of employment and do hereby, voluntarily and of my own free will, make the following statement. This was done without having been subjected to any coercion, unlawful influence or unlawful inducement.

I entered the U.S. Air Force in 1957 as a flight surgeon and was assigned to Walker AFB, NM, in 1958. Following a residency at Ohio State University from 1959 to 1963, I was assigned to Wilford Hall USAF Medical Center, Lackland AFB, TX, where I eventually became the Chairman of the Department of Medicine. I retired from the Air Force in 1977. I am presently a Professor at The University of Texas Health Science Center at San Antonio, and Chief Executive Officer of the Cancer Therapy and Research Foundation of South Texas.

I remember a balloon crash that happened north of Roswell, NM, in May, 1959. I received a phone call from the NCOIC of the Flight Surgeon's office, who informed me of the crash. The NCOIC, Earl Wormwood, came to my quarters and we drove, in an old blue Air Force "crackerbox" ambulance, to the crash site. I remember the gondola laying on its side and the deflated balloon on the ground. The crew members were sitting next to the gondola. I examined the pilots and determined they were not seriously injured. They told me they were practicing touch-and-go's and a gust of wind had dumped them on the ground, and the gondola had struck one of the pilots in the head. Also present were Air Force technicians in trucks who tracked the balloon. The injured pilots were transported to the Flight Surgeon's office at the hospital at Walker AFB.

The injury sustained by the crew member was a head abrasion/contusion and a hemotoma. The hemotoma caused the patient's head to swell; however, it was not serious enough for him to be admitted. I remember receiving a call from Col (Dr.) John Stapp. He was in charge of the balloon project and was quite famous. Dr Stapp inquired about the injuries to the pilots and he wanted them returned to Holloman AFB as quickly as possible.

The hospital was an old World War II cantonment-type building with long corridors and a capacity of fifty beds. I do not recall a nurse assisting me in the treatment of the patient, although a nurse may have been on duty and observed the patient. I was the only doctor in the hospital that morning. There were no visiting doctors from other bases or facilities. I do not remember any altercations or arguments that day. During my time at Walker, I do not recall that any autopsies were performed at the hospital, since we did not have a pathologist on staff. I do not recall any remains brought to the hospital in body bags, or wreckage transported in the back of an ambulance. There may have been remains brought to the hospital in body bags after a KC-97 crash, but that was before I arrived at Walker. Dr Ed Bradley was involved in the recovery of the remains

At no time was there ever any involvement of the Walker hospital with UFO's or "space aliens" I know this to be true because the hospital was very small and had a small staff. If any activity, other than normal hospital functions, had occurred, I would have known about it.

I am not part of any conspiracy to withhold or provide misleading information to the United States Government or the American public. There is no classified information that I am withholding related to this inquiry and I have never been threatened by U.S. Government persons concerning refraining from talking about this matter.

SIGNED:

Charles A. Coltman, Jr., M.D.

Sworn to and subscribed before me, an individual authorized to administer oaths, this 25th day of May, 1995, at

James McAndrew, 1st Lt, USAFR

WITNESS(s):

STATEMENT OF WITNESS

Place Date: 25 May 95

I, Dan D. Fulgham, Col, USAF (Ret), hereby state that James McAndrew was identified as a Lieutenant, USAFR on this date at my place of employment and do hereby, voluntarily and of my own free will, make the following statement. This was done without having been subjected to any coercion, unlawful influence or unlawful inducement.

I entered the U.S. Air Force in 1952 as an aviation cadet. I flew F-84s on 100 combat missions during the Korean war. After a tour as a flight instructor I was assigned to the Aero Medical Laboratory at Wright Patterson. I participated in both the Air Force Man in Space program and Project Mercury. I also participated in the X-15 and X-20 programs and worked as a bioastronautics officer with NASA on Gemini. During my Air Force career, I earned both a Master's and Doctorate degree from Purdue University. I flew a combat tour in Southeast Asia in F-4s as a member of the 555th Tactical Fighter Squadron and flew 133 combat missions. I retired from the Air Force in 1978 as the Commander of the Human Resources Laboratory at Brooks AFB, TX. I am presently the Director Of Biosciences for a research organization in San Antonio, TX.

In 1959 I volunteered for training to become a back up pilot for Capt Joe Kittenger in his high altitude balloon projects. I flew two missions for training purposes with Capt Kittenger and Capt Bill Kaufman from Holloman AFB, NM in May, 1959. On the second flight we were practicing touch and go landings north of Roswell, NM when we "crashed" on one of the landings. The gondola flipped over and my head was pinned to the ground by the lip of the gondola. We managed to lift the gondola off of my head and looked it over for damage. Capt Kittenger was bleeding from a cut on his face and I noticed that my head seemed to be protruding outward from underneath my helmet. Realizing I was injured, I sat down and feared I might go into shock. I was not in pain but my entire head was throbbing and began to swell.

I then remember boarding the "chase" helicopter that was following us and flying a short distance to Walker AFB for medical treatment. I recall walking into the hospital and also stopping on the front step to smoke a cigarette. I remember security personnel escorting and questioning us to determine who we were. Security was very tight at Strategic Air Command bases such as Walker. On occasion surprise inspection teams from SAC headquarters arrived in helicopters just as we did. In addition, a story of three Air Force officers crashing in a balloon was somewhat far fetched. The security people were convinced of our identities when they spoke with Col John P. Stapp, the Aero Medical Laboratory Commander.

While I was at Walker my head had swelled considerably and both eyes were turning black. Later the skin on my face turned yellow. I remember being seen by one doctor and I do not believe any other doctors participated in my treatment. I do not recall any nurses attending to me. I also do not recall that a black NCO was present nor do I recall any civilian men in the hospital. I do not recall that Capt Kittenger was involved in an altercation of any kind while we were there. After I was treated and released we all flew back to Holloman on the helicopter.

At Holloman I was admitted to the hospital and had blood aspirated from under my scalp. I remember my forehead drooping down, I had to use my fingers to open my eyelids, and I had to sleep sitting up. Several days later I returned to Wright Patterson with Capt Kittenger and Capt Kaufman. My wife met the airplane and when she saw me, she burst into tears due to the swelling of my head, the two black eyes, and the yellow color of my skin. When I returned to my office at Wright Patterson, my secretary also began to cry when she saw me. After some weeks my head returned to normal size and I was returned to flying status.

During my Air Force career I was involved in many different scientific research projects including the space program. I can state with certainty that none of them, including the incident described here, had anything to do with UFOs or "space aliens".

I am not part of any conspiracy to withhold or provide misleading information to the United States Government or the American public. There is no classified information that I am withholding related to this inquiry and I have never been threatened by U.S. Government persons concerning refraining from talking about this matter.

SIGNED:

Dan D. Fulgham, Col, USAF (Ret)

Subscribed and sworn before me, an individual authorized to administer oaths this 25th day of May 1995 at

James McAndrew, 1st Lt, USAFR

WITNESS(s):

Rose M. Lucas

STATEMENT OF WITNESS

Place : Date: 28 May 95

I, Bernard D. Gildenberg, GS-14, (Ret), hereby state that James McAndrew was identified as a Lieutenant, USAFR on this date at my home and do hereby, voluntarily and of my own free will, make the following statement. This was done without having been subjected to any coercion, unlawful influence or unlawful inducement.

I became involved in high altitude balloon development while an undergraduate student at New York University (NYU). Following graduation I was hired by the Air Force at Holloman AFB and worked continuously as both a meteorologist and aerospace engineer at the Balloon Branch from 1951 until my retirement in 1981. My job responsibilities were to forecast the weather and fly by remote control, high altitude balloons for many different scientific projects. During this time, I became internationally recognized as an authority on high altitude balloon trajectory forecasting. I have published numerous technical reports and articles.

The first project in which I was involved, while still an undergraduate student at NYU, was the acoustical detection of nuclear explosions. The name of the project, Mogul, was classified and I didn't know this name until several years ago. Based on my experience with this project I am certain project Mogul was responsible for some portions of what has become to be known as the "Roswell Incident".

Following project Mogul I was involved in perfecting high altitude balloon technology and made many test flights with large polyethylene balloons from Holloman AFB. I worked extensively on atmospheric sampling projects and biological flights in which the balloons lifted small animals to altitude for cosmic ray experiments. I also worked on the Moby Dick Project that collected meteorological data and the classified Gopher (119L) reconnaissance project.

I was relied upon to forecast the weather, conduct climatological studies, predict balloon trajectories, and to hit with precision, ground targets both on and off the White Sands Missile Range. Balloon trajectories in New Mexico below the tropopause, are predominantly towards the east-northeast, when launched from Holloman AFB with the exception of July and August when balloons remained over the Holloman area. At high altitude, above the tropopause, trajectories are generally westerly during the summer and easterly during the spring, fall, and winter. As a result these winds, the Holloman balloon branch recovered many, probably hundreds, of balloons and scientific payloads from the Roswell, NM area over the years.

During the time of the year when trajectories were to the east I attempted to drop the equipment near accessible non mountainous areas and paved roads. The main target area was the first large north-south road on the other side of the Sacramento Mountains from Holloman AFB, Highway 285. This road goes north and south through Roswell. The standard procedure was to preposition military recovery crews near the projected point of payload impact. The crews consisted primarily of Air Force members in uniform and they operated military vehicles. I often directed these crews to "standby" along the shoulder of Highway 285, both north and south of Roswell until the balloon was in position. The recovery crews received detailed instructions from tracking aircraft that led them to the exact location of the payload. The recovery vehicles included, depending on the mission, a crane, weapons carriers, communications van, and occasionally tanker trucks to refuel the aircraft that would sometimes land on nearby roads.

During the time of the year when balloon trajectories were to the west, I attempted to drop the payloads in the Rio Grande Valley. I also aimed for another valley, the flat area north of Truth or Consequences that includes the Plains of San Augustin. In addition, many remote balloon launch sites were located throughout the Rio Grande Valley west of the White Sands Proving Grounds. Launch crews were also mostly military and used much of the same equipment as the recovery crews.

I had extensive involvement with Project 7218 that later became Project 7222. This project studied the free-fall characteristics of anthropomorphic dummies dropped from balloons from altitudes up to 100,000 feet. The missions usually consisted of two dummies attached to a suspension rack that I directed to be released at altitude. Depending on the wind conditions and time of year, the dummies, on many occasions, landed in the Roswell area. I recall some difficulties in the release mechanisms of the dummies that resulted in some of them free-falling to the ground while they were still attached to the rack. Someone without a good vantage point or not associated with the project might mistake these dummies for "aliens" due to their odd flesh tones and abstract human features.

I also recall an accident involving a manned balloon flight. I remember this event clearly because I am also a balloon pilot and had an accident approximately two years before. The accident occurred on a flight that Capt Joe Kittenger was "checking out" two back up pilots for his high altitude missions. The balloon was launched around midnight from behind the Balloon Branch at Holloman AFB. I remember that some of the steel ballast used by the balloon caused a "fireworks' display when it contacted some nearby power lines during the launch. I was operating the control center for this flight and I received notification from the communications vehicle that was following the balloon that there had been an accident north of Roswell. I later learned that the gondola had rolled over during a practice touch and go landing and one of the pilots had been struck in the head and injured. I recall speaking to Capt Kittinger about the accident and I saw the injured pilot. Although his injury was not serious, his head had considerable swelling and he looked very odd.

I also worked with Capt Kittinger on Project Stargazer. I also had met several times the civilian scientific advisor Dr. J. Allen Hynek. Dr Hynek was thoroughly familiar with the balloon operations at Holloman and visited the Balloon Branch numerous times. This project experienced some difficulties and only one manned flight was conducted.

Another project I was involved with was the Air Force investigations of UFOs, Project Bluebook. Since I was a meteorologist and amateur astronomer I evaluated, starting in 1951, local sightings of UFOs. New Mexico had alot of sightings because of the good visibility and the many experimental projects of the White Sands Proving Grounds. During my time on Project Bluebook there wasn't any sightings that we could not explain. Nevertheless popular literature still refers to some of these sightings as unexplained.

Another project with which I was involved, was the NASA Voyager and Viking Projects. These space vehicles were tested by launching them from our balloons at extremely high altitude to simulate the atmosphere of Venus and Mars. To utilize the instrumentation on the White Sands Missile Range I elected to launch the balloons and attached space vehicles from the Roswell Industrial Air Center, formerly the Roswell Army Airfield. The Holloman Balloon Branch made approximately eight launches of these two vehicles from Roswell. In appearance the Viking and Voyager probes could be mistaken for a flying saucer. They were both unclassified highly publicized projects and I do not recall getting any UFO reports for these flights. I believe one of these probes is on display at White Sands Missile Range and its known as the "flying saucer".

I am not part of any conspiracy to withhold or provide misleading information to the United States Government or the American public. There is no classified information that I am withholding related to this inquiry and I have never been threatened by U.S. Government persons concerning refraining from talking about this matter.

SIGNED:

Bernard D. Gildenberg, GS-14 (Ret)

Subscribed and sworn before me, an individual authorized to administer oaths this 28th day of May 1995 at

James McAndrew, 1st Lt, USAFR

WITNESS(s):

STATEMENT OF WITNESS

Place: Date: 28 May 95

I, Ole Jorgeson, MSgt, USAF, (Ret), hereby state that James McAndrew was identified as a Lieutenant, USAFR on this date at my home and do hereby, voluntarily and of my own free will, make the following statement. This was done without having been subjected to any coercion, unlawful influence or unlawful inducement.

I enlisted in the U.S. Air Force in 1957 and became a Ground Communications and Electronic Repairman. I remained in this career field throughout my career. I completed three tours at the Balloon Branch at Holloman AFB, NM. I retired from the Air Force in 1977 as the NCOIC of the Communication and Instrumentation Section of the Balloon Branch at Holloman AFB.

I recall an overnight balloon training mission that was conducted in May, 1959. Capt Joe Kittinger was training back up pilots for one of his upcoming projects. I was an airman assigned to coordinate communications and to assist in the recovery of the balloon upon completion of the mission. I followed the balloon in an old Korean War vintage "crackerbox" ambulance that had been converted into a communications van. Another airman and I followed the balloon throughout the night on an easterly trajectory over the Sacramento Mountains to an area north of Roswell. Also following the balloon were recovery technicians in a weapons carrier. We stayed in contact with the balloon crew by radio and also observed flares the crew would light at various intervals so we could visually track them. Just after sunrise I recall the balloon landing north of Roswell and Capt Kittinger offered me some coffee and told me he was going to make one more touch and go landing to complete the mission. I remember that I took some photographs of the balloon and waited for the last landing. Several minutes later I remember hearing a "bang", this was the squib that fired to release the gondola from the balloon. We immediately went to where the gondola landed and saw the gondola laying on its side and saw two of the pilots standing and one lying down. Lying on the ground was a shattered helmet that was worn by one of the pilots. Capt Kittinger told me they were attempting to land to avoid some power lines and a row of trees.

Soon after I arrived at the crash site, a helicopter that was also following the flight landed and transported the three aircrew members to Walker AFB for medical attention. I recall I assisted the recovery technicians load the balloon and the gondola on the weapons carrier and then drove 15 to 20 minutes to the hospital at Walker AFB. When I arrived at Walker, we parked the converted ambulance near the hospital and either the other airman with me or the recovery technicians called the balloon control center to notify them of the accident. I recall waiting near the hospital for a short period of time and then returning to Holloman AFB. During the time I was waiting at the hospital I did not observe any arguments or altercations. I did not observe Capt Kittinger speaking disrespectfully to anyone. I also do not recall any male civilians or any vehicles that belonged to a mortuary.

I participated in many, probably more than 100, balloon recoveries. I often recovered payloads and balloons from the area surrounding Roswell, NM. It was routine to be directed by the balloon control center to an area near Roswell to wait to recover a balloon. We would wait along the side of the road, at small airports, or at the armory in Roswell. It would not be uncommon for our recovery vehicles to be seen waiting to recover balloons throughout New Mexico, Arizona, and West Texas. When we recovered the balloons and payloads sometimes civilians would be in the area and make inquires. We would tell them what we were doing and provide them with a telephone number at Holloman AFB if they wanted to report any damages. We were required to clean up the area and remove all debris before we left. In addition to the recoveries, I recall making balloon launches from sites up and down the Rio Grande Valley. I remember that some of these launches were made from an area west of Soccoro, NM.

Another project I participated in was the testing of the Viking space probe in 1972. These four launches were all made from the Roswell Industrial Air Center, the former Roswell Army Airfield. Approximately twenty Air Force personnel were on temporary duty to Roswell throughout the summer of 1972 to support this project. NASA personnel prepared the spacecraft for launch from the old hangers of the former Air Force base. This project was not classified and was covered by the news media.

I am not part of any conspiracy to withhold or provide misleading information to the United States Government or the American public. There is no classified information that I am withholding related to this inquiry and I have never been threatened by U.S. Government persons concerning refraining from talking about this matter.

SIGNED:

Ole Jorgesen (signature)

Ole Jorgesen, MSgt, USAF, (Ret)

Subscribed and sworn before me, an individual authorized to administer oaths, this 28th day of May 1995 at

James McAndrew (signature)

James McAndrew, 1st Lt, USAFR

WITNESS(s):

STATEMENT OF WITNESS

Place :   Date: 28 October 1996

I, William C. Kaufman, Lt. Col., USAF (Ret), hereby voluntarily and of my own free will, make the following statement. This was done without coercion, unlawful influence or unlawful inducement.

I was drafted into the Army of the United States in 1943, transferred to the Army Air Forces, and was commissioned as a pilot in 1944. From 1950 until 1967, with a break for training for a combat tour in Korea and for educational assignments to AFIT, I was assigned to the Aero Medical Laboratory at Wright Patterson AFB, OH. During that time I was a physiological training officer and worked in the development of early pressure suits. I tested many high altitude pilots and also the first group of astronauts. Later during my Air Force career, in 1961, I earned a Ph.D. in Physiology and Biophysics. I was assigned to the Aero Medical Laboratory for three tours and retired in 1968 as the Chief of the Biodynamics Branch of the Aero Medical Field Laboratory at Holloman AFB, NM.

During my third assignment at Wright Patterson, I volunteered, along with Capt Dan Fulgham, to be a backup pilot for Capt Joe Kittinger for his high altitude balloon project, Project Excelsior. Capt Kittinger instructed Capt Fulgham and me in ballooning in May 1959.
At the end of an overnight training flight, on the morning of May 21, 1959, northwest of Roswell, NM, we (Kittinger, Fulgham and I) had an accident with the balloon. We were practicing touch and go landings when a severe gust of wind overturned the gondola, dumping all of us to the ground with the gondola on top of us. The accident occurred in a small pasture where a pony was grazing next to a small cottage. For safety, we were followed during hours of darkness by a C-131 aircraft and during the day by a H-21 helicopter. We were followed the entire time by technicians in a truck for communications and for the recovery of the balloon and gondola. Seeing the accident, the crews of the helicopter and the recovery trucks came to our assistance, much to the dismay of the farmer who owned the pony, which had run away when the truck broke down the fence to reach the crash site. I recall that a member of the helicopter crew attempted to calm the farmer.

Capt Fulgham sustained an injury to the forehead when the lip of the gondola struck him. Capt Fulgham thought he had fractured his skull but the experimental helmet he was wearing apparently protected him. Capt Kittinger was bleeding from a cut on the face. I was beneath Fulgham and Kittinger and unhurt. Fulgham was loaded into the helicopter and we were taken to the nearest hospital, at Walker AFB, in Roswell. I recall the helicopter pilot called the air traffic control tower at Walker and informed them we were inbound with an injured pilot from a balloon accident. This was quite unusual and I believe the tower personnel might have thought we were a surprise Strategic Air Command inspection team that at the direction of the SAC Commander, Gen. Curtis E. LeMay, sometimes made unannounced visits by helicopter. We landed in front of the tower and were met by an ambulance along with a detail of military police with machine guns. The military police escorted us to the hospital for treatment and to verify our story of the balloon crash.

While Capt Fulgham and Capt Kittinger were being treated I was asked to explain to the Walker AFB Base Commander what had happened. After Capt Kittinger was treated he called Col Stapp from a phone adjacent to the waiting room were numerous military wives were waiting for pre-natal care. Capt Kittinger, as the project officer, was concerned what effect this accident might have on the future of his program. As we waited for Fulgham, Kittinger paced up and down the hall concerned about Fulgham and getting out of the hospital before Walker AFB officials might complicate matters. I do not recall any male civilians in the hospital, nor do I recall Capt Kittinger being involved in an altercation of any kind. Capt Kittinger did not shout or use obscene language, he was simply interested in getting medical attention for Fulgham and leaving as soon as possible. I do recall that one or two nurses were present. I do not recall a black NCO accompanying Kittinger while we were in the hospital.

When the medical personnel were finished treating Fulgham, all three of us returned to Holloman AFB by helicopter about noon the same day. The following day I took my FAA exam and was awarded a balloon pilot license. Three days later, on Sunday, Kittinger, Fulgham and I returned to Wright Patterson via a special C-131 flight. Fulgham looked very odd with two black eyes and protruding forehead; his head was so swollen he could not wear his uniform hat for some time. I later worked with Capt Kittinger on the Stargazer project and and occasionally flew aircraft with him.

During my entire time at the Aero Medical Laboratory I neither saw nor heard anything that would lead me to believe that the Air Force was keeping "aliens" at Wright Patterson. I knew there was a project on UFOs called Bluebook, at the base, but to my knowledge the Aero Medical Laboratory was not involved. Many scientific accomplishments came out of the various laboratories at Wright Patterson but I am unaware of any that might have involved aliens or UFOs.

I am not part of any conspiracy to withhold or provide misleading information to the United States Government or the American public. There is no classified information that I am withholding related to this inquiry and I have never been threatened by U.S. Government persons concerning refraining from talking about this matter.

This is as I recollect those events.

SIGNED:

William C. Kaufman

William C. Kaufman, LtCol, USAF (Ret)

WITNESS(s):

Patricia A. Kaufman

STATEMENT OF WITNESS

Place :   Date: 24 June 95

I, Joseph W. Kittinger, Jr., Col, USAF (Ret), hereby state that James McAndrew was identified as a Lieutenant, USAFR on this date at my home and do hereby, voluntarily and of my own free will, make the following statement. This was done without having been subjected to any coercion, unlawful influence or unlawful inducement.

I entered the U.S. Air Force in 1949 as an Aviation Cadet. From 1950 to 1953 I flew fighters in Europe before being assigned to the Fighter Test Section at Holloman AFB, NM in July, 1953. During my tour as a test pilot I conducted the first zero gravity tests and was the balloon pilot of the first Project Man High high altitude research mission. In 1958 I was assigned to the Escape Section of the Aero Medical Laboratory at Wright Patterson AFB, OH. During this tour I was the Project Officer of Project Excelsior and made three high altitude parachute jumps, the highest from 102,800 feet, which today remains a world record. For these jumps I was awarded the Harmon Trophy for 1960 by President Eisenhower. Following Excelsior, I was the Project Officer of Stargazer, a project that made astronomical observations from a high altitude balloon. I flew two combat tours in Southeast Asia with the Air Commandos. I later flew a tour in F-4s and was the Squadron Commander of the 555 Tactical Fighter Squadron. I accumulated over 1,000 combat flying hours and I am credited with one aerial victory. I spent ten months as a POW in Hanoi. Upon my return I attended Air War College, flew F-4s and retired from the Air Force in 1978. In 1984 I became the first person to make a solo crossing of the Atlantic by balloon.

In 1958 I was made the Project Officer of Excelsior by Col John Paul Stapp, the Aero Medical Laboratory Commander. I supervised and was actively involved in the dropping and recovery of anthropomorphic dummies from high altitude balloons at Holloman AFB, NM for this project. We also dropped dummies, from aircraft only, at Wright-Patterson AFB, OH. The object of the Holloman tests were to study the free fall characteristics of dummies dropped from balloons at altitudes of 50,000 to 100,000 feet. Based on this data we designed a parachute that stabilized the dummies and I later used this parachute on my three high altitude jumps.

The balloons carrying the dummies were launched from various locations in New Mexico and often impacted off of the White Sands Proving Ground depending on the wind conditions. The dummies were outfitted with clothing and equipment of an Air Force pilot. The facial features of the dummies were not as pronounced as a human. The ears and noses did not protrude. I do not recall any dummies with ears or noses. Some of the dummies were not complete; they sometimes did not have arms or legs. To someone not associated with the project or who viewed the dummies from a distance, they could appear to be human or with some imagination a space "alien." In fact, I recall one incident at Wright- Patterson where one of our dummies landed near the backyard of Gen. Rawlings, Commander of the Air Research and Development Command. Gen. Rawling's wife was entertaining officer's wives that afternoon when one of our dummy's parachute failed to deploy and impacted the ground in full view of the ladies at Gen. Rawling's home. I acted quickly to retrieve the dummy and went to the impact site and recovered it by throwing it in the back of a pickup truck and quickly driving away. Later that day I received a call from Col Stapp who informed me that some of the women at the party believed that the dummy was a human and they were appalled to see the careless nature in which the obviously dead or injured "parachutist" was hauled away.

At Holloman AFB recoveries of the dummies were handled by the Balloon Branch but members of my project team, including myself, often assisted. The standard procedure was to track the dummy both from the ground and air to attempt to recover the dummies in a timely manner. On the ground we used an assortment of Air Force vehicles to track and recover not only the dummies but also other scientific balloon payloads. We used trucks, communications vans, converted field ambulances, cranes, and trailers. In the air we used helicopters, C-47s transports, and L-19 and L-20 light observation aircraft. On occasion civilians would observe our recovery operations. We often attracted a crowd due to the odd appearance of the balloon payloads and dummies and also the aircraft that circled overhead or landed on nearby roads. We also used many of the same procedures and equipment to launch from off range locations. During the recoveries weapons were not carried because there was no classified information or equipment. I do not recall any altercations of any kind. At no time did I or any of the personnel makes threats against civilians. We always attempted to maintain good relations with the local civilians and explained the purpose of the project to them if they asked. We were directed to remove as much of the material dropped by the balloon as possible. Sometimes this was difficult because the balloon and payload would break apart and cover a large area. We collected the debris in these cases by "fanning out" across a field until we had collected even very small portions of the payload and balloon. We were particularly careful to recover the large plastic balloons because cattle would ingest the material and the ranchers would file claims against the government. Additionally, there were reward notices that offered twenty five dollars for the return of the equipment attached to each of the balloons. I wrote a book, *The Long, Lonely Leap* (E.P. Dutton & Co., 1961), that completely describes Project Excelsior and my participation.

Also as a part of the high altitude balloon projects, I trained balloon pilots in May 1959 at the request of Col Stapp. Col Stapp was concerned that I might be injured as a result of the hazardous nature of the projects and he wanted backup pilots to be trained. The backup pilots, Capt Dan Fulgham and Capt Bill Kaufman were volunteers from the Aero Medical Laboratory and they were sent to Holloman from Wright-Patterson for training on a temporary duty basis. On our second training flight, Fulgham, Kaufman and I, flew an overnight mission that was launched at Holloman and ended with a crash northwest of Roswell, NM. We were followed on this mission by an aircraft at night, a helicopter during the day, and a ground crew in trucks at all times.

I recall that just after sunrise the weather had deteriorated and I directed Fulgham to land the balloon in a small field. This was the last suitable field before we would overfly the City of Roswell. I remember approaching the field just over the trees and I recall our forward velocity was about 10-12 knots, a little fast for landing. When we touched down Fulgham cut the balloon away and due to the forward velocity the gondola flipped over spilling all three of us on the ground. While lying on the ground I realized that Fulgham was injured and Kaufman and I raised the gondola. Fulgham had been struck in the head by the edge of the gondola and I could see the blood rapidly accumulating under his scalp in the forehead area. We treated him for shock and soon the recovery vehicles and the chase helicopter arrived. I decided to transport Fulgham by helicopter to the hospital at nearby Walker AFB.

When we arrived at Walker I remember that security was tight, as it was at all Strategic Air Command bases, and we were closely scrutinized by security personnel due to the unusual circumstances and early hour of our arrival. I had two concerns once we arrived at the hospital, first to get treatment for Fulgham and second to leave as soon as possible. After I was assured that Fulgham's injuries were not serious I wanted to quickly leave the base before the Walker AFB Flying Safety Officer arrived to fill out an accident report. I didn't want a report filed because an accident investigation would bring unwanted scrutiny to the project. Even though the project was unclassified I did not want any publicity or premature releases of information.

Although Fulgham's injuries were not serious, his head had swollen considerably--- both eyes were black and his face had swollen so much you could barely see his nose. I believe that if someone saw him while we were at Walker they would have been startled. When his treatment was completed we all three returned to Holloman on the helicopter. At Holloman, Fulgham was admitted to the hospital and I made preparations for him to return to his duty station at Wright-Patterson AFB. Due to his grotesque appearance, I did not want Fulgham to fly on a commercial airline. I made arrangements for all of us to fly to Wright-Patterson on a C-131 a few days later. When we arrived at Wright-Patterson, I assisted Fulgham down the steps of the aircraft because his eyes were swollen shut and he could not see. His wife was waiting at the bottom of the steps of the aircraft and she asked me where her husband was. I replied "this is your husband" and she screamed and began to cry.

While I was at the Walker AFB hospital, I do not recall any contact with a male civilian. I certainly did not call anyone an "SOB" or speak to anyone in a disrespectful manner. I did not make any threats or instruct anyone else to make threats. I recall nurses in the hospital but I am not certain if they participated in the treatment of Capt Fulgham. I was not accompanied by a black NCO at the hospital, but there may have been a black NCO on the balloon recovery team. I recall no body bags in the hospital and I am sure there were no "aliens" at the hospital, just Dan Fulgham with a very odd looking head injury.

I was also involved in the joint Air Force, Navy, and Massachusetts Institute of Technology astronomical observation project, Project Stargazer. The object of this project was to make observations via a stabilized telescope mounted atop of a gondola suspended from a high altitude balloon. I was the USAF project officer and Dr J. Allen Hynek was the scientific advisor. I worked very closely with Dr Hynek over a period of five years from 1958 to 1963. Dr Hynek would typically spend a half day working on Stargazer and then the rest of the day participating as one of the consultants on the UFO study, Project Bluebook, that was also conducted at Wright-Patterson AFB. Dr Hynek, as the scientific advisor to Stargazer, was very familiar with the techniques and capabilities of the Air Force high altitude balloon program. Dr Hynek once approached me and we discussed at length, the possibility that Air Force high altitude balloons were responsible for many UFO sightings. We ended the conversation in agreement that the balloons probably accounted for many of the UFO sightings. In other conversations Dr Hynek always gave me the impression that there were very few UFO sightings that could not be explained by good scientific investigation. At no time did Dr Hynek mention or discuss the alleged "Roswell Incident". I was therefore "flabbergasted " when Dr Hynek appeared to believe that some of these sightings were of an extraterrestrial origin.

I am not part of any conspiracy to withhold or provide misleading information to the United States Government or the American public. There is no classified information that I am withholding related to this inquiry and I have never been threatened by U.S. Government persons concerning refraining from talking about this matter.

SIGNED:

Joseph W. Kittinger, Jr.

Joseph W. Kittinger, Jr., Col, USAF (Ret)

Sworn to and subscribed before me, an individual authorized to administer oaths, on this 24 day of June 1995 at

James McAndrew

James McAndrew, 1st Lt, USAFR

WITNESS(s):

Sherry Kittinger

STATEMENT OF WITNESS

Place: Date: 31 May 95

I, Roland H. Lutz, CMSgt, USAF, (Ret), hereby state that James McAndrew was identified as a Lieutenant, USAFR on this date at my home and do hereby, voluntarily and of my own free will, make the following statement. This was done without having been subjected to any coercion, unlawful influence or unlawful inducement.

I enlisted in the U.S. Navy in 1947 and transferred to the U.S. Air Force in 1958. In June, 1958 I was assigned to the flight surgeon's office at Holloman AFB, NM as an Aero Medical Technician. I served several tours in Southeast Asia and retired from the Air Force in 1974 as an Aero Medical Superintendent.

On May 20-21, 1959 I was assigned to provide medical coverage for a balloon training mission that took off from Holloman AFB and ended with a crash near Roswell, NM. Capt Joe Kittinger was training two other pilots, Capt Fulgham and Capt Kaufman. I followed the balloon in an ambulance during the night and at daybreak I followed the balloon in an H-21 helicopter. Just after daybreak I saw the balloon crash and the three pilots were dumped form the gondola. I immediately informed the helicopter pilot and we landed in a field on which cattle were grazing. I recall the rancher was upset because the helicopter was frightening his cattle and some cattle had gotten out of the field.

I assesed the injuries to the pilots and recommended they be taken immediately to the closest hospital which was at Walker AFB, apprximately 5 to 10 minutes away by helicopter. Capt Fulgham's head was swelling due to a hemotoma he received when the gondola struck him. Capt Kittinger was cut on the face and was bleeding, Capt Kaufman was uninjured. At Walker I remember a telephone conversation with a flight surgeon who told me to "go home and sleep it off". He apparently did not believe my story of three Air Force pilots that were victims of a balloon crash. However, I was able to convince him and he treated Capt Fulgham and Capt Kittinger. While at the hospital Capt Fulgham's head had swelled enormously and his eyes were beginning to turn black.

I do not recall that anything unusual occurred at the hospital at Walker. I remember the three pilots sitting on a bench in the hallway waiting to be treated. I do not remember that Capt Kittinger was involved in an altercation with anyone while at the hospital, if he had , I would have known about it. Capt Kittinger was concerned with getting medical treatment for his injured crew member, Capt Fulgham, and returning to Holloman. I also do not recall a black NCO accompanying Capt Kittinger while we were at the hospital. I do not remember a nurse assisting in the treatment of Capt Fulgham or Capt Kittinger. I also do not remember a male civilian or any personnel or vehicles from a mortuary, and I do not recall any remains in body bags in the hospital.

I was present the entire time when the events described here took place. I am certain that this event had nothing to do with "space aliens" or any other irregular activity that would require a cover up. It was a balloon crash and nothing else.

I am not part of any conspiracy to withhold or provide misleading information to the United States Government or the American public. There is no classified information that I am withholding related to this inquiry and I have never been threatened by U.S. Government persons concerning refraining from talking about this matter.

SIGNED:

Roland H. Lutz, CMSgt, USAF, (Ret)

Subscribed and sworn before me, an individual authorized to administer oaths this 31st day of May 1995 at

James McAndrew, 1st Lt, USAFR

WITNESS(s):

Harry C. Aderholt, Brig. Gen., USAF (Ret)

STATEMENT OF WITNESS

Place :   Date: 20 June 95

I, Raymond A. Madson, Lt Col, USAF (Ret), hereby state that James McAndrew was identified as a Lieutenant, USAFR on this date at my place of employment and do hereby, voluntarily and of my own free will, make the following statement. This was done without having been subjected to any coercion, unlawful influence or unlawful inducement.

I was born, raised, and presently reside in New Mexico. I graduated from New Mexico A&M College in 1954. I entered the Air Force in 1955 and was assigned a short time later to the Aero Medical Laboratory at Wright Patterson AFB, OH. At the Aero Medical Laboratory I was assigned to the Escape Section as a project officer and test parachutist. During this time I also had extensive participation in various aspects of the space program and worked on the highly classified U-2 project. I served a tour of duty in Alaska and at the School of Aerospace Medicine at Brooks AFB, TX, before being reassigned to the Aero Medical Laboratory at Wright Patterson. I retired in from the Air Force in 1979 and I am currently and Environmental Specialist for the State of New Mexico.

The first project that I was assigned at Wright Patterson was Project 7218, later changed to Project 7222. This project was first known by the name High Dive and then was known as Excelsior. The object of this project was to study the free fall characteristics of anthropomorphic dummies from balloons at altitudes of 50,000 to 100,000 feet. Following satisfactory dummy drops, Capt Joe Kittinger made a series of high altitude parachute jumps that culminated with a jump from 102,800 feet.

I assumed the duties of Project Officer for the dummy drops in the spring of 1956. I made numerous trips to Holloman AFB, NM, the site of the drops, from 1956 until the end of the project in 1959 (dummies were also dropped for this project at Wright Patterson AFB by personnel from the Parachute Branch). I wrote two technical reports that described the project in considerable detail. The type of anthropomorphic dummy used primarily was manufactured by Alderson Laboratories but we also used Sierra Manufacturing type dummies. Both of these dummies are shown in the technical reports. The Alderson dummy had facial features that were not life-like and ears that were not well defined. The dummies were outfitted with flight suits of various colors, fuchsia, olive drab, and sage green (a shade of gray). We chose the Alderson dummy because it was relatively inexpensive as compared to the Sierra dummy.

We encountered considerable difficulty dropping the dummies from the balloons. I designed the rack that suspended the dummies, two at a time, from the balloon. On numerous occasions the dummies were fouled during the release sequence and the dummy rode a "streamer" all the way to the ground. Other times malfunctions occurred that caused the two dummies and the entire rack assembly to descend to the ground as one package. Both of these instances are described in the technical reports.

I participated in at least two dummy recoveries. The meteorologist from the Balloon Branch, Duke Gildenberg, would determine the best place to launch the balloons depending on the prevailing weather conditions. Duke also predicted, with considerable accuracy, where the dummies would impact. I specifically recall a dummy I recovered near the Jornada test range, between Leasburg and Organ , NM. During this recovery I drove a weapons carrier and I was only able to locate one of the dummies, I never found out what happened to the other one. The next recovery I remember was on a ranch just southwest of Roswell. We were given directions to the area by the balloon branch personnel who had been contacted by a rancher. The equipment had reward notices taped to them to aid in recovery. We went to the Smith ranch, I remember the name because I went to New Mexico A&M with the rancher, I knew him as Smitty. We searched that day from horseback and could not find the dummies. The following day we resumed our search from horseback and again could not find the dummies. I also recall that Smitty asked us for some of the parachute material so he could make a shirt. We dropped many dummies from the balloons and I know many were not immediately recovered, but most were.

I served for twenty five years in the Air Force and most of those years were in the aero medical field. I participated in the space program and the highly classified early stages of U-2 program. Never during this time were "aliens" or "flying saucers" a part of any project. There were, however, countless achievements by the Air Force in aerospace medicine that were the result of dedicated scientific research. It seems likely to me that someone could have mistaken our anthropomorphic dummies for something that they were not.

I am not part of any conspiracy to withhold or provide misleading information to the United States Government or the American public. There is no classified information that I am withholding related to this inquiry and I have never been threatened by U.S. Government persons concerning refraining from talking about this matter.

SIGNED:

Raymond A. Madson, Lt Col, USAF (Ret)

Sworn to and subscribed before me, an individual authorized to administer oaths, on this 20 day of June 1995 at

James McAndrew, 1st Lt, USAFR

WITNESS(s):

STATEMENT OF WITNESS

Date: 25 April 1996 Place: Aztec, NM

I Frank B. Nordstrom, M.D., hereby state that James McAndrew, was identified as a Captain, USAFR on this date at my home and do hereby, voluntarily and of my own free will, make the following statement. This was done without having been subjected to any coercion, unlawful influence or unlawful inducement.

I was on active duty in the US Air Force and stationed at Walker AFB, Roswell, NM from July 1951 until June 1953. During that time I was a pediatrician assigned to the base hospital. Following my tour of duty with the Air Force I attended the University of Colorado as a resident in pediatrics. In July 1954 I relocated to Farmington, NM and began a private pediatric practice. I retired from private practice in 1987 and became the Medical Director of the San Juan Regional Medical Center, which is also located in Farmington, NM. In 1989 I retired from that position and presently reside in Aztec, NM.

I have been shown two transcripts of interviews where an individual named Glenn Dennis described conversations and visits he claims he had with a pediatrician in the late 1940s or early 1950s in Farmington, NM. According to these interviews, Mr Dennis also claims that this pediatrician had previously served at the hospital at Walker AFB/Roswell AAF. Since I am the only physician in Farmington, NM who previously served at the Walker AFB/Roswell AAF hospital, I believe I am the person he is referring to in these interviews. I am confident of this because I know I was the first pediatrician to practice in Farmington, which when I arrived in 1954, was a small community of approximately 8,000 people. I remained the sole pediatrician there for approximately 20 years and I know most, if not all, of the physicians in the area.

Even though I believe I am the person Mr Dennis referred to in the interviews, I do not remember him. I can state with reasonable certainty that I cannot recall any conversations with him, and he, to my knowledge, never visited me in Farmington, NM, in Colorado, or anyplace else. I have been told, however, that a person named Glenn Dennis operated a drugstore in the late 1950s-early 1960s, just outside Farmington, in Aztec, NM. But I do not recall any contact with him there either.

While I was stationed at Walker AFB, I do not recall any incidents that may explain the information Mr Dennis provided in the interviews. To my knowledge there was only one fatal aircraft accident during my tour of duty and that accident involved a Walker AFB based aircraft in the United Kingdom. I was not involved in any aspect of that accident. I also do not recall any other incidents such as automobile accidents or house fires that may be the source of this information. Nor do I recall a nurse named Lt Naiomi Selff or a nurse named Capt "Slats" Wilson. While at Walker AFB I did not witness or hear rumors of anything that involved flying saucers, aliens, or anything else of an extraterrestrial nature.

I am not part of a conspiracy to withhold information from either the US government or the American public. there is no classified information that I am withholding related to this inquiry and I have not been threatened by US government persons concerning not talking about this matter.

SIGNED:

Frank B. Nordstrom, M.D.

WITNESS:

Subscribed and sworn before, a person authorized to administer oaths this
25th day of April 1996 at Aztec, NM

James McAndrew, Capt, USAFR

Appendix C

Transcript of Interview with Gerald Anderson*
Alleged firsthand witness to "Crash Site" Two
(allegedly 175 miles northwest of Roswell)

A: We drove down to the Plains of San Agustin which is west of Socorro, New Mexico in the Magdalena, Datil, area. We were down there looking for banded and moss agate, which according to my uncle Ted and my cousin Victor was prevalent in the area. My brother being an amateur rock hound had wanted to get some of this. That was a way of showing us around the area. They had relatives down in Magdalena that they wanted to introduce us to.

So we had gone down there and we got down in the Horse Springs area and had driven off onto the plains down an old rutted road for, oh, a mile or so and it seemed like a long ways. We parked the car, got out of the car and walked down a hillside.

There's a semi-forest, I guess you could say. It had pinon trees and scrub oak and stuff like that on it and we walked—well, not scrub oak, but cedar—and walked down the hillside into an arroyo, a dry wash, and then walked south down a dry wash toward where the agates were supposed to be at.

As we came around a bend in the arroyo that had pinon and cedar trees growing, we were able to see farther ahead down the arroyo and on the next ridge line there was a large silver disc shaped object was embedded in this side of the ridge line...there was debris and wreckage strewn about the area mainly this thing was intact. I would estimate its size from an adult perspective to something like 35 feet in diameter. I've heard other people who were there say they thought it was like 50 feet. But as an adult, I would say about 35 feet in diameter, quite large. When we got up to it there were four bodies there... not human, there was two of them that were obviously dead, one of them was obviously very badly injured, and one of them apparently suffered no ill effects...or it didn't appear to be injured and was ambulatory, was mobile. It was just setting there next to the one...

Q: Were they right next to the vehicle?

A: Right next to it. Right under the edge of it. And this craft had apparently come in from the east and bounced off one ridge line, plowing through this arroyo area and then crashed into the ridge line and embedded itself. They were sitting back under the edge, it was kind of tilted up like this and they were sitting back under the edge here. And I'm assuming that this one creature that was all right had laid this material on the ground but it looked like unrolled tinfoil that these other three creatures were laying on.

---

* Exerpted from raw footage used to prepare the video, *Recollections of Roswell Part II*, (Washington, D.C.: Fund for UFO Research, 1993).

Like it was trying—like you do a person in shock, you know, a put him on a blanket, that kind of thing. And apparently it had some boxes there around it and had apparently been trying to give first aid or help these other creatures when we first got there.

As we approached, the creature drew back like this, like it was in fear, like we were going to hurt it. And it wasn't very long, you know, we were trying to communicate with it, the adults were. It seemed to calm down and just sat there and kind of looked back and forth, watching them, apparently trying to figure out what was going on...

Q: What did it look like, a little bit more.

A: These creatures, all of them, were, oh, about four foot tall, four and a half feet tall. They had very large heads that were shaped larger on the top and they kind of tapered down, not to a real sharp point but just tapered down where they were thin. And they had very large, very large, oval shaped or almond shaped, I guess you could say, black eyes. The head... They were so shiny, they had almost a bluish tint to them when the light reflected off of them. Their skin coloration, the best way that I could describe that is it was kind of a bluish tinted milky-white. It looked like someone in shock. And the ones that were laying on the ground were really—really looked more that way, more blue in the light, you know...

Q: How about ears, nose, mouth?

A: No, there were no visible ears on the creatures except like—if you was just to cover your ear like this to where there was just a rise there and then a hole without, you know, your ear lobe and the rest of the area...

Q: How about nose?

A: It was—the nose was very, very small, almost imperceptible. It's like two holes, straight in; and the lips were just a straight line. It was like a cut and you couldn't see, just the lips like we have, it was just a slit. And...

Q: What hair color? Sound?

A: Pardon?

Q: What hair color?

A: There was no hair. They were completely bald.

Q: And no sounds?

A: I never heard a sound one, not out of any of the creatures including the one that was...

Q: Did you see fingers?

A: Yes, they had fingers like this. They didn't have a little finger. They just had the thumb and three extra digits except the center digit was longer and the other two were about the same size. They were very long and slender and looked very delicate and I made the statement before and I'll make it again, I think he would have made an excellent violinist because of the structure of their hands.

They were wearing one piece suits. All of them were dressed exactly the same. It was sort of a real shiny silverish gray color.

Q: No zippers, buttons?

A: No, I saw no zippers, no buttons.

Q: Insignias?

A: No, no insignias. The only thing that was different, you know, and they all had this, but the only that was different from the silvery gray thing, the suit, was that down like a seam line, like there was a seam on his shoulder and around the collar it was trimmed in what appeared to be maroon, like cording.

Then the suits were continuous with their footwear. We could see right this area down, it seemed to be less pliable then it was up here, like this was a stiffer area, like they were boots or shoes or something. But they were all dressed exactly the same.

Q: Okay. So you and your family are talking back and forth, wondering what was going on, what did your family say? I mean...

A: Well...

Q: ...did they say anything?

A: Yes, my brother, one of his first remarks I heard him say him say, "That's a god damn spaceship." You know there were bodies up there and, you know, I was told not to go up there, which I didn't. And...

Q: How old was your brother at the time?

A He was in his early twenties, I think, 20, 21, something like that.

Q: He was a lot older that you were?

A: Oh, yes, considerably.

When we got up there I kind of meandered off to one side. This thing was cocked up and I was standing here, the bodies were here, and everybody else was kind of down here except my cousin Victor was over here playing and looking in this gaping hole on the side of this disk. And it was shaped just like a discus except for a round dome was up on top and there was this big gaping gash in there. We could see inside and it looked like a double hull.

Q: How big—explain it? The gash.

A: The dome?

Q: No, the gash.

A: Well, it covered the greater majority from the center of the craft out. It was just like a gaping hole in there. I mean I'm thinking, you know, it's like about 32, 35 feet in diameter so we're talking about 17 feet maybe. Most of that one side was ripped open like that. You could see inside and you could see another double hull, like—in there. And there were just rows of components that was on there.

And there were lights that flashed on and off. Some of them were steady and some were flashing. There was a lot of debris and stuff hanging out of the hole. There was evidence that there apparently had been fire. It looked like it had been burned along the edge there. The gash...

Q: Now this wasn't a gash that could have been caused by the thing coming in for the ground? It wasn't at the leading edge of the vehicle?

A: No, no. This was in the side like—it almost appeared it was elliptical. It almost appeared as if something the same shape as the disk we were looking at had hit that same—you know, like it hit the disk and left an imprint that pretty closely approximated the outside diameter of the disk itself. And it appeared to be caved in looking, kind of like it hit them like this and it just crumpled and caved in and ripped it open.

Q: Okay, so you're there, you take all this in, everybody is mystified. What were the circumstances outside? Hot, cold?

A: Very, very hot. Incredible to me, being the first time in New Mexico and coming from back east. I had dry heaves. It was like the inside of an oven. It was unbelievable to me. You know, the odd part about this was that the closer you got to it, the cooler it was. And standing under it in the shade there next to these creatures' bodies, it was like refrigerated air conditioning. And...

Q: Did you feel air coming out of this thing?

A: No, it was just like it was (inaudible).

And I remember reaching up and putting my hand on the side of it but I think I was afraid I was going to hit my head because there was enough room for me as small child, you know, I was approximately the same size as these creatures, to walk up under there and stand there but I kind of did like that, put my hand up against this thing.

Q: What did it feel like?

A: It was ice cold. It felt like it just came out of a freezer.

Q: Was it smooth? Was it rough?

A: It was very smooth. It had a very smooth texture to it. It was obviously made out of metal. It was very solid and it was very cold, ice cold.

And there was a smell in the area. It smelled volatile, acrid, like acetone. And that seemed to be coming out of that gash, that smell. But the closer you got to this thing, the cooler it was so, you know, I kind of remained there.

And I guess that while they were over here, my father and my uncle Ted and my brother. Uncle Ted was trying to talk to this thing in

Spanish and of course it didn't understand a word he said. And dad tried to talk to it and then they tried, you know, sign language and that didn't work.

And I don't know, for some reason, I just—I reached down and touched it, this one that was laying next to me. When I touched it I realized and I jumped back. It scared me. It startled me because I suddenly realized that these weren't dolls. I thought they were plastic dolls. And I—you know, it was still in my mind that these were dolls until I touched it and then I realized, you know, this was a dead thing.

I'd seen dead relatives before and unfortunately made a mistake one time in touching a relative that was in a casket and I just knew this was a dead thing and it scared me, and I ran around behind my father and my uncle and this thing was sitting there on the ground and it kept looking back and forth. And it just had its hands like this in its lap, and just kept looking back and forth between the three of them and—like it was trying to understand.

And all of a sudden it just turned and looked right straight at me between my uncle Ted and myself. And this is when—it was just like an explosion of things in my head, things... I started, you know, feeling, just terrible depression and loneliness and fear and just, you know, awful, awful feelings that just suddenly burst in to my mind there. I don't know if that meant that it was communicating with me and I was the only one there that it could communicate with because I was a kid. I don't know.

I turned and ran and I ran across the arroyo and up on the area that it had bounced off of during the crash. I was just standing there looking down at this scene, you know, at my family, and off in the distance I could see cattle grazing. I could see a windmill and could see dust trails out on the plains out there.

And, oh, I was there for a while and then I came back down. I guess we were there—Victor was, when I got back down there Victor was up in the craft and Ted yelled at him to get out of there and Glen went over and grabbed him by the belt and jerked him around...

Q: That's your brother?

A: Yes.

And jerked him off, says, "Get out because this thing may explode and kill us all," you know, and then of course he went prowling around in there.

I was kind of standing off to one side looking. That's why I knew that there was—I can look off these rocks that I was standing on and look right into this thing. That's why I knew, you know, about the lights and the components and stuff.

And then I heard other people talking. I turned and there was a group of people coming up the arroyo from out on the plains from the south. They had come up there and of course they walked up and was talking.

Q: How many?

A: There was an older man and five younger students.

Q: Boys, girls?

A: Three boys and two girls. And they were all, you know, introducing, talking to my father and my uncle and my brother...

Q: What did the older one look like?

A: He was a very tall man, a very big man. He was wearing a pith helmet when he first came up, one of those kind of explorer helmets. And he was bald and I know that because he had taken it off and he had, you know, wiped it with a handkerchief and put it back on. He was a balding man. And he had a round face. He was very ruddy completed. A big man, and he apparently was a doctor because they kept calling him doctor and it was my understanding that it was an archeological group that was out there on some kind of summer thing. And they talked and he apparently was able to speak several foreign languages and he tried to talk to this creature several times in different languages, again to no avail.

Q: How did they happen to be there? Had he seen the thing...

A: Well, they claim that they saw—they said they saw this thing come down the night before in flight, you know, and they thought it was a meteorite and they had talked about well, early in the morning, you know, we'll go over and see this, where this meteor came down, because that's what they thought it was.

And when the sun came up the next morning, you know, and they got about their business, got up and somebody looked over and said, you know, they saw this shiny metal and stuff across the plains there and they realized it wasn't a meteorite, it may have been an airplane that had crashed so they all decided to go over there and see if there was anybody left alive, you know, that was hurt that needed help.

Q: They had driven over?

A: No, they walked over apparently, the way I understand it. And it's quite a ways across that plain so it had to take a very long time to do this or they may have had a vehicle, I don't know. That's an assumption, I think, on my part, where they walked.

Q: Okay. So they're around...

A: But they came across...

Q: ...with the family...

A: ...the plains. I don't know why I said that. I'm not sure if they drove or not. I didn't hear any cars.

Q: And then somebody else shows up?

A: Yes, they were down just, oh, 15 maybe 20 minutes tops, you know. And they were picking up things, some of the students. And this Dr. Buskirk, that they called him, this one girl went up and said, "Look, doctor, wouldn't this make a beautiful ring?" And she was holding what looked like a red rod, a red tube that was some kind of silvery-red.

And he kind of snapped at her, you know, "Put that down because you don't know what that thing is. That thing could hurt you. Don't pick this stuff up."

And she kind of said, "Well, yes, okay, doctor." And then he went back to what he was doing and she walked away and put it in her pocket.

And a lot of them were doing this, sort of picking up things and feeling things. I was picking up things and feeling things. It was all kinds of material and metal, stuff like that. I heard it, well, we all heard it, the sound of a motor coming, like a truck. And I went back up the incline area to the ridge line and I could see out there, there was a truck coming up. It was an old pick-up truck. It was sort of a beige color, a tan colored van with an antenna on it. And it stopped and this guy got out and he's wearing brown clothes. He's got boots on and he's wearing a straw hat, just like the kind that Harry Truman always wore, and he had wire rimmed glasses. He was a big man and he looked exactly like Harry Truman to me. You know, I'd seen him in the Movietone News...

Q: He was president then.

A: Yes, I was well aware who Harry Truman was. Everybody was. He was kind of a hero, you know, and he just kind of looked like him except bigger, bigger. You know, I don't think he—and he didn't look as old either. His hair was kind of light gray.

And he walked over there and they got to talking, you know, with everybody and he told them that he worked out on the plains out there and that he made maps and that he had seen the wreckage from out there on the plains and he saw the people and he thought it was a plane wreck and, you know, that something was going on and he came over to see.

And he hadn't been there but just a very, very few minutes when we heard all kinds of motors and engines straining and stuff. And here comes a military car with a big white star on the side of it followed by a six-by which is a military truck with a kind of canvas wagon, kind of a canvas thing over it and it's full of soldiers. They've got guns. And right behind them is what we call a four-by which is like a medium sized jeep/truck situation and it had two big high whip antennas, all kinds of radio gear in the back and a guy back there with ear phones and stuff on and he's, you know, working these radios. And they all pulled up and stopped.

Q: Which direction did they come from, do you know?

A: They came from the north, from the Horse Springs area, right...

Q: So they could have come off the highway there...

A: Oh, yes. I'm sure that's exactly how they got there. They come off the highway, the same way we did. Well, in the meantime, when the stopped, this black soldier, this sergeant, the reason I know he was a sergeant, my brother told me he was, and he got out of this car and then a guy got out on the other side and he was a, Glen said he was a captain, he told me later he was a captain and this guy had orange and red hair. So all the soldiers and them came running over there pointing guns at people, telling them, "Get away, get away, get away," you know? And when this creature saw these people, the military, he went nuts. He went into an absolute panic, worse than what he did when he saw us.

Q: Did he move around or just his eyes or...

A: He just, he just...

Q Oh, okay.

A: ...went crazy. And it was like...

Q: Like he was scared?

A: Yes, like he was looking for a place to run and hide.

Q: But he never got up?

A: He never got up. He never left the beings that were next to him. And this red headed officer, this guy was a real butt hole. He made all the threats. He threatened to have people shot.

Q: Everybody?

A: He went, "Get away, get away," you know, "We'll shoot. Get away from there. This is a military secret." You know, just screaming and hollering. He told my uncle and my father that if they didn't want to spend the rest of their life in prison they would never say anything about what they saw there, if they ever wanted to see us kids again, they'd take the kids away. They'd never see the kids, you know, meaning me and Victor. That we'd better keep our mouths shut because if we did not, this is what was going to happen. They were threatening people and pushing people...

Q: The students as well and Dr. Buskirk?

A: Oh, yes. They were hustling everybody. And one of the soldiers pushed my uncle. He had a rifle like this and he shoved him back like that. Well, that was something you didn't do to my uncle Ted. Ted had a violent temper. And he grabbed the rifle and reached over top and smacked this guy and dropped him right there. And Ted would go out and fight, heck, this guy's a cowboy. He'll hit you in a minute.

And of course when he did that there was bolts opened and I guess cocking, they were cocking their rifles. They were pointing guns at people and everybody Buskirk and Glen and dad grabbed him, you know, pulled him back and got him away. "No, don't, Ted, they're going to shoot. Don't do that." You know, trying to stop this. And I think we came very close to having someone shot.

Then they really started threatening, you know, and they...

Q: Did the redhead do all the talking, pretty much?

A: Pretty much. Except once in a while the sergeant would, you know, chime in and make statements like that to other people in response to the redhead. But mainly it was the redhead...

Q: Was there a name tag?

A: Yes, sir, there was. His name was Armstrong. And I'm not sure if I know that from having read it or know that from remembering it and now being able to read it in my memory, or if someone said that to me. But his name was Armstrong, it was right here on his uniform.

Q: But he chased you guys away pretty quick?

A: Yes, yes, he did.

And they herded us up like cattle and we were just up the arroyo, back in the direction we came from, over the protest of this Dr. Buskirk who said, "No, no, we've got to go the other way. We came from over there."

"I don't care where you came from, get your ass up the arroyo."

And they ran us up the arroyo and...

Q: So you get to your car again?

A: Oh, right.

Now they took us up the arroyo and just over the hill we came down, they broke us off and moved us up the hill.

Now this whole time, no one has ever frisked us down, no one has ever checked our pockets to see if we picked up any of this material and this girl, Agnes, still had that stuff in her pocket and some of the other students had stuff. To my knowledge, up to that point, they had not been searched. Whether they did so afterward, I don't know. They never searched us, ever. They ran us back up the hill and when we got to where the car was parked, where dad had parked the car up there, there's a jeep with a guy sitting in the back and there is a mounted machine gun in the back of this jeep and all of these soldiers.

The jeep pulls out, we're told to get in the car, we follow the jeep, and the soldiers go with us all the way back out to the highway. When we get back out to the highway, they set us right there. They wouldn't let us out of the car. They wouldn't let us move forward. I don't know whether they were making a decision or what.

When we got out to the highway, this place was absolutely full of military personnel, military equipment. There was airplanes sitting out there that they had landed on the highway.

Q: Did you see any airplanes when you were back at the site?

A: Yes, there was airplanes in the sky but nobody thought much about. You know, I didn't think anything about it. I was used to airplanes being in the sky, having been raised in Indianapolis, Indiana, the home of the Norden bombsight, you know, the sky was always full of military aircraft at night.

And when we get back on to the highway, there's observation aircraft, you know, high winged aircraft, and there's one, of what I know now to be a C-47 setting there. And how we didn't hear that land is beyond me and how he landed—well, of course, I guess you could land it if you're a good pilot out there as there were no poles or anything.

And it was—they had torn the fence down on the north side of the highway and all this equipment was setting back up there. The plane was up there and they were taking stuff out of the plane. There was military ambulances and there were trucks with—like wreckers, cranes on them. And there was tankers, like maybe had fuel or water in them. There was just—everywhere you looked there was military.

Q: A major recovery operation?

A: Yes, it looked like an invasion force. It really did.

And they were all wearing these light khaki uniforms. They didn't look like, you know, olive drabs. They were light khaki and they all had the same patch over their—that kind of blue funny patch with the circles on it, was on his shoulder.

And a lot...

Q: Do you have a clue as to where they came from? Did your brother or your uncle?

A: No. I don't know where they came from. No, I don't think anybody ever ascertained that.

There were a lot of MP patches and some of them were wearing nightsticks off of these webbed utility belts. They had night sticks and they had .45's in holsters, you know, the automatics, full holsters. And these were the people that were giving most of the orders.

They had the road barricaded off out there and we sat there for a very long time and, you know, we were getting thirsty and everything and we asked if we could go back to Horse Springs to get some water.

"Oh, no, no. You can't through there."

And right after that, they said, "Now you just turn around and you head out of here now and you go to Socorro," and this is the redhead again, "Keep you mouths shut. Just keep going and don't look back."

Well, as we drove away, you know, dad, "The hell with it, we'll go to Magdalena. We'll get water in Magdalena." You know, because that's where John Trujillo lived, a relative of Ted's.

And so as we drove away, I was looking out the back window and I could see Dr. Buskirk and these kids and that guy, the guy in the pick-up was standing there and this Dr. Buskirk was doing just like this in this redheaded officer's face and he kept pointing back behind him and I guess that meant, you know, we've got to go back that way and he was fed up with this guy or something and he was shaking his finger in his face when they were yelling at each other and that's pretty much the last I saw of the whole situation. I don't know what happened after that because we just kept going.

(END)

Transcript of Interview with W. Glenn Dennis*
(Alleged firsthand witness to events at the Roswell AAF hospital)

Q: You started getting calls from the base mortuary officer is that right, some time in the afternoon on some day in July [1947].

A: Right after noon, yeah.

Q: Do you recall, was that before the story appeared in the [Roswell Daily] Record?

A: I don't know. I'm sure it was. I can't honestly say, but I don't think the paper came out until the next day, I don't think. I'm just assuming that.

Q: I understand. When things like that happen to me way after the fact I try to remember, and I wasn't sure if you had any recollection or not. It was the base mortuary officer who called you, not any of the MDs out there.

A: No.

Q: He was just, the mortuary officer was just the guy...

A: We used to have a standing joke. What did you do that was so bad they made you the mortuary officer.

Q: Exactly.

A: He wasn't a doctor or anything, but he was an officer and he was probably some old boy they was trying to figure out something to do with.

We used to all have them come in, even the officer himself, say, "God, I didn't know I screwed up that bad."

Q: Was this a guy you'd worked with before? Somebody you knew real well?

A: No. Those guys come and go.

Q: I realize that. You don't remember what his name was or anything like that?

A: No. I'm like Bob [Shirkey]. I think if I would see it or heard it or something I might. Those guys, they were in and out. The mortuary officer, usually they would appoint some sergeant or somebody. The only time the doctors were involved is when you'd have an embalming inspection

* W. Glenn Dennis, interview with Karl T. Pflock, November 2, 1992.

or dress inspection where the doctors came in and examined the body to make sure everything was right. You had another inspection to make sure their dog tags, make sure all the medals and everything...

They always had two crews of inspectors. The doctors were only involved in the cause of death or the autopsies or identification process, dental charts and all that. After they did their work, then a doctor would always come in and make sure the body was embalmed because [they] know more about it than the other people. But they were involved before. You know.

Q: The reason they contacted you was because Burt Ballard's funeral home up here had a contract with the base, right?

A: Yeah.

Q: You worked for Burt for a lot of years, didn't you?

A: Yeah, a long time.

Q: When did you first go to work for him?

A: I went to work for him, I was hanging around the funeral home when I was like a freshman in high school. I'd want to make some extra money. "I'll give you 50 cents to wash the hearse." I knew his daughter real well. We were all in school together. That's where I really got involved in the funeral home. I just kind of worked my way in it.

Q: He basically taught you the trade and all that.

A: Oh, yeah. My folks weren't in the funeral business.

Q: The reason I was curious about it was because when I went back... I'm one of these guys that goes to Washington and then gets fed up and leaves and swears I'm never going to go back, and then I go back anyway. But the last time I went back and did that, I shared a townhouse with a guy for awhile who was a mortician from Michigan. But he had to go through all this formal training and all this rigmarole...

A: No. That started in (inaudible). Maybe you don't want to hear this, but I was in the 9th grade, and this teacher was going around and wanted us to write a composition on what we wanted to be when we graduated from school. What were our future plans. I was kind of a wise guy, I guess I must have been, but I said undertaker, and I don't even know why. All the girls squealed, so I got a little attention. Then she said okay, if that's what you want to do then you've got a week, you bring me your composition. I want to know why you want to be an undertaker.

So I went to the funeral home. They didn't have any books in those days or anything, but that's where I went. That's why I got involved in it, started.

Q: How long were you in that business before you... I know you ran the Wortley Hotel up in Lincoln [N.M.].

A: Oh, that was after I retired.

Q: Oh, I see, you retired from the mortuary business...

A: Oh, yeah. I was in the funeral business 33 years.

Q: All the time with Ballard?

A: Oh no, I had my own funeral home over in Las Cruces [N.M.], and one in Soccoro [N.M.].

Q: Oh, okay.
Speaking of that, do you know Norman Todd or his family?

A: His dad and I took the state board together. He was at Clovis [N.M.]. Norman's his son isn't it?

Q: Yeah. He's a lawyer over in Las Cruces [N.M.]. His...

A: Wasn't his dad the funeral director in Clovis [N.M.]?

Q: I think so. The reason I know him is because Mike Cook, who is Steve Schiff's press secretary, and he have been friends ever since they were in kindergarten together. It turns out that Iris Todd, I guess his stepmother, is the niece of Loretta Proctor. So talk about small world.

You got these calls from the mortuary officer who was asking you all these questions. We don't have to go back through all of this. Then at some point you decided to go out to the base. What took you to the base?

A: At some point I didn't decide, that's not correct. Somebody wrote that, but I don't think it's right. The way I ended up out at the base later, we had the ambulance service. The way I got it, the ambulance service, I got a call, was an airman that was hurt. I took him to the base. The best I remember, he wasn't on a stretcher or anything because we walked up the ramp and he sat up in the front seat with me. So he weren't real bad and weren't dying. Anyway... This guy walked in, I walked him in. Where I usually park the ambulance, there was a field ambulance there. I had to go back up to the front. The airman and I walked up the ramps. That's why I went to the base.

Q: The hospital in those days was apparently a complex of buildings, right?

A: Yeah. Kind of like Bob [Shirkey] said, like the officer's club. They're all wooden barrack types.

Q: So the building that's out there now, the rehab center is a completely new building and had nothing to do with that.

A2 [Bob Shirkey]: No. Think of a long walkway, like a tunnel, attached to the front of a series of...

Q: I know just what you're talking about.

A: ...with a little of breezeway between each building, the best I remember it. Isn't that right, Bob?

A2 [Bob Shirkey]: Yeah. Here was the building and you came out the front door and you went down this walkway, which I just said, like a tunnel. You could see from one end to the other, but all these separate buildings which were different wings of the hospital.

Q: This was the infirmary where you took the airman, right?

A: There were some ramps there, I think the old ramp's still there. It was. Anyway, that's the kind of buildings they were. You don't see it today, no.

Q: I knew that the building, most of it, was new, but I wasn't sure if they'd built onto it...

A: That had been worked over two or three times.

Q: When you look at it looks like it's been one of these things where they've added things to it.
So you pulled around behind the infirmary, basically.

A: It was a pretty tight squeeze in there. You couldn't get very many cars in there.

Q: How many of those ambulances were back there?

A: There were three old box ambulances. I call them box ambulance. I guess you call them... I wasn't in the military so I don't know what all the terms were.

Q: Like these old field ambulances.

A: They've got the old square field ambulances, you know.

Q: The airman walked up that ramp with you. Both of you guys went into...

A: The airman and I both went in.

Q: Did he see that stuff in...

A: He wasn't paying any attention because he had, I had a tourniquet and towel over his busted nose, and he went right on in.

Q: Got himself into a little trouble in town, did he?

A: Rode an old motorcycle. The reason I remember it is because he had an old Indian motorcycle, and I'd just bought one. I paid $40 for one and he [rode] one, and I didn't have any fenders, and I was thinking of maybe of...

Q: So you took him in there, and then basically after you got him taken care of you figured you'd go look up your friend, the nurse.
Let's get that straight.

A: Stan Friedman, I think, somebody thought that I was having a relationship with this nurse. I was not. This girl wouldn't even think about going with me, and she was going strictly, when she got her time paid back to the service she was going into an order of the nuns, sisters, and she was going to be in education and later on she changed to the nursing deal. The only reason she was in it, because her folks were in debt and she went in the service to get her education. She got her education and then she was going to pay back the church what they owed her. Her whole thing in life was, from the day she was born, her life was planned that she was going to be in an order.

Q: Did she ever tell you which order that was?

A: It was in St. Paul, Minnesota. That's all I know.

Q: That's where she was from.

A: That's where she was born and raised. She never went out of the city until she went to... My understanding was she never went anywhere and she never lived anywhere. She was raised up from the time... Strictly raised by the church. That was the only life she ever planned. She wouldn't date a man if her life depended on it. She'd get around and talk and everything, but there was no way. But everybody said I was going to marry her and... That's bull shit.

Q: The implication was that she was cute and...

A: She was cute. I could have been interested. If I wouldn't have played second fiddle to the Catholic church, because that's what she would have been.

Q: How did you get to know her, just being out there on the base?

A: The ambulance service. You go out there, and you've got your splints on a guy, you've got first aid, whatever, you can't just throw them off of your stretcher. You maybe help them... Sometimes you're out there two hours or three. Then while you're waiting to get your equipment back you sit in the coat room with the doctors and with the nurse's quarters. That's where we always had our cokes and stuff.

Q: So you'd just shoot the breeze with whoever's around.

A: You get to know these people. That's the only way. See, she'd only been there less than three months. Of course, I'm a crazy son of a gun... Nearly everybody remembered her. She was a good looking little thing, a beautiful little girl. We thought she was kind of lonely.

Q: As you well, know, there's been a major effort to try to find her.

[Skip in tape]

A: She was out here less than three months.

Q: So you went back there. Tell me what happened.

A: I started back there, and that's when I got in trouble. I saw this officer standing there, and I saw this debris in the back of the ambulance.

Two of them was full of debris. Like Bob [Shirkey] saw a bunch little stuff, and there was a couple of pretty good sized.

Q: Two of the three ambulances had stuff...

A: One of them's door was closed, but the other two... There was two MPs standing right out, kind of just leaning up against the back of those. I remember.

Q: Did they challenge you when you tried to go in?

A: No...Evidently because I drove up with that airman, and they just figured whatever.

Another thing, when I was there, all the people that was there, that nurse was the only person I saw that was permanent station. Everybody else was all new in that whole hospital operation. Even in the coke room, there wasn't anybody in there that I knew. I started back and got to the door, and I saw this...

(Pause)

We've been friends for years, but I don't want to talk with him around.

Q: So the stuff you saw, you said it was not aluminum...

A: ...looked like hot stainless steel when it got hot. When you put flame on stainless, see, I do sculpture work and all that, and I know what the stuff looks like.

Q: Oh, you're a sculpture? I didn't know that?

A: Yeah, I've been doing it for years. I had my own foundry... I did. I don't do it any more. I have my stuff done. But anyway, this stuff was a blue purplish, it looked like hot stainless steel, is what it looked like. Steel that got hot. It didn't look like aluminum, it wasn't even melted like aluminum. I don't even think it was melted, just like a bunch of fragments.

Q: But there were some bigger things in there besides the fragments, right?

A: Yeah. There were was two pieces.

Anyway, do you want to go back to the nurse?

Q: Yes, please.

A: I started back, see, and this captain was standing there, and naturally, I just thought we had a plane crash. When we had that, we used to fill up the ambulances and everything else. It would (inaudible) for you to have a hand here or an arm or a foot or something. You know what I'm talking about. Then you've got to get in and take all that stuff and separate it and put those bodies back together with identification. That's what you've got to do. I thought we had a crash.

I saw this guy, I didn't know him. He was standing there at the door.

Q: Just inside?

A: Just kind of standing like in between the door of this room up there. I was going down the hall. I said, "Sir, it looks like we had a plane crash. Do I need to go in and get ready for it?"

Q: This was an officer?

A: Yeah, he was a captain. I remember the bars on his [inaudible]. He said, "Who are you?" I told him I was from the funeral home, and he said, "Wait right there, don't move."

Then he came back, that's when the two MPs came up. When the nurse came out, we started down the hall and that's when somebody in the back of us said, "Bring that son of a bitch back." That's when the redheaded captain asked where the sergeant came in right there. Then they took me on out. As I was going down the hall, she came out of, like Bob said, out of this room, and there was two guys in back of her, and they all had towels over their face.

She saw me and she said, "Glenn, what are you doing here? Get out of here, you're going to get in a lot of trouble. How did you get in here?" She said that two or three times. She was sick.

Q: This is when you were talking to that first officer?

A: Yeah. He just told the MPs to take me back to the funeral home.

Q: He had just told them that, and then she appeared at that point?

A: He told them to take me to the funeral home, and we started down the hall, back out the hall, and that's when she came out of another room with these other two guys. What happened, she told me the next day, they were all sick because those little bodies were in those sacks, and two of them were very mangled and the smell was horrible and one was whole and two of them were very badly mangled.

Q: Did you get a whiff of that stuff yourself?

A: No, evidently not. If I would have, I would have known what it was. I worked on a hell of a lot of stuff.

Q: In that tape you talked about working on floaters and all that kind of stuff.

A: You know.

Q: I haven't had professional experience in it, but I've been involved in it.

A: In New Mexico you've got this hot 100 degree stuff, and you've got bodies out there two or three days, and (inaudible).

Q: This read headed guy, what was his rank, do you remember?

A: I think he was a captain. It seemed to me like he had on some bars.

Q: When he first appeared and started getting, essentially, pretty rough, was the sergeant around at that time, or did he show up...

A: He was kind of beside of him. I think they were standing there... Yeah, they were definitely standing there together. I don't know if they walked in together, because I didn't see them until they turned me around.

Q: Was there a lot of activity at that time? Were there people...

A: People were [fastened] everywhere. And the odd part of it was, there wasn't anybody, wasn't any of our regular people. These were all people that I'd never seen before. That's why I got in so much trouble. I'd never seen these guys.

Q: These were not any of the guys that would ordinarily recognize you as somebody who would...

A: And they sure as hell didn't want me there, you know that.

Q When he says, "Get him out of there," the redhead, did he make any threats to you himself? Did he say, "Don't say anything about this, forget it..."

A: He said, just like that. He says, "Now listen, Mister, you don't go back into town starting a bunch of damn rumors." This guy swore as much as I do. Anyway, he said, "Don't start a bunch of damn rumors, because nothing happened out here. There's no plane crashes. Nothing's happened. You don't go in and start." Then he told the MPs, "Get the son of a bitch out of here."

That's when I said, right then, I said, "Look, Mister, I'm a civilian, and you can't do a damn thing to me, you go to hell." That's when he said, "Listen, Mister, somebody will be picking your bones out of the sand."

Then the black sergeant said, "Sir, he would make good dog food," or something like that. I remember the dog food.

The next morning at 6:00 o'clock the sheriff was out at my dad's house and told my dad, "Glenn may be in a lot of trouble with the base, and tell him to keep his mouth shut."

I never told my story to anybody, but my dad came up, I was living in a room at the funeral home. He came up and got me out of bed and wanted to know what I'd done. He was a very patriotic old man, and he said, "If you done anything against our government, I'll take care of it."

Q: When was this?

A: The next morning.

Q: You were saying what the heck? What's going on?

A: Yeah. I said, well hey... He said, George Wilcox—the sheriff and my dad were real good friends, and he said George tells me you're in a lot of trouble out there. He wasn't going to leave, and I told my dad the story. He got all upset because they threatened me and all this kind of stuff.

I didn't see the nurse, then, until the next day. After I saw her, then I kept calling. When I got back to the funeral home I started calling, because she was in trouble and so was I.

Q: It was the next morning after you'd been hustled out of there that your dad came by to see you.

A: Yeah, 6:00 o'clock in the morning.

Q: He'd been called by the sheriff...

A: The sheriff went to my mother and dad's house, and at 6:00 o'clock... My dad always got up early, sat and had coffee. He was an old carpenter and building contractor. He and George were old friends because he used to go hunting, and dad was making gun stocks, so they were good friends. They used to play some kind of domino games or 42, whatever you call it. They were good friends.

Q: So the sheriff went by to see your dad...

A: Dad said he was there at 6:00 o'clock.

Q: The sheriff came by early in the morning and then your dad immediately came from home and came to see you.

A: After George Wilcox left, my dad came up to the funeral home and wanted to know what I did.

Q: Did your dad say why the sheriff... Had the sheriff been contacted by the base, or...

A: No, he just said, he was concerned about what I'd done, how I'd got in trouble.

Q: Do you remember what he told you about what Wilcox told him?

A: He just said George said I was in trouble at the base, and what did I do.

Q: Then after having this rude awakening, you then... Did you call the nurse?

A: Well, yeah, this was in mid-morning. I remember I finally, I waited until kind of, well, it must have been 9:00 o'clock or so, and I called. I knew the work station that she always worked at. She was a general nurse. They didn't specialize. Just orderlies and everybody was on general duty in those days. I was informed that she wasn't there, she wasn't working. She wasn't working that day.

Q: It was one of the other nurses that you talked to?

A: Yeah, it was an old girl by the name of Wilson., Captain Wilson. I asked her, I said what happened? She said, "Glenn, I don't know what happened, but she's not on duty. I'll try to get the word to her that you want to talk to her." She was wanting to talk to me, but she was sick. She was in total shock.

Q: Did she tell you that later, that she was sick?

A I knew she was sick. She came out with that towel. She said, she and the two doctors were sick. Then at the Officers' Club, she said I want to know what happened to you, and I'll tell you what happened to me. The only way we ever got to the Officers' Club, the old regular group said you don't go anywhere, you keep your mouth shut. [inaudible] said that. The old group, they would have known us. It probably wouldn't have mattered. But these people, hell, these people didn't know us. And of course I had a pass, and I had an associate membership to the Officers' Club, the funeral home did, so I could go as I pleased. I had free access to the base.

Q: Did you meet her at the club?

A: She said she'd meet me over there. She was sick. She said I'll meet you there.

Q: When you got there, she was at the club?

A: She was walking up when I drove up. She walked over. It wasn't very far from the hospital.

Q: She walked from the hospital or...

A: From the nurse's quarters.

Q: Let me back up to the event with the MPs. They physically hustled you out of the hospital....

A: Well, they didn't carry me out, they said, "Come on, we're taking you back," one on each side. They didn't have their hands on me or forcing me.

Q: I've forgotten which one of the accounts has them lifting you right off your feet and all that kind of stuff.

A: No. They may have got me by the elbow, but that was that. They were nice guys. They were doing what they were told to do.

Q: They got you to the ambulance. Did they follow you back to the funeral home?

A: One followed me in a pickup and the other one sat in the seat with me.

Q: Oh, I see, he actually rode with you in the ambulance.

A: He rode with me, and the other one drove a pickup and picked him up. They had a pickup.

Q: Did the guy riding with you say anything about what was going on?

A: He said he didn't know what was going on. That was the first thing I said, "What in the hell's going on?" You know. He said, "You know more about it than we do," something similar to that. I don't know the exact words, but he didn't know anything.

Q: Now we're back to the Officers' Club and you met her there. When you saw her, how did she look?

A: Like a nervous wreck. Her hair wasn't combed or nothing. She said she'd been sick all night crying and everything else, and she was still crying. She was hysterical. She put her hands over her face and said I can't believe it. The most horrible thing she'd ever seen. She was really in bad shape.

Q: You called her and wanted to get in touch with her to talk with her about what happened.

A: I was curious.

Q: Did she seem reluctant at first to talk to you about it?

A: No, she said I've got to talk to you. I want to know what happened to you. She said I've got to talk to somebody, and that was it. You know, I'd see her a lot. I knew all those old girls out there, you know.

Q: Did she give you any indication or any reason to believe that she had been told to keep her mouth shut about it, or...

A: Well, yeah, because I'll tell you what. She had this drawing on the back of a prescription pad, these little bodies, it was on the back, a little small thing on the back of a prescription pad. She said, "I'm going to show you something, and you have to give me your sacred oath that you won't tell anybody when you got this and you won't ever mention my name, because I will get in a lot of trouble." That's what she said. "I will get in a lot of trouble."

Q: She didn't say specifically that somebody had...

A: No, she just said, "I will get in a lot of trouble." She said, "Will you do that?" I said, "Sure."

She showed me that. And she had it written on the back like I had it on the back of that, you have my drawing, where I said note, and all that. That's what she said.

Q: She let you keep that, she gave it to you?

A: Yeah, she said you look at it and you throw it away. I never did. I went and took it back and put it in my personal file.

Q: Which subsequently got tossed, apparently.

A: Well, all the files got tossed.

Q: What happened?

A: Well, the funeral home, I hired some guys, the manager up there now [was there] before I left, and Raymond said that he doesn't know, because when he was working up there was another manager, and he said he thought Joe [Lucas] told (inaudible). Of course Joe and I weren't very good friends and we'd had some problems over the funeral business, and he said Joe found my files. He said I know he went through everything you had.

He and I had a partnership in a business, and I put up all the money and it went sour and so we had problems.

Q: You and Stan Friedman actually made an effort to try and find that, didn't you?

A: We went down there. The old file was right where I said it was, it was still there. But it was, Stan will tell you, we went down in this old basement, and I knew exactly... See, I kept files on every case that I was involved in, murders, anything that I went to court on, that I was a witness on, I kept all that. I called those my personal files. If I ever had to go back with the insurance companies or anything, I had it all right there. That's why I had those.

Q: You found the filing cabinet but there was nothing in it?

A: No. We went through it. There wasn't a thing in it. Stan and I both.

Q: They'd stripped it out, or was there other stuff in there...

A: There wasn't anything in there.

Q: After all of that excitement, then what? Did it just kind of evaporate?

A: It just kind of evaporated. Then of course two or three days later, I was concerned about her because she was sick. I took her back to the nurse's quarters and let her out. I called back the next day and they said she wasn't on duty, and I called the next day and they said she wasn't on duty. Then I went out there, for some reason, I don't recall. I went out there and I asked about the lieutenant, and they said she'd been transferred out. They said, "She was transferred out yesterday." Well, that was the day after I saw her. They got her out the next day.

Q: Who told you she'd been transferred out?

A: I don't know. Some nurses...

Q: It wasn't anybody that you remember?

A: No.

Q: Did they tell you where she'd been shipped to?

A: They didn't know. They said she had been transferred, and that's all they knew.

Q: But then you heard from her subsequently.

A: About three or four weeks later. I got a card addressed to Ballard Funeral Home. It was from her, and inside it just said, just a short note, she said we will correspond later to see what happened to each other, something similar to those words. She said the only way you can contact me is through this APO number, and there was an APO number. It was a New York APO number.

Q: So she'd gone to Europe or some place.

A: Then right on the bottom she says, "I'm in London." That was it. I wrote a note, just a note, that said if you feel like it and you get time, then I would love to know and we'll correspond. Mine came back. That was about three or four weeks later. Mine came back.

Q: That was the one that was marked deceased?

A: Yes. It said return to sender, [addressee] deceased.

Q: Then what did you do?

A: (inaudible)

Q: You didn't try to follow up or see if there was any possible...

A No. I asked (inaudible), at the time we called her Slatts Wilson, a big tall nurse, 6'2", 6'3", big tall skinny girl. We called her Slatts. Everybody called her Slatts. She's the one that told me she'd heard that there was a plane crash and she was the nurse that went down on a training mission. She said that's strictly rumor, I don't know anything about it. That's what I...

Q: No one's been able to turn that one up at all.

A: I guess maybe I should never even mention this. I know no one believes this damn story. Nobody believes this story.

Q: I don't know if that's true.

A: Anyway, it was a hell of a story. I told (inaudible). I said I told the woman, I don't want to give you her name, because I told the lady I'd give a sacred oath and I didn't want to get involved. Well, it's been 45 years, almost 40 years, and I haven't heard anything. He said I will do it confidentially and nobody else will have this name. Well, that's where he broke his promise after that. I got all over him about it. I called him and I was madder than hell. He said well, Bob Shirkey was the one that told everybody, that he was sitting in the back of us. Bob brought Stan [Friedman] up there when he interviewed me. He said, Bob Shirkey was the one that let out her name. To this day, Stan Friedman (inaudible) still says he did not put her name out. I've been on several shows, not several, but two or three interviews, and I'm not going to mention her name. If somebody says is this her name? I'm not going to say it is or it isn't. I told Stan... I was madder than hell about it, because I did give my word.

Q: There's another side to that, too, from the standpoint of those who are trying to get some answers. By not having her name around, it makes it easier to cross-check the stories that you get from people. You have... It's a question of honor, and that's very sound. I applaud you for that. There's not too many people around these days that are concerned about that kind of thing. And it's also, from an investigator's point of view, an advantage, too.

A: I've never read this stuff, I've never watched the videos, I've never read any books, I haven't even read Stan's books, I haven't even read [Kevin] Randle's only what they say about me. Friedman is a lot more accurate, but see...

Q: You mean about...

A: About me. I've read that. That's the only thing I've read. I'm not a UFO guy. I've got another life besides UFOs. But anyway, Stan Friedman's story is pretty well right. But Randle and them was always said I got curious. I didn't get curious. I went out there on a call, just like I told you.

Q: The section of their book that refers to you is really kind of cryptic, anyway.

A: They said the book was already published. Now they had a copy... Friedman sent them a copy of my tape. They had the (inaudible). Hell, they had my tape. They just made that up. Somebody did.

Q: I was puzzled by it when I read their book. That whole section where they refer to you, and it's all very mysterious, and your name is not referred to in the table of contents, but you're in the list of people that's been interviewed, but you're not one of the key people lists...

A: They never did interview me.

Q: They never talk to you at all?

A: Not personally. They didn't interview me until a long time later, a year or so later. They only had Stan's tape.

Q: So when they were actually writing their book...

A: The book was already published.

Q: When they were doing the writing, they were working from Stan's tape.

A: Evidently.

Q: Who was actually the first UFO investigator to get in touch with you?

A: Stan Friedman. When they had Unsolved Mysteries here and different ones. There was a lot of people... I'd get different ones. I had different people come and say we want to talk to you about the UFOs, and I said I don't have anything to say, I don't want to talk about it, and I never did. I've talked to very few people since.

Q: How did Stan come to find you?

A: One of the guys that I went to school with, high school, and Captain Harry Blake, he's a general now, (inaudible).

Q: Is he still on active duty?

A: No, he's retired. He was just a general in the military school, National Guard, I don't know. He never was really a good friend of mine. We lived across the street from each other when we were kids.

So that's how Stan found you. He was the first guy to talk to you.

A: Bob Shirkey brought him up there to see me.

(Pause)

Q: There's a reference in here to you having some years later, I think, talked to a pediatrician that you knew? A guy that was stationed...

A: I can't find his picture, and I don't remember his name. I ran into him when I was fishing up in Colorado and we ran into each other.

Q: This was a guy who was at that time stationed here?

A: He was here, and they called him in. He said that was out of his field and he didn't want anything to do with it.

Q: They actually called him in and asked him to take a look at what had been retrieved or...

A: He said they called him in. I don't know. He said, "But I said that was out of my field and I didn't want anything to do with it." That's what he told me, now.

Q: Did you get the sense that he knew more than he was telling?

A: I would say so, yeah. I'm sure they did. A lot of those guys out there did.

Q: You don't remember his name?

A: I don't remember it. But I did run into him. Somewhere I've got his name.

Q: Have you talked with anyone else? Had you during that time before you got into all this...

A: No, I wouldn't have even talked to him about it. He brought it up and wanted to know whatever happened on the UFO business.

Q: It was at his initiative.

A: I didn't bring it up. I told him I didn't know any more about it than he did. He said well that was strictly out of my field, and I didn't want to get involved in it. That was about it. But he brought it up. I didn't ask him.

Q: He was just curious about what happened.

A: Wanted to know whatever happened to it.

Q: That's about all I've got.

(END)

Transcript of Interview with Alice Knight* (Alleged secondhand witness to "crash site" 175 miles northwest of Roswell)

A: I remember that he saw—one time I went to visit—and I don't remember whether it was before my husband and I married or after, I don't recall the date. But he said that he saw a UFO fall. He was out working in the field and I understood that he was out on the St. Agustin Plains and he went over that way and it fell and he got nearly to the site and there was a group of people on a geological—archeological hunt and they were over there. I don't remember how many people he said.

But they got nearly up to the UFO but it was close enough that you could see some creatures. He said they didn't look like human beings out there.

And along came government cars and trucks...

Q: Now, by government you mean....

A: I guess it was government. You know, as I said it was a long time ago. And someone came along and I understood it, I don't know whether it was army or what. I think he just termed it government trucks and they told him to go on back and forget they ever saw anything, and that's all I recall.

(END)

---

* Exerpted from raw footage used to prepare the video, *Recollections of Roswell Part II*, (Washington, D.C.: Fund for UFO Research, 1993).

Transcript of Interview with Vern Maltais*
(Alleged secondhand witness to "crash site" 175 miles northwest of Roswell)

A: ...he [the eyewitness] had been coming back from one of his field trips, he'd run onto a flying saucer that had burst open and there were four beings on the ground and that he was surveying the site, archeological group from the University of Pennsylvania, telling us that there were about four or five people with this group.

As they were just starting too look things over really closely, the military moved in and gave them a briefing not to say anything about it and keep quiet and it was in the national interest to get out of there.

Q: What was his feeling about what it was that he had experienced?

A: He had no qualms about what it was. He said it was a vehicle from outer space . There wasn't any question. The beings on there were nothing like, not exactly like human beings...

Q: How did you...

A: ...similar but not exactly.

Q: How did he describe them?

A: He described them being about three and a half to four feet tall, very slim in stature, and with—there heads were hairless, with no eyebrows, no eyelashes, no hair. Sort of a pear-shaped head with the top of the head being smaller—larger, I mean.

Q: Any other characteristics about their appearance?

A: Only one thing that he mentioned. The hands were not covered, they had four fingers.

(END)

* Exerpted from raw footage used to prepare the video, *Recollections of Roswell Part II*, (Washington, D.C.: Fund for UFO Research, 1993).

Transcript of Interview with James Ragsdale*
(Alleged firsthand witness to "crash site" north of Roswell)

RAGSDALE, JAMES   EYEWITNESS   Transcript
26 JANUARY 1993

DS: So you were actually out there.

JR: Yeah.

DS: Do you remember the name of the ranch it was on?"

JR: It was on...Fisher?

DS: Was it north of here.

JR: Yes...back out here.

DS: Northwest...Just take your time.

JR: It was Foster. (Some discussison with his wife about who owned the ranch)...Let me see what you've got (referring to the photographs). That's the place right there (identifying the location from the pictures).

DS: What area?

JR: It seemed to me that that place belonged to...Fisher, but it sold to somebody else...somebody else bought that...

That's how come I was out in that area. And we was out there and she's dead and all the guys I showed the stuff are all dead. It's amazing what all went on...

Discuss our book and the Museum.

DS: showing one of the pictures...so you think this looks like

JR: That looks like the place.

DS: As far as the ranches go, driving around at that time, it could have been most any ranch, right? This would have been in '47...You were with this woman?

JR: Yeah. We were camped out out there.

DS: You were camping?

JR: Yeah... I would say half of it...I would say that only about half of it...just half of a...you really couldn't tell what it was...what you could still see, where it hit...I think it was two spaceships flying together and one them came down and the other one picked up what they could and got out of there.

---

* James Ragsdale, interview with Donald R. Schmitt, January 26, 1993.

RAGSDALE - JANUARY 26, 1993 (2)

DS: Is it possible that because it was hit by lightning that it broke up and part of it went down...(discussion of the Mac Brazel sighting)

JR: ...but it was either dummies or bodies or something laying there. They looked like bodies. They weren't very long...over four or five foot long at the most. We didn't see their faces or nothing like that but we had just got to the site and heard the army, the sirens, all coming and we got into a damned jeep to take off. We had to hold a fence up to go onto another ranch to come out from there.

DS: How far would you say this from town here?

JR: Thirty miles...forty miles.

DS: In a nortwesterly direction?

JR: Right up here. (Discuss the pictures again.)

DS: Were there any buildings?

JR: No. You couldn't see nothing. You go up on top of the hill. It was a hill...(referring to the pictures) you could see the stuff right here.

DS: The object...the craft...what was left of it...in these photos...where was the object?

JR: Along this right here...It looked to be about half of around (?) because around the edges...I had two great big pieces. That's what they got when they stole the car...you could take that stuff and wad it up and it would straighten itself out. I never seen anythig like it. Looked like something between a plastic...looked like carbon paper...

DS: That was the color of it?

JR: Yeah. Carbons. That was the color of it. Sure was...between plastic and...hell I don't know...let's see how to describe. One piece we had you could take it and put it in any form you wanted and it would stay there...you could bend it in any form and it would stay...it wouldn't straighten back out.

DS: You picked those up from the ground?

JR: Yeah.

DS: You threw them in the jeep...stuffed them in your clothes...?

JR: Yeah and then we heard all of them coming...

DS: How many vehicles...how much commotion did you hear as they came in?

JR: Oh my God it must have been...it was two or three six by six army trucks, a wrecker and everything...and leading the pack was a 47' Ford car with guys in it...MPs and stuff in it...we had the windshield down on the jeep and we stayed in the weeds and stuff...and we came on back down to where we was camped at.

DS: So you watched for a while?

JR: Yeah. Sure did.

DS: What was their...

JR: They cleaned everything all up. I mean cleaned it. They raked the ground and everything. I mean they cleaned everything.

DS: You didn't stay there that long?

JR: No, but they had a truck. I would say it was six or eight big trucks besides the pick up, weapons carriers and stuff like that.

DS: What kind of guard did they have. Did the surround certain areas...

JR: They had MPs all...they got way out in the field. They had people all along this ridge...they drove up in here. We was back over here. This grass here...

DS: So if you were back here, could you see the activity down here?

JR: You couldn't see too much of what they...you could tell...As soon as they got there they began gathering the stuff up...we were hidden in what you call buffalo grass...

DS: Did you see any behavior around the bodies.

JR: Huh-uh

DS: You couldn't see down to that level?

JR: Yeah.

DS: Did you see any activity near the craft?

JR: No.

DS: The angle of the craft...was it flat was tipped...

JR: One part was kind of buried in the ground... and part of it was sticking out of the ground...about like that (DS: about a 30 degree angle?) Yeah...and I'm sure that was bodies...either bodies or dummies...

DS: Why do you say dummies?"

JR: The federal government could have been doing something because they didn't want anyone to know what this was...they was using dummies in those damned things...they could use remote control.

DS: So you thought that it could have been an experimental craft?

JR: After I came to down showed Frank Willis and his son (he's dead)...the Blue Moon beer joint over on the old Dexter highway. We was there until two o'clock in the morning...I had the jeep behind my car.

DS: Did you still have the scrap in the jeep?

JR: Yeah. I showed it to him. He said I would just keep my mouth shut...he said hell there is no telling where that come from.

DS: So you didn't think it was from outer space?

JR: No. We didn't even think about outer space back then...

DS: When was the first time that you thought that maybe this was something more?

JR: It was about three weeks...it came out that a spaceship had crashed at Roswell...about three weeks. But it could have been out longer than that there but see I worked in Carlsbad...

DS: But you first saw there had been a newspaper article about three weeks after...

JR: Oh hell it was two or three weeks before I caught up on it...a spaceship...what I hear is they guarded that place for a long time out there...because me and another fellow went out there and you couldn't get...they had the roads sealed off...it was a month or so after...

DS: And they still had it cordoned off.

JR: The MPs and stuff were still on the road. They wouldn't let nobody go out there...

DS: If a person were to drive out there today...going north out of town...are we talking 285?

JR: No. Highway 48. You go out 48. You go out here to the truck route, hit 48 and...and it's about forty some miles out in there...(And no talks about the car being stolen in 1951 when the car with the debris was stolen...) ...I would say 18 inches and 30 inches long...strips off the edge of it...it was a heavy material but it didn't have no ridges...it was put together with some kind of solder like stuff...no bumps, no nothing in it...it wasn't...it was about as heavy as duraluminum...it wasn't as brittle...you could take a small piece and it was flexible... (then discuss the stealing of the car with a wrecker and the material was locked in the trunk of the car. And then discuss the break in of the house where the last of the pieces were stolen about eight years ago...1985).

DS: Was there a storm that night?"

JR: Yeah. There sure was. It was a whale of a storm.

DS: Did you hear anything unusual? Did you hear...between the cracks of thunder...

JR: Well, it lit up the sky when it came down. It lit up the damned...we thought at first that it was falling star or something. And electric lightning...man it was something.

DS: You heard something and you saw something...

JR: Yeah, sure did...because we were laying there in the back of the pick up...the whole sky lit up...we thought it was a star falling.

DS: Did you then go to check it out...

JR: Sure did. The next day, sure did. We drove right up on it. She picked up a piece of it and we had the jeep parked a little ways away from there and throwed a piece of it up there somewhere and I have tried and tried to find where she had throwed that piece...she had a piece but when she saw the army coming she throwed it out...she saw them a coming and she throwed it out...I doubt that I could even go back to the place it's been so long. (Now begin to talk about the car wreck that nearly killed him.)

Remainder of the tape is discussion about the car wreck, the ranchers in the area, and the murder of Mrs. Ragsdale's brother.

(END)

Selected Bibliography of Technical Reports

The technical reports listed below are available for sale by contacting:
National Technical Information Service (NTIS)
5285 Port Royal Rd
Springfield, VA 22161
(703) 487-4650
http://www.orders@ntis.fedworld.gov

Publication	NTIS Report Number
Air Force Cambridge Research Laboratories. "Report on Research, for the Period July 1965-June 1967", AFCRL TR-68-0039, 1968.	AD 666484
Air Force Missile Development Center. *Man High III,* MDC-TR-60-16, 1960.	AD 259635
——. *Man-High I,* MDC-TR-59-24, 1959.	ADA 215867
Air Research and Development Command. *History of Flight Support Holloman Air Development Center, 1946-1957,* 1957.	ADA 323526
Bartol, Aileen M., et al.. *Advanced Dynamic Anthropomorphic Manikin (ADAM) Final Design Report,* AAMRL TR-90-023, 1990.	AD 234761
Bushnell, David. *Contributions of Balloon Operations to Research and Development at the Air Force Missile Development Center Holloman AFB, N. Mex. 1947-1958,* 1958.	ADA 323109
——. *History of Research in Space Biology and Biodynamics at the Air Force Missile Development Center, Holloman AFB, New Mexico, 1946-1958,* 1958.	ADA 323170
——. *History of Research in Subgravity and Zero-G at the Air Force Missile Development Center, Holloman AFB, New Mexico, 1948-1958,* 1958.	ADA 323144

———. *Major Achievements in Biodynamics: Escape Physiology at the Air Force Missile Development Center, Holloman AFB, New Mexico, 1953-1958,* 1958. ADA 323127

———. *Origin and Operation of the First Holloman Track, 1949-1956,* 1956. ADA 323573

———. *Research Accomplishments in Biodynamics: Deceleration and Impact at the Air Force Missile Development Center, Holloman AFB, New Mexico, 1955-1958,* 1958. ADA 323097

———. *The Aeromedical Field Laboratory: Mission, Organization, and Track Test Programs, 1958-1960,* 1960. ADA 323166

———. *The Beginnings of Research in Space Biology at the Air Force Missile Development Center, Holloman AFB, New Mexico, 1946-1952,* 1958. ADA 323167

Cobb, D. B. and Waters, M.H.L. Royal Aircraft Establishment Farnborough. *The Behavior of Dummy Men During Long Free Falls,* Mechanical Engineering Note 179, 1954. AD 060052

Firestone, James R. and Patterson, Jack H. *Recovery of Parachute-Borne Packages by Helicopter,* TDR 62-6, 1962. AD 276477

Flight Summary, Non-Extensible Balloon Operations, 6580th Test Squadron (Special), June 1950 to October 1954. ADA 323108

Gildenberg, Bernard G. "General Philosophy and Techniques of Balloon Control", in Lewis A. Grass, ed., *Proceedings, Sixth AFCRL Scientific Balloon Symposium,* AFCRL-70-0543, 1970. AD 717149

———. *Capacity and Fatigue Tests on Three Mil Polyethylene Balloons,* HADC TN-55-4, 1955. AD 066092

———. *Crane Launch Techniques for Polyethylene Balloons,* HADC TN 57-3, 1957. AD 123732

———. *Development of Shroud Inflation Techniques for Plastic Balloons,* HADC TN-54-4, 1954. AD 039440

———. *Investigation of Inflation Techniques for Nonextensible Balloons,* HADC TN 54-7, 1954. AD 067595

———. *Meteorological Aspects of Constant-Level Balloon Operations in the Southwestern United States,* AFCRL-66-706, 1966. AD 644895

——. *Summary Report Project Moby Dick: Covered Wagon Balloon Launcher Development and Test Results*, HDT-21, 1952. AD 001124

——. *Techniques Developed for Heavy Load Non-Extensible Balloon Flights*, Report No. HADC-TN-54-3, 1954. ADA 030902

Greer, R.J., et al. *Development of a Balloon-Borne Manned Vehicle,* WADC TR-59-226, 1959. AD 227244

Hertzberg, H.T.E. *The Anthropology of Anthropomorphic Dummies,* AMRL TR-69-61, 1969. AD 706411

Hess, Joseph. *Determination of Parachute Descent Times and Impact Locations for High Altitude Balloon Payloads,* AFCRL 63-885, 1963. AD 421021

Holloman Air Development Center, Weekly Test Status Reports, Project MX-1450B/7218 (High Dive), June 1954 to January 1956. ADA323823

Madson, Raymond A., 1st Lt. *High Altitude Balloon Dummy Drops, II. The Stabilized Dummy Drops*, WADC TR 57-477 (II), 1961. AD 270880

——. *High Altitude Balloon Dummy Drops, Part I. The Unstabilized Dummy Drops*, WADC TR 57-477, 1957. AD 130965

Mazza, Vincent and Wheeler, R.V. *High Altitude Bailouts*, MCREXD-695-66M, 1950. ADA 323449

Nolan, George F. *Balloon Ascent Trajectory Dispersion Over the United States at 60,000 and 100,000 ft,* AFCRL-66-98, 1966. AD 631502

Redmond, Kent C. *Integration of the Holloman-White Sands Ranges, 1947-1952,* 1957. ADA 323574

Ruffner, Kevin C. (ed). *Corona: America's First Satellite Program,* 1995. PB 95928007

Simons, David G., Lt. Col., (MC) *Stratosphere Balloon Techniques for Exposing Living Specimens to Primary Cosmic Ray Particles,* MDC TR 54-16, 1954. AD 075812

——. Man High II, MDC TR 59-28, 1959. ADA 230805

Stapp, John P., Maj., (MC) *Human Tolerance to Linear Deceleration, Part I. Preliminary Survey of the Aft Facing Seated Position*, Air Force Technical Report 5915, 1949. PB 100871*

——. *Part II. The Aft Facing Position and the Development of a Crash Harness,* Air Force Technical Report 5915, 1951. PB 106572*

*Available from:
Library of Congress
Photoduplicating Service
Washington, D.C. 20540
(202) 707-5640

Index

G

H

I

J

K

L

M

N

O

P